COLLECTING GARBAGE

dirty work, clean jobs, proud people

COLLECTING GARBAGE

with a new introduction and
epilogue by the author

Stewart E. Perry

with a new foreword by
Raymond Russell

Transaction Publishers
New Brunswick (U.S.A.) and London (U.K.)

Copyright © 1998 by Transaction Publishers, New Brunswick, New Jersey 08903. Originally published in 1978 by The University of California Press as *San Francisco Scavengers: Dirty Work and the Pride of Ownership.*

This book is printed on acid-free paper that meets the American National Standard for Permanence of Paper for Printed Library Materials.

Library of Congress Catalog Number: 97–23173
ISBN: 0–7658–0410–7
Printed in the United States of America

Library of Congress Cataloging-in-Publication Data

Perry, Stewart E.
    Collecting garbage : dirty work, clean jobs, proud people / Stewart E. Perry : with a new introduction and epilogue by the author and a foreword by Raymond Russell.
        p. cn.
    Originally published: San Francisco scavengers. Berkeley : University of California Press, c1978. With new front and back material added, based on 1997 interviews.
    Includes bibliographical references and index.
    ISBN 0-7658-0410-7 (pbk. : alk. paper)
    1. Refuse collectors—California—San Francisco. 2. Cooperative societies—California—San Francisco. 3. Employee ownership—California—San Francisco. 4. Italian Americans—Employment—California—San Francisco. 5. Industrial sociology—Case studies.
I. Russell, Raymond, 1946–   . II. Perry, Stewart E. San Francisco scavengers. III. Title.
HD8039.R462U546 1997
334'.082844'0979461—dc21   97-23173
                                                                CIP

This book is dedicated to the
Men of Sunset,
partners and helpers

Contents

Foreword to the Transaction Edition

Raymond Russell

I N 1963, Stewart Perry took up residence in San Francisco. He wasn't there long before something unusual caught his attention. There was something different about the garbagemen in San Francisco. Whereas refuse collectors in other cities looked away from passers-by and kept their attention focused on their work, San Francisco's "scavengers" looked you in the eye, and said hello to you.

Perry decided to find out what made San Francisco's scavengers so special, and soon encountered the colorful people and unique occupational culture described in this book. In 1966, he tape recorded his first interviews with Leonard Stefanelli, and took his first ride on a garbage truck with Fred Fontana. In 1973, Perry obtained a grant from the

National Institute of Mental Health that made it possible to study the scavengers in a more systematic way, and hired me to assist him in the research.

My first aim in this foreword is simply to support Perry's observations and impressions with my own. Between 1973 and 1977, I spent many fascinating days on garbage trucks in a number of U.S. cities, but it is the time spent with the Bay Area's scavengers that I still recall most vividly. The scavengers I encountered exuded warmth, intelligence, and tremendous pride in their companies and in their own individual strength. I have hefted the can that each scavenger carried on his back, but never succeeded in hoisting a full one onto my own shoulders. I had so many good interviews with so many scavengers that, like Perry, I have been unable to forget about them, and still make efforts to find out what's new among the scavengers whenever I find myself in San Francisco.

For Perry, the scavengers demonstrated that there is honor in "dirty work." For me, what was even more interesting about them was that they showed that worker ownership could work. Here were businesses owned and controlled by their own employees, and apparently doing well. Even more impressive than the economic viability of the scavengers' unique form of ownership was its durability. Unlike most worker-owned organizations that preceded them, the scavenger companies had not "degenerated" over time. Their workplace democracy had not surrendered to the "iron law of oligarchy," and they appeared not to make increasing use of the labor of nonowning hired workers, as so many worker cooperatives before them had done.

Since completing our formal study of the scavengers in 1977, I have spent most of the ensuing years investigating the extent to which the scavengers' successes have been or can be duplicated in other firms. Perhaps the most important fruit of this search for parallels has been to teach me how truly rare the scavengers are.

In the United States, prospects for worker ownership have ridden since 1974 on a federal program of support for "Employee Stock Ownership Plans" or ESOPs. In 1995 such plans were estimated to be in operation in about 10,000 U.S. corporations, and were making at least nominal owners out of about 10 percent of the U.S. labor force (Employee Ownership Report, March/April and May/June, 1996). Most of these plans, however, have not had the kind of impact on the governance of their workplaces that Stewart Perry observed among the scavengers. A survey of 860 corporations with ESOPs conducted by the U.S. General Accounting Office in 1985 found that in only 27 percent of them was the ESOP perceived to have had any impact at all on participation in decision making by nonmanagerial employees (U.S. General Accounting Office, 1986). The failure of most ESOPs to involve employees is doubly unfortunate, because the GAO also concluded that it was only when they are accompanied by employee participation that ESOPs lead to measurable increases in labor productivity (U.S. General Accounting Office, 1987).

Looking outside the United States, Whyte and Whyte (1988) have described a group of worker cooperatives in the Basque region of Spain whose success has been even greater than that of the scavengers, by at least some criteria. From a single cooperative in 1956 with a labor force of 23, the "worker cooperative complex" of Mondragon had grown by 1986 to embrace over a hundred worker cooperatives with 19,500 employees. The Mondragon cooperatives are financed by a central bank, the Caja Laboral Popular, which provides support to its member cooperatives on the condition that they retain democratic structures and make minimal use of nonmember labor. Although their economic successes have been impressive, the Mondragon cooperatives have struggled to make their decision-making processes as democratic in practice as they appear to be on paper, and their use of hired labor has also begun to increase in recent years (Greenwood, Gonzalez Santos et al., 1992).

Both economically viable and long-lived populations of worker cooperatives have recently been described in a number of additional countries, including France (Estrin and Jones, 1992), Italy (Bartlett, Cable, Estrin, Jones, and Smith, 1992) and Israel (Russell, 1995). The small nation of Israel contains one of the world's most diverse assortments of labor-managed firms, ranging from the rural kibbutzim and moshavim to the two large urban bus cooperatives, Egged and Dan. Among these the kibbutzim have long stood out as the most far-reaching, the most successful, and the most long-lasting. In response to economic and social crises that they experienced in the late 1980s, the kibbutzim have recently abandoned their traditional restrictions on the use of hired labor, and the proportion of nonmember laborers in kibbutz factories rose rapidly from 30 percent in 1990 to 47 percent in 1993 (Russell, 1996). In other respects, however, the kibbutzim remain remarkably faithful to their democratic traditions. For example, most kibbutzim continue to insist that managers rotate out of their positions upon the completion of their terms, no matter how successful they have been, or how much unique skill they may have acquired (Getz, 1994).

It was in Israel that I found a set of organizations whose experience struck me as being most similar to that of the scavengers. These were the bus cooperatives, which currently consist only of Dan in Tel Aviv and Egged everywhere else, but in the 1930s and 1940s constituted a much larger population of firms. Like the scavenger companies, Israel's bus cooperatives were formed through mergers of smaller, previously independent operations, and long after the mergers that created them, they still required their employees to play an entrepreneurial role—dealing with the public, collecting money, and so forth. As in San Francisco, members of Israeli bus cooperatives claim that drivers discharge these duties more conscientiously because they are co-owners of their businesses. Such thinking neutralizes or at least reduces the temptation to substitute cheaper hired labor for the labor of worker-owners, which otherwise leads to an ever-growing reliance on nonmember labor in most worker cooperatives, according to the theory of Ben-Ner (1984). As in the case of the scavengers, the Israeli bus cooperatives' opportunities to profit from hired labor have also been limited by the fact that their costs and rates are regulated. Thus, any cost savings that might result from substituting hired laborers for owner-members would hypothetically be passed along to consumers, rather than increasing the incomes of the owner-members. Until the Likud electoral victory of 1977, Israel's socialist government always encouraged the bus cooperatives to minimize their use of hired labor, keeping it at all times below the politically sensitive threshold of 50 percent. In 1988, members continued to outnumber hired employees in both remaining bus cooperatives, 4,692 to 3,400 in Egged and 1,811 to 1,508 in Dan.

In Israel's bus cooperatives, as in the scavenger firms, the number of worker-owners increased proportionally, as each company grew in size. During a sabbatical leave that I spent in Israel in 1989–1990, I also found decision making within the Israeli bus cooperatives to be remarkably democratic, given their large size and advanced age. The kind of democracy that I observed in these bus cooperatives was similar in many ways to what Perry had seen among the scavengers. Oligarchical tendencies were clearly present in both cases, but in the Israeli bus cooperatives, as in the scavenger firms, leaders who alienated their constituents could quickly be swept from power by palace coups or rank-and-file revolts. Periodic campaigns to reassert the threatened democratic traditions of labor-managed workplaces have also been described by Batstone (1983) in a study of French worker cooperatives. Batstone sees such renewal movements as mechanisms that make possible the "regeneration" instead of the inevitable "degeneration" of the democratic practices of many labor-managed firms.

In short, one can indeed find democratic workplaces in the world today whose successes equal or exceed those of the scavengers, if you look for them hard enough. On the one hand, I am disappointed that the total number of such organizations is so small, and that the conditions under which they appear to flourish are narrow and rare (Russell, 1993). On the other hand, I am encouraged that they exist at all. They show by their example that we can indeed have democracy in modern work organizations, in at least some places and some times.

I therefore envy those readers who are about to encounter Leonard Stefanelli, Fred Fontana, and Perry's many other Sunset scavengers for the very first time. Note them well, for you are about to behold free men.

References

Bartlett, Will, Cable, John, Estrin, Saul, Jones, Derek C., and Smith, Stephen C., "Labor-Managed Cooperatives and Private Firms in North Central Italy: An Empirical Comparison," *Industrial and Labor Relations Review* (1992) 46: 103–118.

Batstone, Eric, "Organization and Orientation: A Life Cycle Model of French Co-operatives," *Economic and Industrial Democracy* (1983) 4: 139–161.

Ben-Ner, Avner, "On the Stability of the Cooperative Type of Organization," *Journal of Comparative Economics* (1984) 8: 247–260.

Estrin, Saul, and Jones, Derek C., "The Viability of Employee-Owned Firms: Evidence From France," *Industrial and Labor Relations Review* (1992) 45: 323–338.

Getz, Shlomo, "Implementation of Changes in the Kibbutz," *Journal of Rural Cooperation* (1994) 22: 79–92.

Greenwood, Davydd J., Gonzalez Santos, Jose Luis, et al., *Industrial Democracy as Process: Participatory Action Research in the Fagor Cooperative Group of Mondragon* (Assen/Maastricht: Van Gorcum, 1992).

Russell, Raymond, "Organizational Theories of the Labor-Managed Firm: Arguments and Evidence," *Research in the Sociology of Organizations* (1993) 11: 1–32.

Russell, Raymond, *Utopia in Zion: The Israeli Experience with Worker Cooperatives* (Albany: State University of New York Press, 1995).

Russell, Raymond, "Individual vs. Collective Forms of Sharing Ownership in Israel," *Journal of Rural Cooperation* (1996) 24: 67–86.

United States General Accounting Office, *Employee Stock Ownership Plans: Benefits and Costs of ESOP Tax Incentives for Broadening Stock Ownership* [GAO/PEMD-87–8] (Washington, D.C.: Government Printing Office, 1986).

United States General Accounting Office, *Employee Stock Ownership Plans: Little Evidence of Effects on Corporate Performance* [GAO/PEMD-88–1] (Washington, D.C.: Government Printing Office, 1987).

Whyte, William Foote, and Whyte, Kathleen King, *Making Mondragon: The Growth and Dynamics of the Worker Cooperative Complex* (Ithaca: ILR Press, 1986).

Introduction to the Transaction Edition

WHEN I originally chose to study that archetype of the so-called dirty-work occupations, the garbage worker, I especially wanted to explore how one's status and self-respect in such work might be protected and enhanced. The work patterns of San Francisco scavengers in reputation and reality were a magnificent example of dirty work so enhanced. With them I had hoped to gain insights that would be helpful in the organization of other dirty work occupations. Indeed, as the United States in the late 1990s enters an era in which the unskilled or lesser skilled will often be compelled to move from welfare support to jobs paying less or little more, the questions inherent in recruiting and maintaining people for lesser skilled jobs (which tend to be dirty-work occupations) become more intense. The vaunted training goals that various state and federal government leaders claim will upgrade those on welfare are simply not going to be fulfilled. Mostly people will be going into jobs that do not require a lot of training and that are lower on the rungs of economic and social status.

Further, in the burgeoning field and varying forms of nursing care and of living arrangements for more and more senior citizens, more and more jobs will be created at what are usually considered the lower levels of skill (whether or not that is really the case for such work), and these are jobs that often fit the dirty-work label. At the very same time, some American businesses are exporting a great many dirty work jobs (as in the clothing industry) because some people abroad will do the jobs for less than American workers demand. So the issue of dirty work remains at least as significant in our society today as when I began to study the work of garbagemen thirty years ago.

As a participant observer over several years, periodically going out to work with the garbagemen on the trucks and interviewing them and the managerial officers they had elected, I got caught up in many questions in their company history. True, the work of the San Francisco scavengers has evolved further over the past twenty years. Some of it is more complicated and demanding. Yet the scavengers' experience does in fact still cast light on the general problems of dirty work in our society, and it still also raises questions about the structure and operation of business firms that depend upon low status work.

As a function of the passage of years and continued technological development, the story of the continual evolution of the work and of the company itself becomes more prominent. So too are issues of worker-ownership. Indeed I might well have written another book and necessarily a very different type of book just to report the evolution, but I believe the new facts can be adequately presented in the context of the original history, by an epilogue written for this edition.

I have not otherwise revised the text of the original publication despite the lapse of years. While some parts have been reprinted a number of times in various textbook readers, others could have done with some revisions, I am sure. Certain social and economic developments in our society would have made me take a slightly different tack in some passages of chapters 9 and 10; certain statistics could be updated though not changed in direction or significance; and of course the further evolution of the company might put a few earlier events in a different light. Nevertheless, I have chosen to use the epilogue approach. In a sense this editorial decision also offers the new reader, who begins at the beginning, a certain suspense as to what has happened to this unusual cooperative of unusual garbagemen. The story has not ended even yet. That is true of most, perhaps all the significant, ever-changing formats of human life.

My earliest colleague in studies of garbage collection, Raymond Russell, now professor of sociology at the University of California, Riverside, has provided this book with a foreword to recall the literature on central issues of cooperative and worker-owned companies, a topic on which he has published frequently over the years. He was a key researcher for a thorough review of Employee Stock Ownership Programs, conducted by the General Accounting Office some years ago, and his recent book analyzing worker coops in Israel, *Utopia in Zion*, is particularly insightful. But over the years he also kept track of events at Sunset, as they appeared in San Francisco papers. By a series of interviews in the late 1980s he assembled a brief account of tumultuous changes occurring in the company during that period and presented it at the American Sociological Association meetings in San Francisco in 1989. He has made all his materials available to me for this edition and thus aided my task immensely, both intellectually and otherwise. I am newly indebted to him in many ways and recognize again the value of his friendship and collaboration.

In February 1997 I visited San Francisco to conduct a new round of interviews and observations for the purposes of this new edition. That kind of visit had for 10 years been my practice for the original book, and I found the same generosity in the informants I managed to talk to again. Some, of course, were gone, and I missed them: Pasquale Fontana, whose marvelous picture, by George Chobanoglous, appears as the frontispiece, has died, so has John Molini, and Gal Campi, and others, too.

Some of my former sources of ideas and information remain as vital but changed, like their old company. Ever my helpful friend, Freddie Fontana, in retirement now, is a Santa Claus in his pink cheeks and white hair, and Emily, his wife, helpful too in thoughtful conversations, moves around with a walker. This time Freddie pushed me to look also at a different sort of garbage company, a small enterprise, a family affair, owned by his sister and brother-in-law, now in their eighties, and run with their son, daughter, and a grandson in nearby rural and exurban Sonoma County. I have not been able to make full use of that brief but exceptional experience, but I want to thank all the Crotto family.

And some of my informants seem unchanged: Lenny Stefanelli, at 63, is still as energetic and full of productive ideas as ever, now as a full-time vice president of another Bay Area garbage company. He was also as candid and helpful as ever, but I can't resist mentioning tape-recording one hair-raising interview with him while he was simultaneously driving pell-mell down U.S. 101 and talking into two cellular phones at the same time! And also: his vivacious and insightful wife, Virginia, gave me a significant new perspective without which I would not have properly understood the story I tell. And I want to thank especially my old friend Ernie Samietz, now in retirement, whose candor in a telephone interview was very important.

Other absolutely essential and enormously helpful interviews were the gift of people I had not previously met. Some of them have had long histories with the company, some were relative newcomers. All were indeed generous in their time and interest on my behalf:

Bennie Behrmann (a customer service representative

with more than 30 years with the company), Rich Borghello (an area supervisor and former board member, both of whose grandfathers helped found the company), Livio Cristanelli (former Envirocal president, now retired), Art Cooper (roll-off truck driver, recycled instruments band leader, and an almost 20–year veteran despite himself), Joseph La Mariana (manager of services for commercial clients, who was a thoughtful commentator), Paul Giusti (operations manager after many years on the trucks, in all 18 years with the company, who has a special gift for putting things in perspective), Joyce Hume (a thoughtful and outspoken commentator, a grandmother with 10 years on the trucks), John Legnitto (manager of the Sanitary Fill subsidiary and trustee of the ESOP), Donnie Lopez (dispatcher for the debris box subsidiary and a trouble-shooter for the company), Leo Maionchi, Jr. (a route supervisor of 26 years with the company), Joe Pesce (a 43–year veteran, former board member, and now yard supervisor at the company's transfer and recycling grounds), Robert Reed (manager for corporate communications, who, among other helpful tasks, arranged for the photograph by Larry Strong of the wonderful Sculpture Garden), Kenny Stewart (transportation manager and a restorer of antique garbage trucks), and Jack Sullivan (retired, with a son who is a long-haul driver for the company). I thank them all for their warm collaboration on my task, and I want to thank particularly Mike Sangiacomo, grandson and son of scavengers, now the president and CEO of a company that continues to be a San Francisco fixture. I also received helpful information from Robert Morales, secretary and treasurer of the Teamster Union local to which all the scavengers belong, Sanitary Truck Drivers and Helpers Local 350.

In my 1977 acknowledgements I expressed my appreciation of Helen Swick Perry's intellectual and other help and support. Twenty more years surely deserves another kudo and more loving thanks.

Preface

GARBAGE (and all that is connected with it) holds a peculiar position in our society these days. On the one hand, we seem to consider that garbage in the context of "Ecology" is a perfectly appropriate topic of discussion and thought. On the other hand, the dirty work of garbage collection and all it requires have generally received minimal attention. The practitioners of this occupation are virtually unknown unless they go on strike. Generally, people pay as little attention to them as possible and, indeed, probably try effectively to avoid the whole topic. After all, who likes to take out the garbage? And if no one likes to take out the garbage, no one seems particularly interested in *anything* to do with the mess—at close quarters. Oh yes, ecology is a fine topic, but garbage . . . ? Yet, if we primitively and protectively try to shut ourselves off from this very fundamental, integral, and complicated part of the society and its work, we lose the chance to learn something very important about our own way of life in this country.

Our way of life depends upon various practitioners of dirty work. And by dirty work I mean the tasks (and sometimes whole jobs or occupations) that are offensive to the

senses, personally demeaning, or even morally reprehensible
—or any combination of these.

As I complete this book, I find myself wondering whether or not it may not be necessary for each citizen, as a young
person, to have the experience of an apprentice in the kinds
of dirty work that are basic to the services that a complex industrial society relies upon—in hospitals, on the streets, in
the slaughterhouses and factories, on the farms, and in the
alleyways and dark corners of this country. Perhaps universal
conscription for military service has been a way of bringing
young males, at least, up against some of these tasks, but the
definition of that service seems all wrong. Why should it not
be extended and redefined so that, as a part of everyone's
educational process, we can all begin to better appreciate the
tasks of everyday life and how they form the warp and woof
of our society—indeed form the fabric of much that is good
in our society.

I want in this book to present the work of garbagemen
as real and significant—not as a target of condescending sym-
pathy, chic concern, or humorous curiosity. The men doing
the work are my center of focus. I do not invade their private
lives. I simply examine their daily work activities and work
problems, which indeed are human enough. These are the
men who make up the Sunset Scavenger Company of San
Francisco, one of the two licensed firms that have picked up
the city's refuse for fifty-some years.

I deal here only with that one organization. But just that
one organization and its men offer profound insights into
many different aspects of the American social order. (Later,
with colleagues, I studied other private companies and municipal departments in a comparative investigation, which we
shall report on elsewhere.) Garbage work seems to be pretty
much the same all over America—and for that matter,
around the world. So the Sunset experience can serve for now
as an introduction to the dirty work of garbage collection.
Yet, Sunset is unusual in many ways, the most important of

which is that the company was organized as a cooperative. Also important is the fact that historically it has been a business for Italian-Americans. The special nature of this cooperative firm and particularly its recent history give additional tools for examining our social order.

As the book lays out the work routines and their rewards and discontents, two uncomfortable questions arise: (1) What are the human costs of doing our dirty work for us, as we now require it to be done? And (2) can a creative solution to minimize those costs (as Sunset has tried, via its cooperative structure) survive in the competitive business context of modern "solid waste management?" These questions are neither overly technical nor idle. As I shall show, we have widespread and increasing amounts of dirty work to do in our society. Moreover, refuse removal is becoming more and more salient among the problems of our cities and their workforce. And strangely enough, our biggest city, New York, has been considering an experimental program of turning over specific sanitation districts to cooperatives of refuse workers drawn from current municipal work rolls. Even in its unusualness, then, the Sunset Scavenger Company has an immediate relevance.

My inquiry into this unusual company of Italian-American workmen began as a peripheral interest and only much later assumed the shape of a book-length study. It spanned a period of ten years, 1966 to 1976, an era of tumultuous change in our society, in the refuse industry, and in Sunset itself.

From time to time, I would work on the trucks on different routes throughout the city. I came to find the most insights with a crew that serviced the Haight-Ashbury district, before, during, and after it was a hippie haven. I also learned much from long interviews with the young progressive president of the company. When I first met him, he had just been elected to serve at the same salary as any one of his other partners still "carrying the can" (pulling out and loading refuse), as he himself had for thirteen years previously. Today, he and his colleagues have transformed the company into one of America's most important firms in the industry.

The transformation has not been without some costs, and examining the process of change as well as the early history of the company leads to issues of social policy. I introduce these issues in the concluding chapters. I hope I have by that time demonstrated that the garbageman's work can be meaningful not just to students of ecology, resource recovery, and the like, or even to those concerned with the quality of work and the nature of business firms in our society, but also to all those who seek to understand the possibilities of alternative orders in our society and the human responses to them.

For myself, the experience of learning about the work (together with whatever else was going on, of course, in my life and in my country in the same period) made a difference. I went from my initial research on the company to spend a couple of years in the planning section of the War on Poverty, and then spent about five years as director of the Center for Community Economic Development. In these contexts, and at the Institute for New Enterprise Development, where I now work, I have been able to put to useful ends the richness of what the work of the refuseman teaches, yes, but also the basic critique of our social order that must come to anyone who looks deeply enough into it. Deeply enough pursued, the study of the Sunset Scavenger Company, like the study of any aspect of our society, leads, I believe, to a better understanding of what our social order is and where it can go.

Acknowledgments

MY greatest debt is to the men of the Sunset Scavenger Company, and I hope the dedication of this book will tell them how much I appreciated (and enjoyed) the chance to learn about their work and their company. I owe the most special debt to Leonard Stefanelli, president of the company, who was always generous with his time and patient with my need to know.

Fred Fontana has been my friend and instructor in the tricks of the trade over the years; his interest and warmth have meant an awful lot to me. I feel lucky that, with the limited time I had, I got to know and work with him and Ernie Samietz in the Haight. Gal Campi, unofficial company historian, generously got me some basic facts. And I found the same kindness in John Molini and his crew, who gave me my first introduction to the work, and in any of the other men of Sunset, like Lou Pitto, Julio Goggiano, Joe Renati, or Al Macari—I can't name them all, but they were all helpful and interested in my problems of understanding their work.

When you have been doing something for as long as this research has taken me, you run up a long list of generous folk who have helped and encouraged along the way. I want particularly to mention the colleagueship of Arthur Hochner and

Raymond L. Russell, III. Rusty conducted a couple of days of interviews and observations at Sunset, so I had a chance to get some outside correction and confirmation. He also dug into city records and newspapers and legal files. Even more significantly, Art and Rusty have both sympathetically read my drafts and contributed excellent suggestions, leads, and orienting information from the other researches they are engaged in with me. Jerry Sanders and Charles Vidich wrote case studies of other garbage collection organizations that broadened my perspective, and Joseph Dewhirst made a case study and puzzled over general issues of alienation and status for the refuse worker. I also want to thank Carlessia Warren, a former graduate student at the University of California's School of Nursing, San Francisco Medical Center, who searched out bibliographical items in an independent study that was useful to me too.

As I was concluding this book and needed some consultation on general business issues, Alexander L. M. Dingee, Jr., the president of the Institute for New Enterprise Development, read a draft of the book and discussed what else I needed to include. His expertise and support at that point were generous and crucial, and it was generous and crucial also when he offered the Institute's sponsorship of a research grant proposal to the National Institute of Mental Health.

I am very grateful for grants from the Center for the Study of Metropolitan Problems, National Institute of Mental Health, without which I would not have had the chance to complete the work. However, I want especially to say how much I have appreciated the professional interest and support of Elliot Liebow, chief of the "Metro Center." He is a rare combination of gifted social scientist and correct but unbureaucratic administrator. His understanding of the meaning of this research was as much a psychological support as (ultimately) a financial one.

Finally, let me emphasize the value of having a long-time companion-colleague to share the problems of study and writing in this field. My wife, Helen Swick Perry, has made helpful suggestions all along the research and the writing and was a friendly goad to completing the task. In addition, she was very tolerant when I came home smelling of the garbage I was around! I am, as always, grateful for her intellectual and emotional support.

I have presented the story of Sunset in a discursive narrative rather than in a systematic expository analysis with extensive footnotes or other scholarly embellishments of the text. But I do owe debts to other students of the same problems, and a section at the end of the book provides publication references and documentary citations as well as an occasional commentary on the text. I hope by these means I have satisfied the necessary standards of scholarship without interfering with the interest of the story itself.

I want to thank Kate Bramer for her friendly and careful job of typing this manuscript.

Photo credits. With three exceptions all photographs are courtesy of Leonard Stefanelli and the Sunset Scavenger Company; and Stefanelli took the pictures of John Molini especially for this book. The three photographs not furnished by the Company are courtesy of Gerald L. French Photography of San Francisco; they appear at pages 73, 95, and 116.

One

A Personal Inquiry

PREVAILING westerlies, fresh from flowing five thousand
miles across the wash and swell of the Pacific Ocean,
scrub the air of San Francisco sweet and clean. The city seems
immune, even in a nation apparently intent on burying itself
in its own wastes. Air pollution is only rarely a problem at the
Golden Gate. Occasionally an atmospheric inversion will trap
the big-city smog of industry and freeway for a brief period.
But mostly the sun shines clear or the cool refreshing fog tum-
bles over itself coming in almost every summer afternoon,
bathing the greenery and passing through to drench the
mountains farther east. And in the rainy season, each neighborhood gets an extra scrubbing, so that when the sun re-
appears after a shower, the city again flashes its resplendent
whites and pastels, apartment towers or stucco and frame
houses, vivid against the deep blue of the bay.

In such a city, who would worry about garbage collection? And indeed that service in San Francisco probably seems
as effortless to the citizenry as the natural air conditioning
borne in on the Pacific westerlies. The daily work of the garbageman should have provoked no more interest in me, a
newcomer to the city in the mid-sixties, than it would in

someone else. If at all, I had thought of the work of refuse collectors only momentarily—until I moved to San Francisco.

I had lived in a good many other cities up to that time, and in the mobile pattern of many Americans had visited a good many more. But something about the cleanness and color of this air-conditioned city probably made me open to noticing that, among the many special features of my new home, the garbage collectors seemed different. A sense of that difference provoked me enough to ask others about it. Did they think the garbagemen here were, well, more good-natured or perhaps more . . . related? The response I got was only ''maybe,'' but then in such a city who would be thinking about garbage collectors when there was so much else to engage one?

Wherever I had lived before, however, whatever went on between me and garbagemen was pretty minimal. Indeed, as I came to think about it, I could not remember the same kind of conventional greetings that generally pass between one's self and others like the mailman, the gas-meter man, the delivery man, or whomever—people whose routine brings them regularly into one's neighborhood. I recalled no cheery ''good morning'' or ''whaddaya say?''—none of the usual interchanges with which we conventionally recognize each other as people. In fact, the garbageman and I did not have anything to do with each other if we happened to meet in the course of his work. There was not even apt to be any eye contact, that exchange of recognition that I am here, and so too are you. Until I moved to San Francisco, to me (and I do not think I am so unusual in this respect) the garbageman was virtually a nonperson.

As the days flew by in my new job as a sociologist at the San Francisco Medical Center, I did not have enough time to pursue this tag-end observation, a tiny event in the host of novelties of a new home city. But I did learn very early that in fact the garbage-collection system of San Francisco was quite different from almost anywhere else in the country, and the whole business stuck in my mind. It stayed in the back of my mind because garbage collection is so clearly dirty work, and because my job dealt primarily with nurses, who, since they are low on the totem pole in medical settings, get a lot of dirty work to do. The garbage worker, then, symbolizes intensely that sort of problem in the job of the nurse.

A few facts can set the stage for the search that I finally came to make in order to trace out the significance of my initial impressions of the San Francisco garbagemen. In the whole of North America, 64 percent of the cities of 50,000 or more in population have a municipal sanitation department (and in cities of San Francisco's size, perhaps 80 percent). In all the others, either the city contracts with a firm to pick up household refuse, or the residents must make their own independent arrangements. Boston, for example, lets city contracts, but San Francisco is one of those in which the resident must deal directly (and pay directly) for the service.

The direct relationship between resident and refuse collection firm characterizes about 12 percent of all North American cities—although almost none near San Francisco's size. In the particular case of San Francisco, there are two refuse collection districts, each serviced by a firm licensed by the city to pick up the garbage of a resident householder and to charge her or him for it. This direct-user charge system, as it is called in the trade, allows the householder to contract for the number of 32-gallon household-size cans and the number of times per week that he or she prefers. The two San Francisco firms, then, operate much like the telephone company or the electric company—like public utilities, regulated by the city and state.

For more than fifty years, the Sunset Scavenger Company and the Golden Gate Disposal Company (it used to be called Scavengers' Protective Association) have served the city and its residents. And throughout those years, the men "carrying the can" have been working partners, not employees. I discovered on my first visit to the offices of Sunset Scavenger

Company, for example, that the president was paid the same as the other partners and had himself "worked the trucks" for thirteen years.

Was this unusual type of organization the reason for the difference in my casual interactions with the San Francisco scavengers? We are often told that the business of America is business, which is one way of saying that businessmen have high status in our society. If the scavenger is a businessman, a partner in a big corporation, he would have a different standing than an ordinary garbageman. There would be less chance that you would mistake him for a nonperson. Conversely, there would be less chance that he would fear being thus mistaken—and more chance for good-natured interaction with the casual passerby. Self-esteem at Sunset would be higher, and all the various indicators of self-esteem—in how one behaves with others, in health, in family relations, in reliable work performance, and so on—would presumably show up in the scavenger's life. And the explanation for all of this, apparently, might be traced back to the special feature of their business organization.

However, even if this rudimentary explanation were true, does it matter? My work at the Medical Center had sensitized me to the basic issue of who does the dirty work and how it gets done, so I should begin the explanation there. In the hospital particularly, there is a curious reversal of the importance of different types of work, such that much of the most significant and intimate care of patients is somehow defined as the lowliest of tasks.

Consider, for example, that nursing traditionally is the women's profession, a job for the second sex. Consider also that the increasing professionalization of nursing has included the delegation of more and more of the bedside care, while the better and better (and longer and longer) educated nurses (now with doctorates) move into the office suites of administrators, or at best occasionally roam the wards as troubleshooters for problems encountered by the lower-echelon personnel.

The hospital patient today depends more and more on the attendant or the licensed practical nurse for the kindness and concern that may mean the difference between life and death. The technically trained nurses monitor the machines that are hooked into the patient and serve him most efficiently and significantly that way, but it is the machine they are tending, not the patient. At least that was my worry, and it was the worry of many of the nurse teachers, my colleagues, at the Medical Center.

Taking care of a patient sometimes involves one in some very distasteful tasks. The dirty work in medicine all too often gets passed along the line. The surgeon may prefer that the nurse remove the smelly dressings of the wound, so that he can quickly drop by to look at it. The nurse may prefer that the attendant fetch and empty the bedpan. (And perhaps the attendant goes home and asks her husband to punish the children—for not taking out the garbage: "After all, it's the least you could do.")

For the responsible leaders in nursing and medicine, there is truly a serious problem in all this. How can the basic patient-care task be recognized as important and rewarded appropriately? How can organizational forms, recruitment channels, training opportunities, pay scales, and the like be fitted into a pattern that will make patient care in its most intimate and even distasteful forms both dignified and high in quality? This, of course, is a problem that I will not deal with in this book, but it is a fundamental issue of *all* work in our society. And the fate of the garbageman can teach us something about it.

Dirty work is probably a part of any occupation, as the sociologist Everett Hughes has suggested. In English justice, for example, the division of labor between the barrister and the solicitor protects the barrister who must go unsullied into the presence of Her Majesty's judges. The office-based solicitor does the potentially undignified tasks of dealing directly with the homicidal accused or with the grasping plaintiff seeking filthy lucre from the sued party. Here in the United

States we ask policemen to protect us, but we do not want to know about their unseemly interactions with informers. Moreover, the police are to keep order, but we may get mad and call them ''pigs'' when they order us.

In short, society everywhere encompasses a number of dirty tasks which are considered necessary and indeed generally *are* necessary—for someone else to do. Certainly the refuse worker performs a critical task for us. Today, it appears that there is a growing sector in our economy of those performing dirty work. For example, in 1960, there were 33,000 unskilled refuse workers, by 1970, 72,000. The number of hospital attendants and building maintenance workers is rising fast too. For instance, those in cleaning service, such as charwomen and janitors, have increased almost 50 percent. These occupations are among the swiftest in growth in our nation. They are a base of activity on which much else must rest. Despite our much-vaunted technological advances and perhaps even because of them, the lowliest services remain important.

We expect the dirty work to be done, but we do not recognize the full costs. There are high human costs in dirty work for the person who performs it. When one is engaged in work that others consider demeaning, it is bound to have an effect upon the way one interacts with others. As Erving Goffman has insisted, the sense of one's self can be expressed by the minutest behavior, such as eye contact patterns. I believe that something like a difference in eye behavior initially affected me unconsciously in my initial encounters with the San Francisco scavengers.

Different types of eye behavior have a large set of accepted meanings in our country. One is supposed to be able to judge the sincerity of another by looking into his eyes. A shifty, wavering glance under interrogation suggests falsehood. ''Eyeball-to-eyeball'' is a contest of strength and courage. Yet, under other circumstances, one must avoid looking too long or too deeply into another's eyes if one does not want to suggest a sexual interest. And what does one do when ashamed? Look down; avoid the other's eyes.

The eye behavior of shame or low esteem can be as complex as the shuttling circuits of the telephone system. The shamed one avoids looking into the other's eyes partly because to meet and lock in a gaze runs the additional danger of reinforcing the shame. This is bad for the shamed one, but it can also be embarrassing for the other. The other would ordinarily wish to meet one's eyes only in order to rub the shame in or with the opposite motivation to invite one not to worry. Usually, however, the situation is neither of those, and the other is almost as comfortable as the shamed one. In such a case, it is even more important for the shamed one to exercise a little eye discretion in order not to embarrass the other person and add that unnecessary ingredient to an encounter that is already potentially excruciating for both.

Thus, those with a serious, long-standing sense of shame and unworthiness often choose never to seek another's eyes. Such people are called shy, at best. But if it is not shyness, there is a common agreement that the person is or believes himself to be fundamentally unworthy. The mental hospital houses many of those who seem to have given up the effort to be worthy, and whose eyes dart away for fear of being caught in that effort and discredited for it.

If a garbageman feels stigmatized by his dirty work occupation, humanly his eyes may show it. He may enter into collusion with us to avoid contaminating us with his lowly self. Our eyes do not meet. He becomes a nonperson, and passersby ignore him partly because he makes sure that they do.

Predictably, there are dire consequences for someone who feels stuck in an occupation that robs him of his personhood or, at best, continually threatens his personhood for eight hours a day. It is not hard to understand that the demeaned worker is often an unreliable worker. Those in the lowliest tasks seem to have the highest rates of absenteeism, the most sick days, the most need for "just taking the day off," and the most emergencies at home that prevent them from showing up at the job. In a medical school and other settings, I have heard the explanation of the poorer health and life performance of those in lowly occupations as simply due to their "poor protoplasm." That is, somehow the body cells are made of low-grade materials, and the bodies drift into low-grade occupations. Perhaps that explanation soothes the conscience of otherwise conscientious citizens.

The National Safety Council has recently reported that refusemen have nine times the on-job injury rate of all other industries combined. Their statistics reported that no other occupation had a higher risk of injury. Coal miners are subject to more serious injuries (as measured by the number of days of absence per injury), but even in respect to more serious injuries, refusemen are a higher risk than most other occupations. Moreover, Joseph Cimino, a public health physician, has determined that the New York City refusemen he studied have higher rates of heart trouble and other general health problems than comparable working populations.

The statistics are suggestive and tantalizing, but they do not explain anything. At this stage they merely provide insurance companies with a good reason to charge garbagemen more for their health and life insurance. Is the garbageman a higher risk because he does heavy work, all year long, unprotected from inclement weather? He is also unprotected from other special stresses like the social stigma of the job. In repeated surveys of occupational rankings, Americans have consistently placed the garbageman's work at the bottom. Only shoeshining or streetcleaning is ranked lower. The "hidden injuries" of this status system may be linked to the apparent injuries that public health and safety experts can document.

It is true that variations from one group of garbagemen to another ought to help locate where the explanations are more likely to lie, and how strong each influence is. Unfortunately, there simply is no good and reliable information at present to make the statistics work for an explanation. Again, there are only tantalizing and suggestive leads.

The Sunset Scavenger Company, for example, has reported a workmen's compensation rate which is 40 percent lower than its industry average. That is, it claims fewer cases of on-job injury, for which each state provides the worker with financial assistance. Assuming that this figure is solid—and no trained statistician would take that assumption for granted—there are still a lot of unanswered questions. It is not safe to jump to the conclusion that this cooperatively organized garbage collection group is in better shape because it is cooperatively organized.

In order to consider comparative statistics on injury rates, all sorts of other matters must be checked out. Variations in equipment (some truck models are safer than others) may make a difference. The kind of service provided can be important. Is the refuse carried out all the way from backyards to the truck or is it picked up at the curbside? Also, one would want to know something about the training programs (are there any?), recruitment programs (do they screen out less healthy applicants?), and such things as the age and experience of the workers. And so on and on.

The problem here is that one needs to know a lot about the world of garbage collection before going off half-cocked with any swift explanation of the scattered statistics, including the possible significance of a cooperative organization. Yet, as might be imagined, there is not a whole lot written and published about that world. Systematic studies are just now beginning to be done on accidents, for example—under the impetus of federal and other interest in environmental protection. But in 1966, when I first went out on the trucks of the Sunset Scavenger Company, no one except the workers could tell me very much about the industry.

The point is that it is necessary in an undeveloped field to begin at the simplest level with the simplest explorations. And so, in the beginning, I merely wanted to experience and learn as much as I could about one garbage collection organization, the men and their work. Certainly, I had an idea in mind. My ideological bent and the values I held about participatory decision-making encouraged me to believe that the Sunset Scavenger Company had a key to the transformation of dirty work into clean jobs.

I had some preconceptions: The sturdiness of standing as one's own boss in a society that prizes self-reliance surely enhances the self-respect of the scavenger shareholder. The basic structure of a cooperative must encourage a sense of working together rather than working competitively; and the composure of that kind of team relationship would be likely to reduce the stresses of a work career. But all these were simply conjectures. If there were some evidence for them, I thought it would be necessary to look closely for it in the day-to-day experience of the occupation.

I began, therefore, a personal inquiry, what is called in social science a participant observation study. I shared the work life of the scavengers while I tried to be observant of its details and meaning. I interviewed the men and observed what went on in the company headquarters and in the round of life throughout the day on the trucks. I never played at being a garbageman, but I knew that I could only understand their work if I spent long hours side-by-side with them throughout the work day. I was a social scientist, and they knew it. I was trying to do a study, and I told them so. I had a job to do which was different from theirs, and they understood that and generously helped me do my job. In return, I tried to help them do theirs or at least keep as much as possible out of the way, while at the same time making notes, asking questions, listening to their directions to each other, watching what went on. (For more detail on the research methods for this study, see the Appendix.)

From 1966 onwards, I have had intermittent, sometimes intense contacts with the men and their company. (I will call the company "Sunset" for short, as they often do.) At first, for a period in 1966 and 1967, I had fairly frequent contacts, within the constraints of my university duties, in order to begin what I hoped would become a systematic study. But then I moved to the East Coast, and distance and major responsibilities elsewhere kept me from completing my study in the way I had hoped. Nevertheless, periodically I would return to the city on other business, and each time I would make sure to renew my acquaintances and catch up on the latest news. Sometimes I would call ahead and make an appointment to see the company president. Other times I would simply appear at the all-night doughnut shop where I knew some of my scavenger friends would be gathering at 5:00 A.M. to await the arrival of their truck from the company yards; and I would go out on the truck again. This pattern of contacts was inevitably episodic, but the experience was intensive enough and over a long enough period of time that it is not a slice of life here and there but a relatively continuous record of change.

Now I can tell the story of the Sunset Scavenger Company in enough detail to make it the first step in a long process of getting insight and information not otherwise available. In the fascinating book, *Blue Collar Journal,* * there is described a college president's sabbatical year working as a garbageman and on other blue collar jobs. And Studs Terkel has provided a couple of marvelous snapshots of sanitationmen in his *Working*. These brief accounts serve admirably to introduce one to the work of the garbage collector, but more extended attention than that is needed to recognize the social implications of the garbageman's work for all types of work, but most particularly to find the significance in our society

---

*Full references for all cited or quoted works appear in a section of "Notes and Sources" at the end of the book.

of organizing their work and business in a cooperative structure.

The time span of my inquiry (which actually continues to this day) makes what went on with the Sunset Company and its men reflect and illuminate some of the social history and economic events of the society in that period. It has been a period of tumultuous change in the society, in the refuse industry, and in Sunset itself. Particularly important have been the rise of the ecology movement, technological changes in equipment and job design, and an evolution in the financial structure of the industry and of Sunset. In addition, although I went out on different routes throughout San Francisco (and later in other cities), I gained the most insights working with a crew in the Haight-Ashbury. That district, of course, went through a meteoric process of change, as it rose and fell in that period as the barometer of hope for a new way of life.

In a strange and fortuitous coincidence, much of the meaning of the counter-cultural experiment of the Haight-Ashbury has a curiously close relationship with the social meaning and course of the cooperative structure of the Sunset Scavenger Company. That is, much of the earnest efforts at reform that went on in the Haight in those days aimed to decrease the competitive and conventional business attitudes of the surrounding society and increase the level of service and cooperation. For example, a shop in the Haight, in the flower child era, was not supposed to make a profit as much as it was to offer something of genuine value and provide its worker-owners with a sense of importance in life as well as a living. In the ideology of that "brief moment in time," when one took one's "place on the great mandala," what choice one made in the matter of a calling or occupation was defined somehow to be more excruciatingly important as a matter of personal values than was or is now usually the case. The early history of Sunset, analogously, shows it as a place where immigrant Italians found a new dignity in a cooperative with each other in which they took the greatest pride in both the service they provided and their business ownership.

The Haight-Ashbury experiment in the cooperative ethic ended disastrously for that particular neighborhood, partly because of the newer chemical dimension that the counter-culture substituted for the traditional chemicals of the society. Whatever was spun off to the rest of America and however alive it may be in various forms elsewhere, the special view of a cooperative ethic disappeared in the Haight under the pressures of a social and economic order that had little place for it. (However, that order had a definite niche for the new chemicals, which seemed to fit more easily into the old established channels of social and economic interaction; that is, the drug trade fitted in all too easily.)

Similarly, as I shall try to demonstrate, the fifty-year-old Sunset Scavenger Company underwent an evolution in response to the surrounding society which placed unbearable strains on its cooperative structure and the old patterns of work that the scavengers had followed. For example, without much structural change, the company had evolved from 92 partners at the beginning to about 320 in 1966. That growth in itself represented a major transformation of the city population and the demands of the work. In the meantime, the technology of refuse collection and disposal began to change drastically, and those changes joined others in modern business methods and the general growth of the refuse collection field in a growing economy. Thus, in 1965 the group was finally forced to shift managerial gears, in the election of an entirely new board of directors and a new president who would express more effectively the aspirations of the worker-owners. That shift, in turn, was to require still other changes in the organizational structure, until in 1973 each of the partners exchanged his share of the company for an equal share in a new conglomerate holding company which they set up to own and control a variety of related firms. The questions raised for work and business in our society by this extraordinary evolution are part of the reason for this book.

In presenting this picture of the work of the garbageman in the Sunset Scavenger Company, I hope to do two things simultaneously. Most particularly, I want simply to tell in detail what it is like to do this dirty work, and I want to show what it costs the man doing it under the best of circumstances, even where his rewards seem greater than usual. Secondarily, I want to trace the evolution of the company in recent years, so as to examine the effects of technological and social change on the men and the company. Thereby I hope to be able to raise broader questions about whether and how the performance of dirty work can be rewarded appropriately in our society; whether and how the self-respect of a cooperative structure of equal shares of work and rewards can survive in a society like ours that prizes business growth and profit expansion.

Two

"In the Old Days"

A HORSE, a wagon, and a gun were standard equipment for many a San Francisco scavenger in the years before the Sunset Company was organized. Competition was fierce and aggressive between the independent scavenger entrepreneurs. Several wagons and their owners might be picking up refuse from the same city block, each coveting the other's customers on that block—and any other block. Even a man with his son or brother-in-law or other relative working beside him had to protect himself from the aggressive business practices of the other independent scavengers.

"In the old days," as the men still say, jobs were scarce for an Italian immigrant, even at the laborer's daily rate of only $2.50 in 1912, for example. "He came from the old country and he didn't know how to read or write," explains Leonard Stefanelli, Sunset's president today, "so he went into the garbage business." Scores of immigrants moved into the trade, perhaps working with relatives at first until they could save enough to buy a wagon and a horse for their own. Then they would strike out independently. Ties with friends and relatives and from the same or nearby villages in the old country probably restrained a man in his choice of potential

customers to canvass and concomitantly increased the ferocity
of his competition with those with whom he had fewer ties.

At any rate, in a city with no municipal sanitation services, scavenging became a way to make a living, particularly
if one carefully sorted out the refuse to save everything that
might be saleable—rags, bottles, seemingly irreparable furniture, whatever. And of course, true garbage or swill was
especially valuable; it could be sold to the pig farmers on the
outskirts of the city. While a householder would pay a scavenger to take away the garbage, the scavenger probably would
have to pay for the privilege of carting away the garbage of a
hotel or boarding house, because that would be an immediately re-saleable quantity.

The recovery, sale, and resale of the city's refuse did not
dispose of it all, of course. In the period before World War I,
much went to the municipal incinerator. Just after World
War I, the city fathers struggled ineffectively with the problem of the old smoking incinerator that everyone detested
and with the problems of refuse collection as well as disposal.
A special committee of the city council in 1918 reported on
the hodgepodge of the private collection system: the over-
lapping routes of the individual scavengers, the variation in
charges made to householders for the same services, the rise
in costs to the scavengers for horseshoeing and feed grain,
and especially the astounding rise in the wages for laborers,
at that point $5 a day, as a result of the war-time economy.
The committee concluded that while some scavenger companies might be making a living, others surely were losing
money in the long run, paying out for such costs.

There was a curious slant to the report, leading one to
suppose that scavenging was a matter of substantial companies with many costly workers to be paid. Actually, the
firms were very small, and the wage rates were undoubtedly
being kept down by the family enterprise practices among
the immigrant scavengers. Even pre-teen sons could drive
the wagons while their fathers hoisted the refuse, and if the

horse was gifted, the sons could hoist the garbage too. But the city fathers seemed to be worried more about employer problems than any child labor issue. In any case, their worries were impotent then.

As is all too often the case in municipal affairs generally, the city fathers of San Francisco were belatedly getting to problems that some of their constituents (in this case the scavengers) were already taking action on. In 1921, the mayor and the city council finally decided that a strong hand was needed, and they passed an ordinance outlining collection districts and setting lawful rates for collection. But by that time some of the Italian immigrants had already taken matters into their own hands.

By 1920, the first scavenger cooperative (Sunset) was formed. Everything points to the leading role played by Emilio Rattaro—who, incidentally, was still attending company celebrations in 1973, when he was over ninety years old. He had started his own business in 1916, but in 1920 he was the leading figure in bringing his competitors together to form Sunset. Why did a cooperative and rational pooling of resources occur, instead of the usual gradual growth in hegemony of a few powerful firms which finally force everyone else out of business? What made ferocious competition among the scavengers give way to a major consolidation of interests? The answers to these questions have so far escaped my historical search. All that can be said is that at that point, at least, the usual course of business did not take place. Perhaps part of the reason was the charismatic influence of Rattaro, part was the ethnic and family ties of immigrants in a strange and often hostile land, and part was a general citywide recognition of an intolerable chaos in a critical service. How strong each of these influences was is hard to evaluate.

Other aspects of the early days are also hard to pin down. Sunset itself has published in advertisements both 1912 and 1916 as the dates Rattaro started his own business, and some sources say 115 men merged forces to form Sunset, while the best evidence suggests that there were 92 original members. In any case, Sunset was incorporated on September 20, 1920, a response by the scavengers themselves to what the city had yet to find a solution for.

The next year, the city announced that it was prepared to receive bids from competent private companies for contracts to pick up refuse in city-outlined collection districts. Perhaps this led to further consolidation among the scavengers. Another Italian-American group amalgamated that year to become a second cooperative, the Scavengers' Protective Association (SPA). SPA tended to work the central city area, as contrasted to Sunset, which tended to serve streets further out. Yet, neither cooperative bid on the city contracts, so it would seem that the city council action seeking bids was not a crucial influence.

In fact, much to the city's consternation, nobody bid for the municipal contracts. This led to the unusual pattern which still exists. As a substitute, the city established a system of licenses, rates, and regulations, which are still administered by the Board of Health, although by now the city has its own Department of Public Works for other similar city services, such as street cleaning.

The city council was no more successful at that time in carrying out plans for refuse disposal. It had earlier bought up the old incinerator from the company that had been operating it and had hoped to be rid of it. But there had been no real alternative to its continued use, so it was leased by the city to a scavenger group in that part of town, and the old brick stack continued to belch smoke and blow fiery ashes all over. The city contracted to build two new incinerators on an improved model, but when the first was completed it would not work, and the city refused to take possession. (It finally became a warehouse.) The second one was never built.

In the midst of this municipal ineptitude, Sunset moved ahead. Eleven men had signed the incorporation papers; they became the board of directors. Their signatures were firm and clear, from the first name on the document, Emilio Rattaro, who was to become the first president, to the last to sign, Paolo Bianchi. So was their main purpose: "To gather, remove, dispose of, buy, sell and otherwise deal in garbage, swill, bones, scrap iron, bottles, sacks, boxes, waste paper and other waste materials." They also intended to have an incinerator and for good measure to engage in manufacturing, commerce, and real estate deals. Actually, the first purpose was the only one they acted upon for almost fifty years.

The bylaws spelled out the aims and procedures of the company in a great deal of detail. In fact, in a kind of wrap-up of amendments to the 1934 bylaws, this is recognized:

The foregoing amendments to the bylaws are much longer and diffuse than bylaws ordinarily are, and they contain much matter and discussion usually foreign to bylaws. They, however, have been so framed advisedly, in the first place, to suit the educational attainments of the average shareholder; in other words to make them and the reasons for their existence, comprehensible to the average shareholder; in the second place, to assist in the interpretation and construction of them not only with respect to their meaning but also with respect to their reasonableness.

In addition, the bylaws were available in an Italian translation, though everyone was warned that the translation was only for convenience and could not be cited formally.

Among the matters spelled out, the following is illustrative:

Article 49.—It is the policy of this corporation, as it shall be that of the Board of Directors, to pay, as it has in the past, as high a salary as possible to boss scavengers in order to accomplish the purposes, aims and objects heretofore mentioned, wholly regardless of the reasonableness of that salary. This corporation must protect itself against competition and from degenerating into drones of useless shareholders.

In 1965, lawyers pointed out to the scavengers that modern corporations need a more detailed and broader charter in their articles of incorporation, but that the bylaws could be somewhat reduced. So the Assembly of Members voted certain technical changes in the purposes of incorporation— such as an intent to remain in operation in perpetuity, instead of the original provision for only fifty years. And at the same time, they began a long review of the bylaws that were formally amended in 1967 to a shorter but still rather detailed form.

For ten years or so after the city had finally formalized its refuse system, a number of other companies took out licenses for a share of the dozens of little collection districts throughout the city. In 1932, for example, after some tightening of city regulations, 36 companies competed for permits to provide service in 97 collection districts. However, by 1935 only SPA and Sunset remained in the formal competition, and Sunset bought the last operating company, Mission Scavengers, in 1939. From then on, Sunset and SPA divided up the city into two more or less unified areas, which only slightly overlapped in a couple of sections. The cooperatives had taken over.

Gal Campi, now a company officer and nearing full retirement after 44 years, most of them pulling out garbage, described the feeling of the men in those days:

They were very, very service-oriented and willing to do anything for the public to increase their image in that respect—because they didn't have anything when they came from Italy, and they were big businessmen in their eyes here, because nobody bothered them. They obeyed every little rule and regulation that was set down, whether it be a municipal employee, some organization or governing body—they obeyed it, tipped their hats.

On the matter of relations with the public, the old bylaws were explicit:

Article 36.—Every stockholder and every employee must scrupulously and strictly obey and respect the by-laws, rules, regulations, customs, practices, orders, commands and directions of the corporation, its officers and/or the bosses appointed by it or any of its

When a horse and wagon were standard equipment, even a young boy could help out. Freddie Fontana (foreground) at age nine was already proudly working with his brothers Dominic and Pasquale.

officers. He must perform with great care and diligence the work assigned to him or which he assumes to do or which he is expected to do or which it is his duty to do. He must not only do that work in a way to please and satisfy the customers of the corporation, and above all things he must use the greatest care and diligence to avoid complaints on the part of customers both respecting his work and his personal demeanor or conduct toward them and he must avoid the doing of anything both with respect to his work and his relations and contacts with the corporation's customers or the public which has a tendency to bring the corporation or its stockholders into disrepute or to be disliked or which will harm or prejudice the corporation or the body of its stockholders.

The "big business" was just plain hard work. Campi tells how he and the others managed to heave their carrying cans up the side and into the bed of the horse-drawn wagons.

A man would be balancing the free can on his back with one hand and holding onto the wagon with the other, to begin "the seven steps to heaven"—because "you saw stars by the time you got to the top."

They'd have to put their foot on the spoke [of the wagon wheel]; and then they'd have to come and put that other foot on the middle of the wheel; then they put it on the top of the wheel. That's three [steps]. Then they'd put it on the bottom of the wagon platform and go up about four more steps, going up there.

The thing that made it difficult was that, first of all, the steps were uneven [in height]. Secondly, you put your foot on the spoke of the wheel, and the horse may move and turn the wheel. And you are over there balancing the can on your back, and it was terrible, terrible. One of the things about carrying weights: If your step is equal all the time, it makes it a heck of a lot easier. But these were all uneven. The hardest thing to do is to make the first step when you carry a weight. If that is close to the ground, it makes it easier. So if your spoke was off or something, it was hard. But the biggest fear was the horses—that they would move. . . .

Yet, of course, the horses were dear to the men. "Let me tell you something," Campi said, "they used to take care of those horses and their wagons better than they used to take care of their wives. You went and touched any of their horses! If they were off from work, and somebody else was driving their team, and if he used a whip on them, boy, you heard it! You'd think they would all but crucify you. And they used to argue in the [monthly] meetings about that: 'This fellow here abused my horse,' and so on and so forth!"

Article 11.—Any member, shareholder or employee who mistreats, misuses or neglects a horse shall be fined and otherwise punished.

Article 12.—All who have horses in charge must take good care of them and while those horses are being fed or eating or resting they must be securely tied to a post; he who violates this bylaw will be fined.

The monthly business meetings changed little as the
company developed, except a man would complain that his
truck rather than his horse had not been properly taken care
of when he was off. And all sorts of personal issues that might
have relevance to the business and image of the company
could still come up: for example, did the man dress properly
when he went to collect his bills? Even after I became acquainted with the company, the bylaws forbade vulgar language in the meetings. Earlier bylaws also provided:

Article 10.—Threatening, slandering, abusing, striking or
attempting to strike a member or stockholder or employee or officer
of the corporation, or fighting, or attempt to fight at a meeting or
where the offended or injured member, employee or officer is at
work or going or coming from work or to or from a meeting, is
very strictly prohibited and any stockholder or employee violating
this bylaw shall be severely fined and otherwise punished; if the
offense or violation occurs at a meeting or in the presence of the
president, the fine is to be imposed by the president, if elsewhere,
by the Board of Directors. Directors are and shall be deemed officers
of this corporation.

Although the bylaws changed and became more formal,
they explicitly retained a provision that required the working
partners to carry on the established practices of the company.
So the old bylaw provisions relating to behavior became a
kind of attachment or Exhibit A, so to speak, of the formal
new code. The old code, of course, was relaxed a bit in the
process, and old-timers could laugh about the standards that
used to be—about, for example, a new partner who was
roasted in a meeting for driving in an improper car when he
went to collect. The poor guy had gotten his first big pay-
check as a partner and had gone out and put a down payment
on a red convertible—which was considered excessively gaudy
and conspicuous. At the next meeting, an old gentleman got
up to complain in grave Italian about a "certain car with one

of those paper tops,'' and everyone was very solemn and re-
proving. The new partner shortly resigned from this incom-
patible group and went on to become a millionaire in the
sausage business.

In 1920, ninety-two men had signed (some with a cross
mark) the Sunset agreement which is today framed and hanging in the corporation's headquarters. That agreement bound
them to turn over their horses, wagons, and certain other
equipment (guns not mentioned) to the company, and each
promised not to deal in garbage on the side. For a long time,
each man who joined up stayed basically on his own original
route. In a sense, he probably still felt that he owned that
route, much as before, and of course he would always use
the same horses, as far as possible, even though the horses
belonged to the company. So initially things did not change
too much. The ''boss scavenger'' even paid his helpers (including family members) out of his own receipts, collected
from the householders along his route.

More than fifty years later, Gal Campi described the
business practices of the time:

My father spent just about all his time—forty-some years—working in what they call the Noe Valley area. In the 'thirties, I went
and worked with my dad. My brother worked with my dad. . . .
And after my dad retired, we still worked in that same particular
area. . . . This company was built upon maybe not a lot of formal
education but a lot of common sense. . . . Some of the antiquated
methods that they used to operate the company—it was quite a
kick. And I was a boy, I remember, when my dad and his partner,
when they had the horse and wagon, would sit around the round
table [at home] and do their bookkeeping.

They'd get together at the round table, and they'd ask one another, ''Did that house, that red house with the big gable roof,
pay?'' And he'd say, ''Yes.'' And they'd signify payment by
putting the money in the middle of the table. And they'd go
through all their routes. What a knowledge they had! They knew
their customers and all by some incident, whether it's a redheaded
lady, a lady that was lame, or one that wore glasses or something.

And they put the money on the table, and then they went through all their route, and they'd have that money there. And they'd say, "Okay, how much we got then?" And they'd count the money, and then they'd say, "How much bills we got?" And they'd say so much bills: "Well, pull that money aside for bills." And then they'd split the balance, and that's how they used to do their bookkeeping. I wasn't a part of it then, because I was young.

. . . When they were organized a little bit better in the corporation, the collector of the so-called wagon used to go out and collect the money. And he had to pay his partner X number of dollars at a certain date of the month, which was, say, a salary. And he had to go out and collect it to be sure he had it to give to his partner. If he didn't have enough for himself, his partner got it. And at the end of the month they'd make the recap again, and say, "Well, I already gave you this, and this is what remains."

By the time I began this study in 1966, the 92 original Sunset partners had grown to 320 working shareholders. There were also 120 extra people to work in the offices, the salvage shop, and the repair shop—as well as on the trucks as substitutes, helpers, and apprentices. The number of residential and commercial customers had increased to about 160,000, representing a $6 million a year gross.

The other big cooperative, Scavengers' Protective Association, had made similar strides. For ten years it had operated the city's incinerator while the council dithered in making some other arrangements. In 1932, a citizens' suit against the pollution of the incinerator was finally being pressed to a successful conclusion, and that year SPA also proposed a new solution, a new concept in refuse disposal—the so-called sanitary landfill operation. This was not the ordinary pestiferous open dump that towns, cities, and villages all over America were used to. Here the refuse was to be covered over every day with several feet of dirt, disposing of the refuse with the minimum of unsightly, polluting, or unsanitary results. There would be no smoking incinerators and none of the major capital investment that incineration requires; at the same time, the refuse would be efficiently disposed of. With this innovation for the city, SPA began a new phase in the tradition of outstanding service and concern that the cooperatives have maintained and which have given them a special place in the pattern of municipal services for San Francisco.

In 1935, when Sunset and SPA finally picked up the permits to collect all residential San Francisco refuse, it was partly because between them they were prepared not only to collect but also to dispose of the refuse, in a way that satisfied the city. In that year, SPA and Sunset organized the Sanitary Fill Company as their jointly owned subsidiary to handle disposal at a tidelands site south of the city. Each corporation still owns 49.98 percent of that company. The remaining fraction is owned by the Scavengers' Protective Union, which is a sort of fraternal organization for all SPA and Sunset shareholders, who get illness and death benefits from it.

Becoming one of the favored two for collecting San Francisco's garbage had a certain cost for Sunset. The expansion of its activities probably spurred the Internal Revenue Service to take legal action against it. The IRS insisted that Sunset was not a cooperative and that it was liable therefore to taxation as an ordinary corporation. Sunset contended that it was structured as a cooperative. But federal tax law then barred industrial and service cooperatives from the kind of favorable tax treatment that agricultural cooperatives were receiving. By the IRS definition, Sunset was liable for five years of back taxes, to the amount of $350,000, including penalties.

Apparently, the federal action had not come totally unexpectedly. The company had been warned that it did not conform to the legal definition of a cooperative for federal tax purposes. But change came hard to the scavengers, and the Assembly of Members took no action until finally the IRS gave them no choice. (This experience, incidentally, fed the fears of the partners about what sort of image they had as excessively affluent—especially in those Depression-era times. That added force to informal pressures about what sort of car one was to drive when collecting bills from customers. In one of the other Bay Area cooperatives, there came to be an explicit rule against owning a Lincoln or Cadillac.)

Occurring as it did in the midst of the Depression, the IRS liability might have been disastrous for another group, but Sunset had two financial advantages that permitted it to survive this blow. First, of course, was the trend of increasing demand for its services, and second, it could raise capital by selling more shares. There was more work to do in the 1930s than in the 1920s just because there were more people. So there could be more partners to share in that work and its rewards. The partners decided, therefore, to reduce the number of stocks to which each was entitled and make up new equal allotments of stock to be sold to new partners. The proceeds from that sale were used to help pay the IRS debt.

Sons and other younger relatives and friends of the partners working on the trucks as helpers then had a chance to buy into the company, purchasing the new shares instead of waiting for an existing share to come on the market by retirement, death, or some other cause. The number of partners approximately doubled, and the money was thus raised to pay off the taxes and penalties. At the same time, Sunset adopted new bylaws to conform to the new state license that they were required to take out as a conventional corporation. The new bylaws, however, did not essentially change the structure and operation of the organization; they merely put new names on an existing pattern and set of relationships. It was not until 1966 that the bylaws underwent a thorough review and were thereafter updated to conform to American ideas of how a modern corporation should be publicly described. The bylaws now are no longer maintained as private information for members only, and, for example, warnings in the bylaws to members to avoid divulging corporate financial or other information to "our enemies" were dropped.

The IRS challenge could probably be considered a positive influence on the evolution of the company. It opened up

the ranks to a lot of new men, and although some of them
(in the eyes of the older scavengers still today) were not seasoned enough or able to do the job well, nevertheless the
company benefited from the new blood.

In the late 1930s, the partners became union members
as well as owners. Local 350, Sanitary Truck Drivers and
Helpers, Teamsters International, was organized as part of
the Teamsters' strategy in Northern California to sew up all
California truck drivers in preparation for a major strike at the
Los Angeles trucking terminal. However, the partners came
into the union only reluctantly, pushed by the non-owner
employees of the two San Francisco cooperatives. In fact, until
the late 1940s, the local was actually under trusteeship rule
by the International, as a protection against the preponder-
ance of local members who were also owners of the two companies with which the local had contracts. During that period,
partners from the two cooperatives were elected to most of
the official posts (Gal Campi, for instance, was the first secretary of the local), but the power of the officers was curtailed
by the trusteeship arrangements. Partners continued to make
up the majority of the members until very recent years, when
garbage workers in San Mateo County were organized into
the same local. The complexity of partners as owners negotiating with themselves as union members is difficult to
comprehend, especially as some partners apparently think
of themselves very much as union members and others as
owners—at the time of contract negotiations. So far, it has
not caused a crisis, however.

In 1940, there was a crisis of another kind: some adverse
publicity about friends at city hall. But the company weathered
that too, and today enjoys a remarkable public relations
image based upon the level and costs of its services. In 1971,
for example, a writer in *Solid Waste Management,* an industry trade journal, reported that Sunset carried out its services
"for what generally is recognized as probably the lowest
charge of any major city in the United States." In this and

other trade journal articles, the Sunset recycling program and the sanitary landfill operation (run jointly with Golden Gate Disposal Company) have both been singled out for praise. The business as a whole, the rates, and the quality of service are very much public matters dealt with regularly in public commission hearings. For instance, in 1967 the co-operatives requested and received first-stage approval of a long overdue rate increase, and only one citizen objected. But, by city regulations, even one objection requires a full public hearing, and thus the public interest was protected. In the 1967 case, the scavengers used sweet talk and diplomacy to get "a certain little old lady" to withdraw her objection in order to avoid a prolonged hearing, and she finally did. Thus, the city took swifter action to permit the rate increases than might have otherwise happened.

Nothing like political connections, for example, can any longer be central to the status of the cooperatives. In 1971, for example, the two companies together were making 177,000 pick-ups a week. On these the city received an average of 30 complaints, about 12 of which, according to city inspectors, were apt to be valid. Sunset itself directly received about 200 calls a day from customers who had some problem to be solved. The men themselves termed these "complaints," but most of them, more accurately, should be considered general service calls (such as a change in order for service). Or often it would be someone calling to say that his garbage had been missed. Usually, as I could judge from my own experience on the trucks, this was a matter of the householder's not having put his can out in time, or a car blocked access, or the like. And a special pick-up service the next day would handle the problem. As quality control, the number and type of complaints indicate a very good record, and that assures city satisfaction more than having friends at city hall could.

The next major influence, historically, that Sunset underwent was the impact of World War II. The scavengers, if they wished, could get draft exemptions as essential workers, and that could be an attraction for a family man. Even so, the competition for able workers in a war-time economy was keen. The shipyards and military installations of San Francisco attracted many men who might otherwise have looked for jobs as garbage collectors. The bylaws complained of this situation, citing

the eagerness of many of the corporation's employees during this war to desert this corporation for more lucrative jobs, thus threatening, in view of the inroads made by the draft, a complete breakdown of garbage collection.

Scavenger wages were virtually frozen during the war, while other wages went up. To meet that competition and the expanding needs of a growing city war-time population, Sunset grew also. It issued more shares for more working partners. Before the war, there were perhaps less than two hundred partners, but after it there were more than three hundred.

One significant effect of the sale of shares was to open the company to other groups. What had originally been very much an Italian-American affair widened its horizons to include other ethnics in greater numbers. For example, Mexican-Americans not only worked as helpers but finally bought in as partners. A few blacks also signed on as helpers, although only a half-dozen or so ever stayed with Sunset very long, and none ever became a partner. Other ethnics in smaller numbers also joined up, some to become partners, others to move off eventually to other jobs. The war brought new ideas as well as new people into Sunset, but this influx was not to have its full effect until the 1960s, when the civil rights ferment combined with technological change to press the company to further evolution, as I shall show in later chapters. However, before moving further in this historical review, it is useful to shift from the wide-angle view of company events to a close focus on the man who had just been elected president of Sunset in a company revolution a few months before I met him.

Three

The Scavengers' New Broom

I FIRST met Leonard Stefanelli in 1966, in his office at the company headquarters, located in the southernmost part of San Francisco. The building in which the office was housed was modest and low-lying, erected on land already created by the refuse of the city. The fill had not been entirely successful, for subsequently Stefanelli would point out to me that its settling had cracked the foundations of the office building in several places. His own office was large but rather bare then; a couple of deerskins from his hunting trips were on the floor, thrown over a green wall-to-wall carpet. There were a couple of pictures on the wall: one of them, an amateur but pleasing oil, showed garbagemen working in a dark rainy street; the other, inscribed "To Lenny, keep up the progressive new ideas, Pete," was a photograph of "the first wagon built in San Francisco after the fire of 1910." The wagon was of course a scavenger's wagon.

Lenny, a handsome, athletic man, was then in his early thirties. Usually dressed in a conservative business style, he had a direct, self-confident, but not aggressive manner, much at ease in the president's job that he had entered only ten or so months before I met him. He was in command of facts and figures and dates, and threw them out to me at a great rate.

He quoted the pay scales of the city street cleaning department and compared them to what the scavengers got. Sunset drivers, for example, were then getting $3.30 per hour, which was $1.29 less than those driving the street-cleaning trucks who "don't pick up the stuff; they don't even get out of the truck." (Lesser paid workers toss in the street rubbish.) He snorted at the difference between the "real work" of the scavengers and the easier job of the municipal drivers. "Three of our men do the work of nine on civil service," he claimed.

Sunset pay is formally set by a union contract, Lenny told me. All scavengers (partners as well as helpers) are members of Local 350, Sanitary Truck Drivers and Helpers, Teamsters International. He explained that the pay scale for all partners was the same; the officers and other management-level partners received the same hourly compensation as the partners on the trucks. Helpers who were not partners received $2.69 an hour compared to the partners' $3.30 an hour. The seven management-level partners were not permitted union membership, though they got the same benefits as if they were members.

Lenny himself had "worked the trucks for 13 years" before he became president. His salary in 1966 as president, about $10,000, was the same as the men on the trucks, but he complained, "Now [as president], I work from seven in the morning sometimes until ten at night, but no overtime pay. I am not complaining. But if you're president, you get every wedding announcement and you have to send gifts!" The company informally recognized the special costs its president incurred for a variety of things such as entertainment and other necessary expenses by awarding him (through a subsidiary) a special additional salary of $250 a month on behalf of the company. This informal expense account and the use of a company car probably equalized his effective salary with that of the scavenger carrying the can.

The figure of $10,000 in 1966 represented for each scavenger about $200 in dividends and the rest in regular

and overtime wages. Lenny announced to me that he expected
to apply for an increase in rates to up that pay. He justified
the increase by pointing out that if the city street cleaners
worked as many hours as the scavengers (including overtime)
they would make more than $17,000.

At the time of my first contact in 1966, there were 315
active partners, with 297 of them on the trucks. The rest were
in the salvage operations, the repair shop, and management.
There were also 120 other employees, almost all on the trucks
as "extras" or "helpers." An ordinary crew size was three
partners and a helper. Each partner was responsible for a set
of accounts on his route, and his wage rate amounted to
about $100 a month more than a helper, specifically for "col-
lecting." Regular overtime gave a partner perhaps an additional $100 per month.

"Collecting," as I shall have occasion to describe in
more detail, was a particularly important task assigned only
to a partner. "Collecting" did not refer to collecting the
garbage, but to collecting the payment for the service from
the householder whose garbage had been picked up.

San Francisco licensed its two scavenger corporations to
charge certain specific rates. These were based on the number
of standard-size cans picked up and the location of the cans—
that is, the difficulty of reaching them—for the householder
did not have to put his refuse cans out on the sidewalk. He
could pay standard extra charges for the scavengers to go to
his basement or backyard or wherever. The partner had to
keep his own rough accounts for the route, including charges
for any extra trash not part of the householder's regular
amount, and had to either present the bill in person and
receive payment or provide the office with the appropriate
information for mailed bills. The responsibility was considerable, and for many partners quite onerous. It was, however,
the financial backbone of the corporation, and thus the shareholder's special responsibility. For Lenny the shareholder's
collection responsibility probably had not been as hard as it
was for many scavengers. Meeting the public in that way must

have been his metier, for even while he was "carrying the can," he was also employed as an insurance salesman—a job he had had to give up when he became president.

Lenny himself had bought into the company in 1954, paying $12,000 for his share. Just before he became president, a share had sold for $17,000. He insisted then that this kind of capital growth in the worth of his own share was much less than what was occurring in AT&T, for instance, but it was obviously one of the advantages of partnership.

If a man wanted to become a partner, he first had to spend at least several months as a helper, usually on a number of different routes, working with a variety of crews and partners. The people he worked with then gave their evaluations to the membership as a whole. If a man was subsequently approved by the membership, he bought a share at the price being asked by the partner who was retiring at that time or otherwise leaving the company. There was a kind of consensus among the partners about the price of a share, so that the owner's demands were tempered not only by the buyer's offer but by what other Sunset partners thought was appropriate.

The buyer could virtually count on a 90 percent loan from the Bank of America, secured by his stock, so he did not have to have a lot of cash. From the bank's standpoint, the stock was readily marketable to the company if not to another individual would-be partner, so there was really no risk in the loan. Additionally, the company arranged a check-off of the loan payments from the man's monthly wages, so there was little chance for arrears in payments to the bank. (Even if a man's general finances got in bad shape, as Lenny reported had happened recently to one of the members, he would be able to sell the share.) Moreover, of course, the value of the share was apt to appreciate over time. Within a year or so after Lenny's election, the sale price of a share rose to $21,000, "although there's nothing to warrant it, such as dividends or income," Lenny told me at that time. The rise was apparently an optimistic reaction to his new leadership.

In our first contacts, Lenny took pains to counteract any impression that the scavengers were living on easy street. He pointed out that the company was tied to a rate structure set by the city and that even the approved maximum rate of profit (5 percent) had never been achieved—at least in recent years. He told me, "Last year [1965] the profit was one percent of the revenues," which, with the earnings retained, permitted a dividend of about $200 per partner. The dividends were distributed in December each year, much as if they were a Christmas bonus.

According to Lenny, people generally felt that the scavengers made a lot of money because they had been in better shape than other working people during the Depression. They had steady work then and made about $6–$8 a day—which was good for the times. (The average wage nationwide in 1932 was $14–$15 a week, though considerably more in urban areas.) Many partners saved as much as they could and invested it, especially in property, so some of them had reaped considerable benefit from having a job in the Depression era. But that was all. "The job's not fat city," he insisted. He pointed out further that this kind of work aged a man very fast: "Take a look at some of the men on the truck, and they seem like 70 even if they are only 50."

After this kind of general orientation to the financial status of the company and its shareholders, Lenny took me for a tour of the entire operation. We began by poking our heads into the room next to his where IBM billing equipment was being installed; and he introduced me to several officers in the company as we encountered them in the main office building. Outside we walked around the salvage and paper-bailing area and viewed the outlying buildings, including the meeting halls where, as Lenny told me, "what you would call pizza is served during the meetings."

At that time the dump-and-cover site was virtually adjacent to the Sunset office building, although by 1970 the garbage was being trucked many miles away from the office buildings. Lenny took me in his car for a drive around the cutting area—a hill nearby which was being gouged out and pared down in terraces—to provide the dirt and rock for covering the garbage. The view from the hill over the bay was lovely, and Lenny told me that when they were finished with it they would be able to sell it to a developer for a housing site. It had been a bargain when they bought it, and they would be able to sell it in a few years for a considerable profit. (Actually, ten years later the company had a major office and apartment development proposal underway for which, with an associated developer, they were seeking zoning variances and financing.)

While we were parked talking on the site, one of the people engaged in the cutting operation came up to us and scolded Lenny and me for driving improperly in the area. Lenny took this criticism seriously and apologized. I took his response as illustrative of his success in getting elected by his co-workers.

In our tour, Lenny showed me the area where the fill-and-cover work was then going on. While we watched a truck spill its cargo in front of a bulldozer, he insisted that the local citizens would need to recognize that "it's not *our* garbage, it's theirs" to do something with. Sometime this area would be full, and the city would have to make other arrangements. He explained the cut-and-cover fill process, noting that it was conducted so that, on the one hand, there were no rats whatsoever around the actual site. On the other hand, he pointed out the sea gulls that "we can't do anything about." (They snatch food from the garbage before it gets covered.) I frankly did not see anything to complain about so far as the birds, or even the odors, were concerned—it was a cool day.

I wondered aloud about his concern over the gulls. He reported that some bird-lovers had recently been aroused against Sunset by someone's story that the gulls were poisoned by eating the garbage while it was being dumped and covered by the bulldozers. "The only thing they die of is eating too much," Lenny snorted. "They get so fat they can hardly fly. But they fly around here, and they can be seen from the highway, so people know there is garbage over here."

The real problem with the birds, apparently, was that they gave away the secret of a fairly well-masked operation. Lenny pointed out trees planted and fences erected along the tideland fill area, arranged to screen the operation thoroughly. Indeed, from my own observation I could not believe that people in the distant hills of the next town could even see what would be going on, much less be disturbed by it. (I had driven many times along the highway and never noticed the disposal work going on, because it was virtually invisible from the highway.)

As we drove out of the area, we passed some of the trucks bringing in the garbage. Lenny knew most of the drivers and waved to them, occasionally telling me their names and backgrounds. One, a Mexican-American, had only a couple of months before bought into the company. At one juncture, a truck flew down the road with papers from its load blowing off into the wind and littering the area. Lenny muttered angrily about the "stupid S.O.B." The open trucks are supposed to have a tarpaulin for cover when travelling, he explained to me, but sometimes it is not put on tightly enough. I learned later that each crew shared the expense of its own tarpaulin. While this had the effect of ensuring better maintenance of a given tarpaulin by the crew, it also tended to encourage them to extend its life too long at times, so that sometimes a tarpaulin would be too ragged to be effective enough.

The company was then changing over from open trucks to covered compacters, from which such wind-blown littering could not happen. All about us were scraps of paper caught in the bushes and fences. Lenny explained patiently that every day they have a crew to clean up around the fill area, but it was not possible to maintain it completely neat. Still, he was quite unhappy at the truck that had lost some of its looser refuse; but he seemed to be more disturbed for himself than because I saw it—the muttering was mostly under his breath.

At one point, I asked him a vague question about possible new methods of refuse disposal that envisaged re-use of everything in a closed system, "as with the astronauts," I said. He replied, "You mean composting. But even with composting, you still would have some materials to get rid of." As far as any compost is concerned, Lenny argued, it is not fertilizer itself, but must be enhanced with chemicals in order to be saleable. Even then it has a bad image, he claimed. "Any way you look at it, people consider it's garbage and people won't buy it"—although in consistency and appearance it would look like any other commercial organic fertilizer material. "It's a funny thing: those same lamb chops and French fries that people will have on their plate and eat, as soon as it goes into the cans for us, something terrible happens to it, and it becomes garbage and something awful." He shook his head wonderingly.

My notes on my first encounter with Lenny highlight the problem for the garbageman, even for the president of the company, to reassure the public of the propriety of his ways of dealing with the mess that garbage seems to mean. Juggling the public questions about him and his work is a central social and psychological task that faces the garbageman, and I shall return to this later.

In my first contacts, Lenny was reticent about the finances of the company and the internal politics that brought him to the presidency. Later he was freer. "In the old days," he told me, "competition was so fierce that you were not even supposed to talk with your wife about the scavenger business." (The old bylaws enforced this rule with fines. One passage warned of "our enemies." Even in 1966, proposed new bylaws still warned of helping "rivals" in "their war on this corporation.") Later on, as we got to know each other better, he filled me in with considerable detail on any topic. Also, in the course of our interviews, he gave me the equivalent of a private course in the technical problems of refuse collection and disposal.

The events that led to the scavengers' selecting Lenny in 1965 as their new broom would not have happened, or so it seemed, if the old president had not demanded a salary raise to $30,000. This request raised questions in the minds of many members. As Lenny put it, a $30,000 salary might have been appropriate if the idea had come from the membership and if the company were up to date. A good president would be worth $30,000, he felt (doubtless thinking of whether he would someday be worth it), but such a salary implied an operation that was more modern than Sunset was. Indeed, Lenny's own thrust was modernization. Only ten months into the job, he had already made a lot of changes, which he ticked off to me. It was partly his recognition of the need for such changes that had led to his election as president. The following tape-recorded interview in 1966 gives his view of the story:

We were behind the times. If we were up to date, I didn't think it would be out of line that the president of the company *should* be paid $30,000, but on the same token, he should be *worth* $30,000. And to see our company fall so far back, you know, from what other companies were doing—modern equipment and everything —and we were still packing garbage like we did 20 years ago, except we had a motor in front where the horse used to be. It just didn't make sense to me, and our salaries hadn't been growing from what they had been years ago when the garbageman was making $8 a day in the '30s. In all reality, he should be making $70 or $80 a day, in corresponding ratios to our cost of living index having gone up. But I mean, that amount of money for a garbageman to make is out of the question—I mean, to try to make that overnight. But regardless of that, we stayed behind time.

So we had the revolution and what we had in mind, primarily, was the idea that we would elect a new Board of Directors that would project new ideas for the betterment and growth of the company. But it didn't dawn on me what we had set up.

I won't go into all the details of the revolution. (I use that word, ''revolution,'' but it was just a revolt of the stockholders. I guess

Leonard Stefanelli.

that *could* be classified as a revolution.) Anyway, we asked for a
new board. We had 235 of the stockholders demand immediate
withdrawal or resignation of the present Board of Directors and a
new Board would be elected. [By our plans,] the new Board would
agree to appoint the very same officers into their respective positions. All you would have is a new Board of Directors. . . .

My suggestions were that we keep [the former] president because
he had 30 years' experience in the job, and you just don't come in
and replace presidents overnight. And we felt that a vice-president
should be working with him in conjunction so he knows what's
going on. The way the rumors were in the company was that our
president was the only guy who could run this company. If he died
tomorrow, we'd all go broke. And this was my thinking behind it:
We would keep him as president because he was due to retire; and
in three years' time a new man (as vice-president) could catch up
and learn what the different facts of the business were.

It didn't dawn on me until the last day when the election was being held, on August 27, and I said to my wife, "That man [the president] is going to walk out as soon as this is over, and leave us with the keys." And just as sure as hell, after the election was over, we came back to the Board of Directors' room; we had to sit down; we talked; he came in and dropped the keys right on the table and said, "You want it—it's your company," and out the door he went. I looked in the desk—I work on the garbage truck and what the hell do I know about running a business of this size? Telephone numbers are gone; all the files are cleaned out; there's nothing. The only things that were in here were the books. No personal contacts—*everything* was gone.

"Holy Criminy," I said to myself, "What the hell is going to happen now?" You know, it's Friday night [and all the other officers and administrators had walked out with the president]. We had to send the trucks out Saturday morning, and we didn't have a work list of who the hell worked where, or anything. We stayed down there and called down one of the girls in the office—the bookkeeper. She came down and showed us things that had to be done. We didn't know where the payrolls were; there was *nothing*! Well, she came down and set us off.

Saturday morning we looked through everything. We found the work list, but it wasn't given to us. It was buried underneath some drawer. (We heard later that they were saying, "Those guys will be crawling for us to come back.")

Well, right about then and there (on Saturday) I said, "Holy Christ, we've got to do something," I said. "I'm not going to back down now. We've gone this far, and we've got to do something." So Saturday we got the men out on the regular work assignments. Saturday afternoon we spent down here until about ten o'clock at night; and we were back here at five or six o'clock Sunday morning. We didn't have any trucks going out Sunday: we had to prepare the work list for Monday morning. The guys phoned up and one thing or another. Most of the stockholders just came in and pitched in. [For example,] they didn't moan about being short a man [on a crew], you know; they just pitched in wonderfully.

And then we had a meeting with [an attorney, officers of the other scavenger company, and bank officers, who] set us up . . . [and] told us the first thing to do Monday morning was to go to the bank and get signature cards changed, and all this type of stuff, going down the line. We set it up. The Board of Directors elected me to be President.

So one week went by. Oh boy, I'm telling you I had headaches coming out of my ears, you know. Then the newspaper got wind of it. "What happened?" a reporter asked. I'd never talked to a reporter before. The next day there's a big splash with a picture . . . that says "Scavenger President Ousted."

I mean, you could imagine how stone cold it was to come into an operation of this size—a six-million-dollars-a-year business—and come off a garbage truck and more or less take the reins of it. So I had obstacles to overcome. I mean, out of the eleven members of the Board, I am the youngest one in the company. All the others had 25–30 years' experience in the company, but nobody wanted it. Everybody was, pardon the expression, crapping in their pants. I had to put on a false front where I had to show that I wasn't scared, you know, to give them the confidence that they needed to carry on. But I was going home, and you can't imagine the headaches I was going home with. I mean *headaches.* Christ, I couldn't get to sleep at night or anything. . . . So after about a week, things started to straighten out. . . . There was a lot of hardships and hard feelings that I tried to overcome. . . . Most of the [old] Board of Directors came back—I mean, they stayed. But the key figures [did not]. . . .

But I didn't want to cause any hardship or malice against anybody; that was never the intention. And I wanted these guys to come back, and I've tried to pour oil over the troubled waters during the year that I've been here and tried to bring everybody back together again. And I think we've accomplished this, in most cases. There's a few die-hards hanging out. One has still got his share here, [and works the trucks] because he wants his pension, but we didn't have the same pension then [that is, after the election, pension rights were improved].

Now, since then, we've made God knows how many improvements with just the income we had. We've increased pension benefits. Now, twenty years after a man has worked in the business, he's eligible for a pension. Before, they had to work till at least age 55. If he got hurt on his 54th birthday, he wouldn't be eligible for a pension. We've increased . . . [the] collector's compensation [for his special work]. I mean, just little things, but, you know, you stop and read a list this long if you want to write them down— little things that mean a lot to the company.

The previous president always had the philosophy that we're all a bunch of dumbbells. He once made the statement in the union meeting that garbagemen are not intelligent people, and, not being intelligent, have to be ruled with an iron fist. Well, I have a different philosophy. I believe that if you respect a man for the job he does, you're going to get more out of him. If he doesn't do it, *then* you give him a fine or something if he's a stockholder. Lay him off work or something.

You have to have *some* means of enforcing the rules and regulations. If it was just a private company with hired employees and the man didn't do his job, it fires him. But here you have a company where you have stockholders. They've got an investment in the company; but for the protection of the other stockholders, you either fine him or lay him off. You have to get hard on *some* of them. They're all not—I won't use the term ''unintelligent''—but some of them have got their own mind and you have to try to run a uniform business. We have a system of fines, but if you look at our balance sheet, the number of fines dropped off 50 percent of what it used to be.

For example, if a man tried to run for the Board of Directors, [he was apt to get into trouble]. . . . Nobody was ever supposed to run for the Board of Directors, you were picked or selected. It wasn't democratic at all. A man who had any brains (or any incentive to get out and improve himself so he'd be an asset to the company) couldn't run because it was a sewed-up clique. For example, if you ran, they would call the guys on the telephone: ''That guy's an S.O.B. The company's going to go broke if he's elected. He's a boat rocker, and we've got wonderful plans,'' and this stuff. And they'd swing him.

A man would have an awful handicap knocking out an incumbent, because he's got to get 156 of those votes to overcome that handicap. And if you swing 156, chances are you *still* might not get in because of a, you know, vote scattering.

So what we have now is a democratic form where a guy can come in and run for the Board of Directors. Of course, a guy already on the Board won't like to have anybody running against him; it's just human nature to say, "Well, that guy's just trying to put me out of my job." At the same token, you can't look at it that way. I mean, we've now got three new guys signed up to run for the Board this year. One's a mechanic. They now sign up to run every year.

But if you lost the election in the years before, the previous president would get to you, one way or the other. He'd fine you; he'd catch you on some damn thing—any little infraction of the rules. You'd get a big fine, and it would make anybody else who wanted to run for the Board hesitate. They would look in your account book for errors. . . . Freddie Fontana [a long-term partner] was an example of that.

Now Freddie's been in the business a long time. His uncle was once president of the company, but Freddie spoke out against the last president one time. Freddie's always outspoken—even against his own uncle, who during World War II wanted to send $1000 to Italy, you know, to help the Italian government. Freddie got up and said, "For Christ's sake, relatives or no relatives over there, they're our enemies—we're fighting them." (Nobody, during the war, got drafted in this company but Freddie; or *maybe* a couple of other guys got drafted.)

Freddie is outspoken. He spoke out against the president, and they went through his books and found $86 or something over a 42-year period [Stefanelli is exaggerating for effect] that he couldn't account for, so they humiliated him by saying he was a crook, and they suspended him indefinitely. Now *that's* a way of getting rid of your boat rockers. But that type of attitude catches up with you after a while. They let some guys off . . . but with Freddie—they threw him out, and his whole family suffered. He had to go work as a helper. But we brought him back as a partner and fined him $200 for the shortages in his book. I mean, we had to have him make restitution to the company—it wasn't a fine—it was a form of restitution, because he could not find where that money was supposed to be in his accounts.

Actually, by the time of this interview I had already gone out on the trucks with Fred Fontana, and I knew him as a candid, open person. Lenny had spent much of his growing-up years with the Fontana family (although they were not related) and so was especially likely to be sympathetic to Freddie's situation. This sort of close connection, however, was common among partners. Indeed, perhaps 150 of the partners were related to each other in some way, by blood or marriage.

Membership in the corporation was thus complicated by all sorts of cross-cutting allegiances. Under such circumstances, it is perhaps understandable that when change finally came to the organization, it would be fairly abrupt. That is, Sunset seems historically conservative, and the close ties of the members to each other, both ethnically and by family, would serve to mute change, until tensions would have built to such a point that a slight disruption would finally shift an entire pattern.

These sorts of arrangements must be understood in the context of the traditional ways of administering the company, as expressed in the bylaws. On the matter of injury, the 1934 bylaws used to be extremely strict:

Article 53. — The experience of this corporation clearly shows that its insurance of boss scavengers against casualties has encouraged boss scavengers to a marked and alarming degree to disregard ordinary prudence and precaution in doing their scavenger work, and, in consequence, the corporation is compelled to pay an excessively high rate of insurance and is threatened with the situation that no casualty company will write its insurance.

Said experience also teaches that all the injuries sustained by boss scavengers are the result of lack of care on their part and could have been avoided by them if they had but used ordinary care. This corporation, principally to prevent said threatening situation that no casualty company will write its insurance except at confiscatory rates, and to compel its boss scavengers to exercise ordinary care in doing their scavenger work, does enact this bylaw:

Every boss scavenger or employee who sustains or receives a wound, laceration, contusion, wrench, fracture, infection, rupture, or other injury or damage while engaged in the work of the corporation or while doing anything within or incidental to the scope of his employment, or who contributes to the causing or occasioning [of]

any accident, injury or damage while he is doing anything within
or incidental to the scope of his employment, shall be fined and/or
temporarily suspended from employment. The usual fine shall be
2½ dollars for the first time, but that fine, even for the first time,
may be greater if the Board of Directors in view of the circumstances
impose a heavier fine. Ordinarily, there will be no suspension of
employment for the first time, but the Board of Directors may, in
view of the circumstances, impose suspension of employment even
for the first offense.

This bylaw was not included in the version that was
prepared after Lenny took office. He also relaxed the rules for
calling in sick, but he did not institute a change in the company's policy of *no sick leave.* Considering the various improvements in fringe benefits that he had brought about, one
might have expected that formal sick pay would have been an
obvious innovation. Sunset has never given sick leave, either
for injuries or illness—although by earlier bylaws the Board
of Directors or the President had the right in their judgment
to approve absences with partial pay for each day off. Yet,
Stefanelli was adamantly against regular sick leave.

"Sick leave makes bums out of people," he insists to
this day. And he cites the Philadelphia municipal sanitation
department, where he was told that in order to maintain a
workforce of 1,400 on duty each day, they have to have 2,100
people, particularly to take care of the Monday morning
no-shows as well as other absences. "And in reality, if they
operated the same way we did, they should use only 700
people, because all the garbage is right on the curbs." Sunset
regularly maintains ten percent more men on the payroll than
are needed on any one day; that is sufficient to cover sickness,
vacations, and any other absences.

When a scavenger is sick, he simply does not get paid,
or more usually, the days are chalked against his vacation
leave. Company policy has become liberal on vacation pay—
starting at two weeks and increasing to five weeks, depending

on length of service. And many men do not use all their
vacation leave, forfeiting at least some of it every year. So the
dispatcher will usually ask a man if he wants to charge a seige
of sickness to his vacation days. Perhaps occasionally, a man
may not formally report being sick and off work for one day
or may work only part of a day, and his buddies on his crew
will carry the work for him, perhaps even with some help
from another crew. Also, a benevolent society, the Scavengers'
Protective Union, provides some partial sick pay for long-term
incapacity or illness up to six months. And of course the
Sunset Board or President could always make some special
arrangements for a man in special circumstances. So there
are certain cushions in the situation, but there is no sick leave
as such.

The company rules used to be even stricter about taking
off for sickness. When Lenny worked on the trucks, the dispatcher was really tough, he said:

If you went out and got a heat on [a drunk and hangover] or you
got sick, even legitimately sick, on a Wednesday morning, and you
phone up and say, "I can't come to work," and for some miraculous
reason you could go back to work on Thursday, he wouldn't put
you back to work. You lost Wednesday, Thursday, and Friday, and
there was *nothing* you could do about it. So you didn't get sick. I
went to work with fevers. [As a young single man] I've gone to
work *so* hung over—say, I really would want to *die*! But I knew
that if I didn't go to work that next morning, I'd be off the rest of
the week.

Sick leave would have made a bum out of *me*. Maybe it wouldn't,
but I mean it would have helped. . . . Many a time I'd have liked
to crawl into a hole and died, [but] you carry that can. Maybe that's
what made a "Christian" out of me: You *had* to work; you reached
down and picked up that thing, and you felt like a bowling ball
was rolling around in your head, and you smell a can of dead fish,
and you liked to puke, heaving your guts out. . . . [So you say to
yourself:] "I don't want to go out and get a heat on and do *this*
again; I've got to be stupid [to get drunk that way]." But if I had

had sick leave, I wouldn't have hesitated to phone up and say that I was out. The only time I missed a day of work was on my honeymoon, and the dispatcher found out I was in town [back a day or so early]. It was raining, and I heard the phone ringing. I knew who it was. Who else is going to phone you at 4:40 in the morning? So I didn't answer the phone. [Later,] the dispatcher really ate my ass out. He says, "I needed you out there." But I said, "I didn't hear the telephone." "Bullshit!"

The old dispatcher is no longer around, and the new one recognizes that it makes his scheduling problems easier if he is not so punitive. But the no sick leave system still survives.

Stefanelli's feelings about sick leave as a fringe benefit were apparently founded in a general consensus among the partners about a workingman's human nature. Reading the state of opinion of his members was naturally an important part of the president's job, and only because he was able to do it fairly accurately was Stefanelli able to move some changes into being. For example, it was a firm policy that everyone was paid equally, and for breaching that policy the previous president was censured and left. But considerations of equity also suggested that there be something of a graduated pay scale, Lenny felt, and he successfully proposed one that met the members' views about equal pay for equal work. For example, a partner who collected bills and managed accounts on his route got, under the new system, more than another partner who had not been able to carry that responsibility and had had to be assigned merely to carrying the can or, at best, driving a truck. Such differentiation had to be clearly justifiable, recognized as fair by everybody. And Stefanelli could express the common view of those who elected him. That common view included the opinion that the president and other managers were due no more than any other hardworking partner who collected the dollar bills that paid everyone.

Yet, with all his plans for changes and improvements, Stefanelli did not have a direct answer for the fundamental routine public image of garbage that each man had to juggle —"those lamb chops and French fries that . . . become garbage and something awful." Stefanelli's approach was to modernize the company, open it up for more participation by members, improve benefits, and take generally conventional contemporary business approaches for efficiency and a better return in dollar terms. Some of these changes affected the day-to-day life on the job very little, but some made a great deal of difference. What was the work like, and where would it make a difference that the partners had chosen a new man to change the pattern of their lives?

In the next two chapters, I want to present in full detail two different days on the trucks. The first will offer a basic introduction to the routines of work, the daily technical problems that are solved without much difficulty, the equipment and how it is handled and how it focuses a man's work, the relationship among the members of the crew and how they divide the tasks among themselves, the pace of the work, and so on. The day is relatively uneventful. The route travelled is mostly through a pleasant middle-class area of level blocks of neat small stucco houses and well-trimmed lawns. This day will contrast strongly with the other to be presented, when I had asked to go out on another crew's hardest day in a lower-income area. But the first day, actually my own first day of observations in this study, will offer a foundation of information from which to base a general perspective on the work.

Four

A Day of Routines

THE natural playing out of the rhythms and routines of that quintessentially urban activity—refuse collection —had almost a slow-motion rural quality to it that first day I followed along with a garbage crew. Not that the crew moved lazily down the streets—far from it—but the predictability of their movements came at first to seem like the patterns of a country dance or the repetitive chores that a farmer and his wife deal out to each other. The themes of that first day steadily and inexorably built up and played themselves against each other unremarkably; but then, unexpectedly, somehow what had seemed so unremarkable, the simple weaving of simple tasks, took shape as something very different, stressful, and dangerous. And yet, it *was* just a routine day.

The "boss scavenger" on the route was John Molini, about 55, a very quiet solid man, short but strong. He was reddish-haired with cheeks flamed by patches of broken capillaries. The other regular man, Ron, about 24 years old, was a tall, brawny, handsome fellow of mild and friendly disposition, also Italian. The third, Ed, was as short as John but thin, wiry, and younger, about 30 perhaps. Although Ed was new to the route that morning, he had worked other routes for Sunset for eight years. John had worked for twenty-five years, and Ron for two.

Blanket Work

As I would learn later, on almost every Sunset route, the morning usually began—as this one did—with "blanket work." Blanket work means doing some preliminary chores, using great burlap squares, called blankets, to carry out the refuse before the company truck arrives with each man's carrying cans. One goes around to scattered pick-up locations, where the refuse production is heavy and requires more frequent attention, such as at apartment houses or commercial establishments. There one retrieves the refuse for later collection by wrapping it in the huge burlap squares. These are tied (and carried) by the four corners and bundled to be left inside an apartment house basement or left outside on the street corner; or they are collected in the scavengers' own private pick-up trucks and untied and emptied into the company truck when it arrives on the route from the garage.

In those days, the blanket work could start as early as 4 A.M. unless people in the neighborhood complained about the noise. (Now there is a city ordinance against beginning before 5 A.M.) In any case, it is a way of saving time; it means that the company truck does not have to stop at scattered pick-up locations and wait outside while each retrieval is being made. A crew that wanted to finish earlier would do a lot of blanket work, but they were not required or paid to use their time or personal pick-up trucks for the task.

When I waited for the crew in the dark at 5:30 A.M. on a street corner in that outer oceanside district specifically known as "the Sunset" (from which the company got its name, of course), two of the crew (John and Ron) arrived in their pick-up trucks. Then, suddenly, Ed was also there with the company truck, a compaction model with an opening or "hopper" in the rear into which the refuse is tossed. The contents of the blankets were emptied into the hopper, and one of the crew pulled the lever to compress each hopper full of the refuse tightly into the recesses of the truck. Then, without any consultation or discussion, each of them grabbed his own aluminum carrying cans ("barrels") from hooks on the back of the compacter and proceeded into the yard of each house along the block where we had met. I hurried along behind them. My notes for this day recorded my introduction to five or six major routines, besides blanket work.

The Route Map

Overall, there was the task of keeping the route clearly in mind—where to go, where to pick up at each house, and how much to expect, in order to decide whether to go singly or together. For example, only some houses had their cans on the curb; for others, the crew man would have to find his way into the backyard or garage or somewhere else. A good boss scavenger would have to have the details of the district in his head and also a mini-map of each backyard. First off that morning, I heard John call Ed to close and latch the garden door through which he went to pick up the first batch of refuse, apparently a firm and long-standing demand by that householder, but that was about the most that was said among the three of them as they began work. John knew the route absolutely by memory. He had been assigned to it for seventeen years. "They are not there," he would call, when Ed or Ron would start in to a household for its can. He knew when the people were on vacation, where every can was kept, and how much refuse service the householder had contracted for. John gave any necessary directions with the minimum of words—for example, to orient Ed as to whether we would turn the corner at the next cross-street or go straight down the block, and so on. He once told me merely to "grab on," and I was supposed to know I had to jump onto a small platform on the back of the truck, find some handgrips there, and hang on precariously while the truck zipped past a long vacant block.

The Choreography of the Barrel

The carrying cans or barrels the men were using were standard for the whole company. They were 70-gallon heavy-duty but lightweight aluminum containers on small casters that rolled easily so long as the cracks in the sidewalks were not too wide. A barrel measured about four feet high with a diameter of well over two feet and could accommodate the usual contents of two or three regular household garbage cans if the contents were pressed down hard; that was the most efficient handling, to avoid too many trips back to the truck for emptying.

At this point in the company history, each man still bought and owned his own carrying can. These were made to suit with either a right-handed or left-handed hook that fitted over the shoulder. If the can is not full and heavy, it can be carried by the hook over the shoulder, leaving both hands free to grab bundles of newspapers. In flat areas of the city where the barrel could be trundled along the sidewalks, the casters were standard equipment, but for other routes the casters were removed as more trouble than they were worth. By 1973, under a new union contract, a new wheeled barrel would be furnished by the company every eighteen months, but the worker would still have to pay for ''extras,'' the individual improvements that a man might get made to suit himself. Ordinarily, even with the care devoted to personal cans, they did not last more than about two years, and even under these circumstances they often had to be patched with riveted reinforcements.

The process of hoisting one of these cans was fairly standard for each man. There is really only one good way to handle a barrel without high risk of hurting yourself. To watch the alternating smooth then sharp movements used for lifting a barrel is like watching a trained athlete or dancer. The barrel is first tipped on edge by its heavy U-shaped handle or hook. Then, suddenly, it is heaved by that handle, so that the lower edge of the can rests on one knee bent low to accommodate it, and then with another heave the body twists around so that the barrel lands on one's back. The handle now droops over the shoulder like a supporting lip, but it is still held by one hand. Thus, while the man begins by facing the barrel, he turns around while at the same time hoisting it higher, so that it ends up resting on his slightly bent-over back, the weight also being borne partially by the shoulder over which the handle is cupped.

In the Sunset area of the city, which is relatively flat, the barrel is rarely carried, but trundled from house to house, until finally it is wheeled up to the truck to be emptied. At this point, the intricate series of lifting movements occur. Then the man, having hoisted the can to his back, turns to the hopper and, bowing to it, empties the barrel over his shoulder, usually tipping the whole barrel and contents into the opening at once, or sometimes shaking the barrel to distribute the contents along the width of the rear of the truck.

This heavy task is obviously more than a matter of strength. The far smaller and older men, John and Ed, could handle their barrels with less strain than the younger, larger Ron. I was at first marvelling at how Ed could manage, but I came to see that as slight as he was, he was really working with less trouble than Ron. John, of course, flipped his barrel as if it were a mere 20 pounds, instead of the 100–150 that it occasionally must have been. Mostly, I would judge that the full barrels usually must have weighed about 60–100 pounds, depending upon the amount of bundled newspapers or dirt. Ron told me that dirt and stones, yard clearings, are about the heaviest materials they deal with. At the end of a day, each man has handled several tons on his own.

The choreography of the barrel involves more than filling, lifting, carrying, and emptying. There is an etiquette that must be followed at the hopper to avoid getting in each other's way. The first one to the hopper moves in an oval trajectory from curbside towards the middle of the street as he pours out the refuse and returns to the sidewalk, leaving room for the next one to follow closely behind him along the same path at the rear of the truck. This is important, too, from the standpoint of injuries. Awkward, impetuous, careless, or unknowledgeable workers run into each other. National industry sources (as well as internal studies by individual municipal departments) indicate that the organization of work by teams, instead of by individual collectors working small trucks by themselves, may lead to a higher injury rate. How the scavenger handles his barrel is a mark of his capacity to work with others without subjecting them or himself to possible injury. I seemed to be getting in everyone's way until I was patiently informed that there was a pattern to follow, which I had not been observant enough to figure out by myself.

Managing the Truck

As we worked down and around the block on one side of the street only, Ron might drive the truck a few yards ahead, and in the meantime Ed might trundle Ron's can as well as his own, while John was busily loading his from house to house. But each man drove the truck ahead from time to time, and ordinarily each took care of his own can, hooking it temporarily on the back of the truck if he were the one doing the driving at that moment.

I could not figure out how they decided who was to drive each time, and Ron told me, ''The furthest man back takes the truck.'' ''Never walk back to the truck,'' he said, as if quoting a rule. As each was filling and emptying his can into the packer, he moved back with his empty can to where he or another had left off in the portion of the block behind the truck. Usually a man emptied his barrel once or twice for each time the truck was stopped. When two men had moved to houses ahead of the truck, the third man emptied his can, hooked it on the rear, got in the cab, and moved up a few yards ahead of his hurrying fellow crewmen.

The body of the truck, a huge red hump attached to a white cab, enclosed a ''front blade,'' which remained stationary except for periodic adjustments moving it further forward as the truck filled, and a back blade—a kind of maw that gobbled the refuse, packing it tightly against the front blade until it could pack no more. When it resisted packing more, one of the men (usually Ron, who loved to do it) would go to the forward end of the red hump where there were the gears and clutches to move the front blade a bit toward the cab. Then he would go to the rear of the truck and fiddle with the lever for the rear blade to pack the refuse tightly again against the front blade. This complex adjustment process seemed inordinately difficult and, mechanically speaking, poorly designed; it really needed two people in coordination, one on the front blade, one on the rear.

John would raise his eyebrows or somehow indicate mock dismay (with the least possible movement of facial muscles) at Ron's working of the front blade, which was never very expert. Ron, struggling with the front gears, sometimes choked off the motor and had to go around to the other side of the cab, get in, and start it again. (The door on the blade-gear side would not open due to an accident before they were assigned the truck.) It was always necessary to go back and forth from up front near the cab to the rear of the truck, back and forth between the two gears, the one for the front or holding blade and the other for the back or packing blade. To help Ron out, I occasionally stood by the rear gear and operated it on signals from him. Once I was not right there, and Ron called out peremptorily to John, "Loosen the blade a little bit, John." It was rather bossy of Ron, but John just smiled slowly and did the task, and then poked fun at Ron's struggles: "Through playing with it?" John grinned and jerked his head at me, "It's a toy to him, always playing with it."

The blade-moving business was both an irksome task and a chance for humorous relaxation in the day's cycle. It had to be moved perhaps five or six times for each truckload, and it was nobody's particular task. But Ron apparently loved to do it; it challenged him, and perhaps each time he hoped by expert handling to avoid the barely visible funny look John directed at him. (Even when John did the job, it would not necessarily go smoothly, the truck being a balky thing.)

Late in the day, Ron moved the front blade forward again, to provide more room for the refuse packed against it by the rear blade. John objected, because he felt that the refuse had not been packed tightly enough and that later it would be harder to pack it tightly enough to provide room for all they still had to pick up. "We'll make it," Ron insisted. "We better, or you'll have to collect it in your pick-up truck," John warned with another sigh and humorous grimace in my direction.

Ron had instructed Ed in the back-blade process, but Ed preferred to leave the mechanics to me, while he shuttled back and forth with his barrel. The rear lever might have seemed simple—just pull to start, push to stop—but it too could make one vulnerable to John's quizzical doubts about the operator's intelligence. The packing process is energized by a motor that will not operate while the truck itself is in gear and moving. Apparently there is only enough power for one operation at a time with this kind of truck. I learned about the power problem only because, in my eagerness to be helpful, I once started the packing process just as John was about to drive the truck up to the next stop. Of course, the motor cut out. He did not say anything to me or give me instructions for later on; but I did not do *that* again.

Interestingly enough, this truck was regarded as highly efficient. John had informed me that their crew was "short" one man because they had the use of this truck. With a compacter, presumably three men could do the work of four. Lenny had bought it second-hand to try it out as a step in modernization, but it certainly had its own problems—although, as I was to find out on another route with an open truck, it just as certainly was a great effort saver, bad as it was. Learning to use the new equipment was a small price to pay, and more advanced models were on the way.

Truck 24A was John Molini's.

Pacing the Work and Other Mutual Adjustments

In the early part of the morning, it seemed to me that the men fairly ran up the walks to each house, emptying the garbage cans into the barrel as swiftly as possible and hurrying over the small strips of driveway and lawn to the next door-way, or sometimes retreating back down a driveway to the sidewalk and trundling the barrel along for a couple of doors to the next customer who had something outside and waiting. When the pick-up at a house was extra heavy or presented other handling problems requiring help, or when someone would start to go the wrong way, or for all possible other necessities, John might whistle, or gesture, or grunt a single word at the most, to signal directions. He was a most non-verbal person for a job that could well permit a lot of social talking. For that matter, Ron said little also, though the crew-men occasionally passed a remark or two with each other if they met at the rear of the truck to empty their cans.

I could rarely hear or understand any of their conversa-tion. It was brief and elliptical, as if they found it necessary to save breath, and the words did not carry above the sound of the truck's revving motors or the scraping of the blade and the clang of dumped bottles that crashed and were crushed with the beer cans, watermelon rinds, fat-dripping paper bags, and magazines and newspapers drawn into the moving maw. I once heard John say more than one word—to urge Ron on faster: "What are you waiting for?" he kidded, as Ron paused at the truck before heaving his heavy barrel. It was a humorous remark rather than a directive, and perhaps that is why John found more words were necessary. And I heard Ron advise Ed, "You are better off out here—no hills," because Ed had previously been working in the Upper Mission district, an area of winding streets on the side of a mountain. The flat blocks of regular rows of Sunset district houses are surely easier, but it did not mean that any of them wasted breath talking to each other. If they had merely been fast for my benefit, they could not have kept it up. But they did.

I usually stood by the rear of the truck because they each came there, and it offered the best contact and conversation point, and also because I could work the gear shift for the rear blade and thus participate, however minimally, in the task. (To watch people work so hard and just stand and look is very difficult.) But I would also follow one or another of the crew into the backyards or doorways or garages or wherever to watch the process and ask a question about little variations in the crewman's actions. Each would patiently explain, but none really stopped what he was doing to talk. There was always a certain urgency. It was a cheerful urge to get through, and by no means in response to the boss scavenger. I asked once, "You all trying to make a speed record?" and Ron told me, "No, just want to go home. The thing about this job is that you do not put in eight to ten hours a day; when you are through, you're through, and you go home."

Ron kidded me about my note-taking at one point, but otherwise little or no notice was ever taken of my own task. They all acted as if they were accustomed to being studied! "Ever try one of these?" Ron asked, as he heaved a barrel onto his shoulder. "No, and I don't believe I will," I replied in both mock and real fear. "Why don't you?" he said, "and I'll take the notes for a while."

The humor during the day was work-related and usually understated in John Molini's nonverbal mode. At one point, John stood by the truck and watched as Ed took the top off a garbage can at a nearby house and emptied the can into his barrel. A bit of paper that was on the top fell to the ground. While Ed was pushing the refuse down tightly into his barrel, John walked up, without comment, and picked up the bit of paper that Ed had left there—while Ed trundled his barrel down the walk to hurry to the next house. They all tended to be fairly careful not to leave blowing papers or accidentally-spilt coffee grounds and the like; and most of the time the top of the household refuse can was replaced carefully. So I assumed that John was simply being neat, and I marvelled at the sense of responsibility not to leave even a little scrap of paper on the householder's lawn. But something else was at stake in John's mind as he ambled back to the packer and stood there till Ed returned to dump his barrel. Then he opened up the bit of paper, revealing two quarters which had been tightly wrapped. He grinned at me, nodding at Ed's amazement and discomfiture: "She pays each week this way" was all he said to us, and then he rolled his own barrel off to pick up on the other side of the street. Of course, most householders paid when the collector came by in the evening, once a month or every two months.

John told me that today they were working his particular collection route; but on another day it might be Ron's route or the route of the crew member whom Ed was replacing while he was in the hospital. Thus, today John was making all the notes about extra cans and so forth.

John told me, when I questioned him as he made a note once, that a house occasionally had more rubbish for collection than was regularly paid for. "It's too early in the morning to bang on the door and collect the extra, but they pay all right," he said, his eyes twinkling as he pocketed his note and stuck his pencil part way under his cap. Nothing escaped his eyes. But he never seemed to make a note unless there was really a whole extra can at the house. A few items, a box full of trash beside the can—these got by.

Coffee break time came about 8:30 A.M., and we stopped at a diner. During the break, I got some orientation from John about the pick-up trucks they use before they meet the packer each morning. The collection from the apartment houses on this route begins perhaps at 4:30 A.M., or as much before 5:30 as is necessary so that that task is done before the packer arrives. Also before the packer arrives, each man will have taken care of one or more special collections from a private householder who has complained that he was by-passed the day before (usually because he had forgotten to unlock his garage, Ron told me) or who has asked for special extra service that week. John informed me that doing these apartment house and special complaint jobs before the packer arrives is up to the crew's discretion. It is done that way because it takes less time for everyone than to drive around in the packer all together. The scavenger may own a truck for this express purpose, but he is given no expense allowance for using it. Both Ron and John have their own pick-ups, as I had noticed when I met them.

The driver who picks up the packer at the yards (in this instance, Ed) is also responsible for cleaning it up after he has taken it to be weighed and unloaded, at the end of the day. If the day's route has been a short one, Ed told me, he will be assigned to "jobs"—that is, some special pick-ups at a housing project or industrial plant, and so on. The other scavengers are presumed to use comparable extra time on such a day for collecting payments—from customers who do not use the wrapped-coin process.

Route work varied naturally for a whole lot of reasons. This morning, Ed discovered that, unlike other routes, here he was not to save the newspapers separately. The reason: the compacter did not have the side-racks that were on the trucks he usually worked on.

Salvage practices and opportunities were generally a variable matter. At one house, a rug showing considerable wear and a number of holes had been put out. Ed to Ron: "Should we save this?" Ron: "No." So it was dumped in with the rest to be buried at the fill-and-cover operation. Ron said to me: "It's just like throwing money away, but we don't have racks on this truck for salvage, so there's no way to save it. This truck was used in an area of public housing projects, so there's no racks." Some routes are known to be without many salvageable items, and the trucks for them may not be equipped to carry something to be saved. In the Sunset district, however, there is more to scavenge; even so, with this truck they were not even setting aside the bundled newspapers.

About the only salvage on this trip was a group of four *Playboy* magazines that Ed managed to stick on a shelf under the rear of the truck. Ron saved a wooden cigar box: "You don't see those much, these days." Every once in a while, an item would attract someone's attention, but ordinarily nothing was worth saving, or else there was no place for it—as in the case of a bent-up children's tricycle that made Ron shrug his shoulders. John fished out a man's small jewelry box, but when he opened it, there was nothing inside, and he tossed it back into the clutching, grabbing blade, and shook his head ruefully.

With newspapers heavy on this route, there was some more discussion about whether the packer would take what was bound to be coming in the blocks still to be canvassed. Ed told Ron that newspapers packed better if they were watered, and at one stop he started to hose some water into the hopper, dragging up a lawn sprinkler from someone's lawn, but just then he noticed that the water would not collect in the hopper to wet the papers, since something (paint and turpentine) was already dripping from openings at the bottom of the hopper. "Other trucks have plugs you can pull out or put in, so you could do that," Ron remarked to Ed. Ed said that trucks on which he had worked had neither plugs nor permanent holes. Ron told him a story about someone who had once put a lot of water in the hopper with the load of refuse, to impress "the girls." (Women employees operate the scales at the land-fill area where the trucks weigh in, and they record the number of tons.) "So when he was weighed in, they said, 'Oh, you are *really* working out there!'" They laughed together at the story.

Meeting the Public

If working out a daily adjustment with fellow crew members offered opportunities for humor and diversion, dealing with customers, the public, was equally rich in ways to make the day go faster. When someone had apparently forgotten to put out his can the night before, it was sometimes part of the game to bang resoundingly on the garage doors to wake them up so that they would come down and bring it out before the truck moved on. Ed did this more than the others. But I could not figure out when he decided to do that, perhaps just for fun, and when he would merely shrug his shoulders and go on, leaving the householder to worry about it when he woke up too late. In any case, we saw some interesting sights, men, women, old, young, of many different races, and in various stages of sleepy undress, rush out of their front doors to unlock the garages so the crew could go in for the garbage cans.

These sights apparently offered more than humor on occasion. Ed and Ron discussed a supposedly exceptionally endowed young woman who lived on Ed's former route and who "*every* Thursday" indicated her availability for sporting purposes. Occasionally, Ed and Ron would make some loud, salacious double-entendre in the presence of an attractive woman passing by. Ron (as if asking whether there was too much trash for Ed to carry out) would call out: "Can you make it?" Ed: "Yeah, I can make it." Or Ed would snicker: "I need a hand here." And Ron would reply: "You used it too much at home."

Ordinarily, however, the sexual kidding was muted and more innocent. As the morning wore on, more and more people would be on the street hurrying to catch a bus for work, and the women fresh for the day elicited true appreciation.

A pretty young girl came by, and Ed said very formally but with a grin, "Good morning, ma'am." She was startled, but smiled and said, "Good morning." Ron, who observed this exchange, told me in mock seriousness, "We've got to be friendly with *all* the customers." They made sure to make arrangements to cross the path of each attractive woman who could be seen coming down the street.

Relations with the public were, of course, also a matter of conducting business. There were perhaps four or five special written messages or other sorts of householder-scavenger communications along the route this morning. One penned note asked that the emptied can be placed in a recessed corner out of sight from the street. John volunteered an explanation: "You wouldn't believe it, but people do steal garbage cans—full of garbage too!" Another note said only: "Please take this can also. We are getting a new one."

By the time we neared the end of the route, there were, of course, more residents up and about. Some were outside their homes, offering directions to the scavenger or asking for special work—to carry away tree clippings or other garden refuse. One elderly couple had six large bags of dirt that the man had taken out of his little patch of front garden, "to level if off," he told me. He thought I, with my notebook, was an inspector. Ron and I did not disabuse him when he kidded Ron about doing his work well or else I would report him. Ron charged and was paid three dollars in cash to take the dirt. I privately thought that sounded like an awful lot, but it was not, as I found out. I asked Ron how he was able to set a price on such things. "They were old people," he said, "so I let them have it for less. That's pretty heavy." A few moments later, when I had a chance to ask him, I said, "How much would it ordinarily have been per bag, a dollar?" Ron: "Yeah, probably. That stuff is heavy, I don't like to take it, and they could actually do something with it, put it in the back yard. If it had been six bags of garbage, it would have been seventy-five cents for it all. Maybe I am wrong, but. . . ." Setting prices for extra work was not an easy routine. It called out all the potential human ambiguities, because in fact there was, I could see, no way to standardize the charges easily. For Ron, then, in this case, the friendliness of the elderly couple and perhaps their obviously modest circumstances conflicted with his responsibility to bring in the maximum revenue.

Toward the very end of the route, we picked up a lot of wood and debris from a house being remodeled. Some of the wood was so long that it had to be broken before it could be packed. John operated the rear blade in such a way as to break up each length, then release it, so that it could be thrown in sideways for packing purposes. I wondered about the cost of this service, for John did not seem to make a special note on this.

In the last half of the work day after the coffee break, the urgency and scurrying was not as evident. By that time, the work had squeezed out the juices of early morning energy, and even John seemed less casual, less cheerful. At one point, his calm dropped away and he became provoked at Ron: Ron had pointed ahead at a group of overflowing cans and boxes in front of a garage door and complained to John, "Look at this." He made as if to skip that collection, to leave it to John. It was an especially heavy and messy pick-up. John growled, "It won't bite you." Ron laughed: "It won't bite me, 'cause I ain't taking it." John went over and got part of the load, as Ron took the other part. John made a note of the extra amount put out by the householder. Ron said loudly to me: "Wait'll he [John] goes on vacation! Then I'll leave *everything*." John refused the joke and remarked sourly, "They'll pay for it. Don't worry about it."

Perhaps because Ron had only worked at the job for two years, he was actually more visibly tired than the other two. He would pause a moment before slinging his barrel up to his shoulder. Once he pulled his shirt away from his shoulder and showed me a blister, broken and raw from the heavy barrel handle. I asked John and Ed whether the way they commonly lifted their barrels irritated the skin the way Ron's was. John said that knee and shoulder calluses do develop, but after being on the job for a while, "you don't feel nothing anymore." Ed agreed.

Ron, off and on, wore protective gloves, but John and Ed did not. Ron also wore a kind of heavy rubber chaps, which he told me helped protect him and his pants from wear and tear from the barrels. ''Some guys can't wear them,'' he said, because the rubber does not permit enough air circulation and causes rashes. Ron often grunted and sighed, but not the others. He was the first to need water, which he got by turning on the hose in the garden of one household where I had followed him. But all three men were slower as the day wore on.

It was a warm day, and Ed and John also took a drink once or twice from a garden hose along the way. It was a casual use of their customers' facilities, without asking. It was expected, perhaps, but no one offered them a cold drink or otherwise offered hospitality. In particular, I wondered how the ordinary bodily needs for water or for urination could be met in this neighborhood. They never asked for toilet facilities, and I gathered that one trained oneself to wait until the coffee break and use the facilities at the diner to which we drove.

This day happened to work out okay for me. However, not being accustomed to planning the use of the toilet during the day, I would sometimes be in real trouble in the course of this study when I went out on trucks in a neighborhood like this where there were no commercial establishments. Indeed, I learned that the men themselves occasionally faced the same problem, and they would suggest to me a dark corner in an unused basement or in some protected areaway where we could relieve ourselves. That might not be possible, however, when the basements were clean and no other protected areas were available. Once when I was in most urgent circumstances, my best friend among the scavengers offered me the use of his carrying can (because it was a very clean basement). The scavenger thus may have to press his own barrel into use for personal needs.

These homely details illustrate why being a garbage worker could isolate one from the simplest refreshments of life, which are thoughtlessly enjoyed in other occupations. The worker on the garbage truck sometimes gets into trouble with householders who object to his using their garden hose. And sometimes a man returns to work the next day and learns that in the meantime there has been a complaint telephoned to the company because he had urinated (he thought, invisibly) behind a garage someplace.

Such things are, of course, insignificant in comparison with the general physical strain of the work or, worse, the risk of injury. This day with John Molini was uneventful; no one strained his back or cut himself on glass sticking out of a paper bag. But Ed was a substitute this day for a scavenger who was in the hospital.

We were working down a broad street towards the end of the day, where every so often you could get a glimpse of the sea not a half-mile away, and then Ron nudged me solemnly. There were big ugly red-brown stains beside us on the street. That was where the crew member yesterday had been struck down by a city bus as he moved around the truck. There he had lain and bled until the ambulance came. Then suddenly a bus came up to us. The driver stopped it near us, though it was the middle of the block. He called out to ask us worriedly how the man was. It was the same bus driver who had hit the scavenger the day before! "He's on the hospital critical list." The men were not friendly with the driver.

This basically uneventful day that had allowed me to focus on the common routines of the work suddenly revealed a hidden danger of the job. Yet, the dramatic accident was only a very visible symptom of chronic physical stress and danger. We finished up at 10:45, driving around to pick up some more blanketloads of refuse that had been collected while Ed took the first compacter load to the dump; and so we completed the compacter's second load. It had been a short work day, measured in hours, but surely a long day, measured in the life of a scavenger. The pressures they had put on themselves to finish early they would have to pay for somehow, some day.

Moving along with John Molini, Ron, and Ed was a good introduction to the customary round of the scavenger partners and their helpers. Yet, as I was to learn, the work was very much more than an uneventful, plodding routine of picking it up and putting it down. The work has its dangers, unusual rewards, and unexpected disappointments. Indeed, part of the enjoyment of the work (as well as some of the penalties) lies in the realm of the unexpected.

The next chapter, which is virtually an extract from my field notes, speaks to this issue. It is not a typical day; yet it is typical in its exemplification of the myriad opportunities for the unexpected and the rewards and discontents of human events along the way. Partly, of course, the differences in days with different crews are a function of the individuality of the men involved. As the reader will surely see, each crew calls out different things in an observer moving along with them. Freddie Fontana and his crew became especially important to me as they took me into their confidence about the problems and enjoyments of the work.

Five

Encountering the World

AT THE SAME TIME that Molini and his men had a packer, Freddie Fontana and his crew were still using an open truck. True, it was sturdy, well-built, with fine square lines. Painted fire-engine red, it sported decorations like an old-fashioned beer truck or circus wagon. But it was a brutal challenge to the stamina of the crew. It had a set of six corrugated iron steps next to the driver's space, up which the scavenger would dart almost in a run, with his barrel steadied on his back with one hand, and sometimes with something else, a bundle of magazines, for example, in his other hand. He would tip his barrel over the front wall of the body of the truck and then return down the steps to other households until his barrel was filled for another run up the steps. Every so often, someone had to get inside the body of the truck and with a pitchfork re-distribute the refuse away from the spot where they had dumped it in.

There were four men on the crew for this truck—because it was not a packer and therefore required more manpower. They were Freddie Fontana, the boss scavenger, the man basically responsible for the route; Nick Demis and Ernie Samietz, designated as collector scavengers, since each of them shared with Freddie Fontana the task of collecting bills from individual householders or apartment managers; and Ray Rodriguez, a non-shareholder driver-helper, who did not do bill collection work but who, on this crew, had the special tasks of driving the truck from the garage in the morning to the route, driving to and from the dump for two or three loads during the day, and then finally returning the truck to the garage at the end of the day. (In addition, Ray, like all Sunset drivers, whether partners or not, was responsible for the general cleaning of the truck.) Each of the men took turns driving the truck along the street during the time they were loading it up. The allocation of this stop-and-go task went to whoever at that moment had not already passed the truck to collect on ahead of it—as Ron had explained to me earlier, on John Molini's route.

The district that Freddie covered each week was the Haight-Ashbury and included 1,700 customers. In mid-1966, when I began the study of this company, the Haight, as it was often called, was not the nationally known hippie haven it was shortly to become. I had chosen to go out in it on the suggestion of my wife, who had been studying the mental health of the community. In general, the area was pretty run-down, rapidly moving toward slum status then, though it did have some nice middle-class homes and even some fancy apartments way up the hill in what is called Ashbury Heights. An active citizens' association was trying to stabilize the lower area, but the later influx of young people probably did more, in the end, to reverse the trend of deterioration. At first, the enormous increase in the youth population was to make things even worse, but eventually values went up as it became the "in" thing to rehabilitate and live in one of the attractive old houses.

The area was extremely congested. The houses were generally set very close together or even directly connected along the hilly narrow streets. Sometimes, covered passageways leading from the public sidewalk ran between adjacent houses,

offering dingy dark warrens by which the scavenger could go
to the rear of a house to reach the garbage cans. Occasionally the cans would be set outside in front, but not often.
Frequently they would be inside garage doors that opened
directly onto the public sidewalks; or one might pass through
the garage to the rear of the house to find the cans. Thus,
entry ordinarily required the use of keys, and the scavenger
always carried along in the truck a cigar box filled with the
keys for the day.

City regulations require that the scavenger pick up the
garbage from whatever location the householder requests. Of
course, the more complex the procedure for gaining access,
the more work it entailed, and the householder is charged for
it. For example, by 1974 the extra charge for each flight of
stairs was fifty cents. So a resident of a fourth floor flat, for
instance, could have his refuse picked up right outside the
kitchen door on the back staircase, if he wished to pay $1.50
extra a month. (As Freddie Fontana once said, "Look at it
this way: It saves arguments in the family about who is going
to carry it down.")

Although I had already been out with Freddie's crew
before, the day reported on here was supposed to be different. I had asked them to let me go out on their hardest day,
and it proved to be awfully hard work; yet I felt it was not so
different from their other days.

As daylight came, the exhilaration of the out-of-doors
on a beautiful day was some compensation for the hard physical labor—one of the pros in the pros-and-cons of the job
that Freddie emphasized to me as we went along. The physical effort, however, was not the only stress. I got to see and
understand why every scavenger seemed to feel that collecting
the money was the real burden of the job. In the early days
of my study, bill collection was usually still being done in
the evenings, although computerized mailed billing was already being substituted. However, then as now, some bill

Before daybreak on a Haight-Ashbury street.

collection takes place during the day in the process of meeting the householder while picking up the refuse. And I saw some of the tensions in these encounters over bills that day.

Of special interest, also, in this day's work were the breaks in the day that provide a respite from the heavy work: the aggressive kidding among crew members and with customers, and the evaluation by the men of their status as garbage collectors. I have included in this chapter everything I was able to record that day, even including Freddie's irritation at a fellow Italian, a customer whom he called a "typical Dago."

It was cold and black that morning when I joined Freddie at about 4 A.M. at the door to a little basement storage room off Haight Street. (The use of this room was donated by a customer to store the blankets and other equipment.) Freddie was a bit later than I, and for a couple of minutes I stood around, jiggling from time to time to keep warm. Because of the cold, Freddie noted later in the morning, "There are not many of them out today." (He was referring to the hippies.) Despite the cold, when the teamwork began with the arrival of the truck, the faces of the men soon glistened with sweat that swiftly gathered in big drops to run down their cheeks. But since I was less active, I found it necessary to warm myself from time to time by leaning against the hood of the constantly running motor.

Before the arrival of the truck, early blanket work had brought Ernie, Nick, and Freddie together to handle a block of larger apartment houses, in some of which the cans were stored on every landing of the back staircases. We would enter the usual shadowed walkway by the side of the building, and then the men would go off in all directions in a maze of passageways in the back courtyards, sometimes without a word, sometimes with murmured agreements. I might be in the rear courtyard of one house with Freddie, and we would hear Nick on one side, invisibly separated from us by a board fence, tamping the refuse into his barrel, and Ernie, just as audible and invisible in the courtyard of the house on the other side of us.

The streetlights were dim, the night black. The blackness of the night stayed on even after the truck came at 5:30. The men, quietly and swiftly peeling off from the truck into the dark passageways on either side of the street, were ghostly walkers, bent under their shining aluminum barrels like astronauts with huge oxygen tanks. Each was alone and yet each was still a part of a group, even though the darkness of the morning meant less communication back and forth than would be true later on.

The sky was black, yet sharply bright with stars when we began. When the sun came up, it became more beautiful. The hills and houses rise on that route in such a way as to hide the east, so that you cannot see the dawning color if there is any. That day the color was transported in pink clouds almost directly above us. The lightening sky was an unusual baby blue. A gull flying at a great height was caught in the sun's rays, incandescent, rosy, and haloed from sunlight still hidden from us. The gull announced the dawn when the sun had not yet reached the little canyons of the Haight-Ashbury streets. The work was transformed by the beauty of the morning.

We drove our jerky, stop-and-go way through the streets, a morning's momentary interest to the children and adults who wiped the haze from their windows to look out at us from their warm apartments. The air did not lose its chill until the morning was almost over, but the day was fine and stimulating. Yet, as the morning wore on, the cheerfulness of Freddie's expression changed to a strained inwardness, from his concentration on the heavy work. His blonde curly hair was matted with sweat under the cap which he removed occasionally to wipe his forehead.

We were still on the morning's blanket work before the truck had arrived when Freddie and I heard and saw a young man running with considerable speed and shoe-slapping noise across the intersection a half block away. He was remarkable only for the obvious haste he was in. But in a few minutes Ernie came up to us in his truck, got out, and told us the story. "You know Joe's bar up there on Haight? I was going in the alley to pick up their can, and when I started to move it, the guy jumps up and, whoosh, runs right by me! I didn't know what was happening, but I looked around, and there in the back door of the bar his brace and bit still hanging on it! About twenty holes he'd already drilled. A few more minutes and he'd have knocked out the panel and been inside!"

The morning's thwarted burglary offered considerable material for discussion for the next two hours or so. There was interminable kidding back and forth about Ernie's letting the guy get by him without knocking him out. There was much detailed talk about how "I would've dropped the guy" or how "I would've let him have it"—all of which involved great strength and bravery, although they all agreed that actually they would have probably been too surprised to do anything either.

Later on, Freddie and I dropped by and took a look at the door ourselves. And quite a bit later in the morning, Freddie went into the bar to check out what had happened, according to the "swamper," the clean-up man at the bar. Ernie and Freddie had pointed out to me that the clean-up man's arrival for work would have surely surprised the burglar if Ernie had not, indicating the burglar's poor knowledge of his task. Freddie came out chuckling from the bar. "I just asked him if he's seen my brace and bit around, 'cause I'd left them somewhere. You should have seen his face when I asked him that. He thought for sure I was the burglar come back."

Immediately after Ernie's discovery, the crew had hashed over and over whether to report the event to the police. Freddie told me that in the course of his work he had reported a couple of deaths over the years—"once some nut jumped off a roof"—but it had always meant a lot of trouble. "The police ask you why *you* were there. Imagine! I always say, 'Don't get involved,' but I do." For more than half an hour, whenever two or more of the crew crossed paths during the blanket work, they wondered whether to tell the police and how. Finally, Freddie muttered something sententiously about "civic duty," and as we came to a police car, he called over the news to the parked policemen. They already knew about it and said another car was engaged in the investigation.

The job brings the scavenger in touch with the many human problems of a neighborhood. And the continuity of his route means that he keeps in touch on an on-going basis, following continuing stories episode by episode. Later on in the morning, Freddie talked about the owner of a place where I noticed the smell of paint: "Yeah, they've been painting there," he said, as he emptied the can into his barrel. "The poor old guy—the owner—was trying to help them out, did too much, and got a heart attack. He's probably dying. Should have let them do the work by themselves, but he was trying to help them."

More mundane matters also have a day-by-day or weekly continuity. For instance, I would help out a bit by closing and re-locking the garage or passageway doors as the scavenger I was following at the moment emerged ahead of me, his hands occupied with the barrel or loaded blanket. But once, when I made to do so, Freddie said: "No, don't need to. He'll be up soon." But other customers would be staying in bed later and would not want their doors open for the day yet, so I would relock their doors. Freddie seemed to know the different schedules of each customer by heart.

Concern for the customers' idiosyncrasies could be mixed. On a previous day, the crew had explained to me that rain-water collects in uncovered garbage cans, and to prevent this they would often punch holes in the bottom of the customer's cans (with or without his knowledge). It was one of the many "tricks of the trade," as they said, that made the work easier. Early this morning I got to see the hole-punching operation. They used a spike hammer, called a "bit," on one customer's can. The bottom had filled with water from the recent rains, adding a lot of weight as well as making the task of emptying it more messy. In this particular courtyard there were a couple of garbage chutes (one serving each tier of apartments), and so both Freddie and Nick were there working together. Freddie had not made much progress in punching holes in the up-turned bottom of the new can, so Nick took over. Freddie got nervous about the noise when Nick kept making more holes (about eight in all). "Not so hard. This one, she's

crazy''—that is, she often complains about noisy scavengers.
The whole courtyard was reverberating (at 5 A.M.) with the
punched drum. Also, they did not want her to know that
they were ''improving'' her can. ''Every time I come to collect, she has to tell me how much the barrel cost her.'' The
courtyard was a very clean place, and Freddie said that he
tried to keep it clean. They indeed left the place as clean as it
was before, with an improved can. Talking about a more
middle-class district, where I was planning to go next, Freddie
said, ''The Richmond is all like this, and we like it that way.''

The work day was more frequently punctuated by breaks
on this route. It was coffee and doughnuts at 5:00, after the
blanket work was done and before the company truck came;
a rest stop at 7:00, when the men sat on the convenient front
steps of a house somewhere along the way and consumed a
can of beer apiece; breakfast about 8:00, while the driver took
the truck on the first run to the dump; and then a final break
around 9:45, when the work was nearing the end but one
perhaps needed a little extra (whiskey) to get through. The
breaks also offered a chance for exchange of information on
tasks to do that day as well as for needed relaxation. (For me
they were a welcome interruption when I could catch up on
notes or ask questions.)

At the beer break, the men chatted about their company
meeting to be held in the evening. It was scheduled to orient
the men to the new rate increase that was being announced
in the papers that morning, and how to handle the matter
with customers. ''Now we got to get ready for the complaints,'' Freddie predicted. But apparently no one read the
morning papers closely enough, for I heard no customer bring
it up all day. In fact, the only complaint I heard was when
one woman ran up to the crew to ask, ''Did you break my
door yesterday?'' The accusation was denied gently by each
man, no one taking offense.

Working hard and fast, somehow the crew was also easy-
going. The breaks probably made a great difference. And, as

on John Molini's crew, there was lots of humor. Sometimes the ribbing would get pretty aggressive, but most of the time it was pretty good-natured.

"Hey, stupid!" anyone might call out. And any of the others would be apt to answer back absent-mindedly. As seems customary, the flat of the hand would slap a locked garage door to alert the occupants to get out their refuse can immediately, but if Nick banged the door, Freddie would groan: "Go ahead! Break the door, Nick!" But it was not only Nick who got ribbed. Once Freddie was so loud and vehement with Ernie—I heard only Freddie's loud voice, Ernie's being quite low—that I thought surely they were seriously quarreling. Then they emerged from a passageway. "I'll drop yah," Freddie snarled. Ernie grinned and ducked his head, and Freddie chuckled, and only then did I realize that it was all a game, as usual. Freddie once told Ernie that the load needed some distributing, but Ernie said, "You're not going to get *me* to go into that truck!" But of course he did.

At the 5 A.M. coffee and doughnuts break, the doughnut man announced loudly (and falsely) that Ernie was paying for "coffee-and." This of course occasioned loud plans to order several dozen doughnuts, though actually in the end only Nick and I picked out one or two from the assortment at the counter. (And Ernie treated us.)

During the whiskey break, Freddie gave Nick a hard time over a live young pigeon—a "squab"—that Nick was given by a customer to take home for cooking. Nick did not want to touch the live bird any more than necessary, owning up to a fearful aversion that was apparently well known to the crew. They put it in a bag for him, with air holes, so that he could carry it home that way; but he had to suffer some jokes as a price for their help. Freddie, for his part, took a few remarks from the others from time to time—Ernie once loudly demanded my notebook to write about Freddie's laziness—but maybe Freddie felt he had been a little too hard on

Nick about the squab, because he poked fun at himself a few moments later, some remarks about his own family.

As usual, fun was also poked at passers-by as well as fellow crewmen. Sometimes the passer-by was aware and joined in; sometimes not. A tremendously large woman walked down the street, and I was told that she was married to a very tiny Filipino. He was not in evidence, which occasioned the remark that he had to have a rope tied around his ankle and then to the bed post, for safety purposes, while engaging in marital relations. In another incident, which I did not observe in its entirety, three crewmen somehow all ended up in the backyard of a woman customer to do some special service. They came trooping out together carrying a large cast-off rug pad. I laughed to see all three of them carrying something together that one would ordinarily handle; and they were laughing too, about the lady customer's swearing in a comradely fashion with them. Freddie said: ''I told her, 'Being as you talk our language, lady, we'll do it for you for nothing.' ''

At the breakfast break, I learned to wash my hands with Ajax scouring powder, but, mercifully, Freddie suggested that Ernie let out the black water that they had used jointly so I could get a new basinful. ''We've used that enough,'' Freddie said soberly.

The little restaurant where we had breakfast was about as appetizing as the washroom, but we all ate heartily in a back booth that was conveniently reserved for the crew. Across from us at another booth, another scavenger crew was finishing up. We had a few remarks with them, but they soon left. As we finished our own breakfast, I was asking questions— one of which was perhaps too probing, as I will describe presently—and first Ernie and then Nick got up and went out to do some blanket work until the truck returned. But Freddie wanted to talk, and he and I lingered on still longer over our coffee.

Freddie got to thinking about the "old regime and the new regime." "I guess Lenny told you about what happened," Freddie began. I replied that Lenny had been very tactful, and I had not been told all the details, but I had gathered that the previous president had really been voted out. "After nineteen years! That guy really had us all believing that we couldn't do any better. He was all for getting it himself but none for us. He pulled something on me personally, and got me suspended. I was *out*! Can you imagine that? Oh, he found some mistake in my books, going back over them for five years or so. Everybody can make a mistake, but he was looking for one, and you can always find a mistake if you are looking for it. And that was his excuse. The Board suspended me, and I had no job. I had to work as an extra man. Then finally I got back in."

Freddie told me that the former president was a "bulldozer," and no one would stand up against him. "He would just fool them. Let me tell you, one time at Christmas he said that there would be enough for a little dividend, maybe four–five hundred dollars—not much, but it would have been nice. And you know what he said? He started telling them that it would be taxed twice, once as corporation income and once as their own personal income, so that it would really cost a lot of money to distribute it as a dividend. He said, 'I am going to do you fellows a favor, I am not going to distribute it, so you won't have to pay the tax on it.' And they clapped for him! They didn't know what he was doing! I tried to tell them. That's when I got into trouble with him."

There have been a lot of improvements since then, Freddie averred. But there were a lot of changes that still would have to be made. He mentioned one boss scavenger, pointing out that the man's work illustrated one thing still wrong with the company. The man worked hard, was honest and a fine fellow, but he just didn't know how to maintain the rate schedule for his customers. "If I had his route, I would get

six–seven hundred dollars more out of it." Freddie detailed
for me the unsophisticated "deals" that the man would make
with customers, in which, for example, they got regular
double service for much less than other customers on other
routes. "That's the kind of thing that will make trouble."
When a customer moves from one route to another, they will
not understand why they cannot get the same service from
the new route boss for the same price.

"We can't get enough good people," Freddie noted.
"For instance, we have to depend upon men from the old
country. Not that they are dumb, they just don't know the
language; and they don't know how to figure things. Now, if
we had it set up simple, like we *have* to eventually, it would
solve a lot of problems. If we charged only by the can, anyone
could at least count the number of cans; and it would be
definite. Also, there needs to be some schooling." As he saw
it, when each new man is brought into the company—as an
extra man, in the early stages of his employment—he should
get a standard indoctrination on how to work. The way it is
now, he will go from crew to crew to get oriented, and he will
see that people do things differently everywhere. But when
he is permanently assigned to a crew, he will of course do it
the way that crew does it, and he will come to think that that
is the right way. Moreover, he'll pass that on to the next one.
"That's the way it gets kept in the old, wrong ways," Freddie
explained. "Naturally, you work the way the other guy shows
you. You wonder, 'Will I get along with the guys on the
truck?' And you do it their way. But it's not necessarily the
right way."

Our breakfast that morning was very leisurely because
Freddie took time to orient me to a lot of things. But perhaps
one of the most illuminating interchanges took place while
Ernie and Nick were still there, when I asked about the public
standing of the scavenger. I had broached the topic of how
outsiders view the scavenger. I reported that one scavenger
on another crew had said that when he told people what he
did, they did not want to have anything to do with him. Since

this was different from my idea of how San Francisco felt about scavengers, I wondered whether any of them had ever had that sort of experience themselves—say, when talking in a bar. I addressed this question to the three of them, but really made it so that Freddie would take the lead in answering it. Freddie agreed that there was a problem with some prople. "I'll tell you the truth, and we ought to speak the truth now, fellows, if there was ever a time. I was ashamed all those years when I had to tell my friends in school that my father was a garbage collector. But I don't feel that way about the job now. Yet, let's face it, we stick the colored [that is, disparage black people], but *we* pick up their garbage."

Maybe both my question and Freddie's response were too open and too anxiety-provoking. At any rate, I could not get anything from the other two at the time. Ernie shook his head, became quite abstracted, and then got up from the table after a moment or two and left. When I asked Nick, "What about you? Did you ever have any of that experience?" he evaded me with a smile and said, "I never go into bars." I tried to get around his evasion, but he merely put me off. "You don't find much of that. I never have." (Later he talked more.)

Nick stayed with us only for a while, as Freddie talked on about the history of the company, but then he too moved out, presumably to do a little work; and, in fact, when we finally joined Ernie and Nick, they grumbled mutinously about Freddie's staying so long at breakfast and leaving them all the work to do. Their grumbling was all in good fun, of course, but it was significantly tension-relieving, as became clear when Ernie said to me, "Gimme that note-pad! I want to put down how that guy is fucking off." Freddie nodded sagely, "You see, Stew? No respect for the boss." I told them I would make a note on all of this, and proceeded to do so.

Freddie must have kept on thinking about some of the things he had told me, about the way the former president had run the company and the status of the scavenger, for, later on in the day, he made some spontaneous remarks: "I told you about how we had the idea that being a scavenger wasn't too hot? Maybe that's the reason: *He* kept us down. It was his attitude toward us. He'd say that garbagemen are dumb, and that people wouldn't accept our getting better pay. He said a garbageman should not make any more than $10,000, so he would not ask for more pay for us—wouldn't ask for a rate increase. I wonder if it wasn't the way he made us feel. Because, actually, except for when I was a kid and embarrassed about my father, I've never really been ashamed of this work.''

I asked Freddie what he most liked about this work. "You're your own boss," he replied. "You're out in the open. Of course, this is all I *can* do, now; but I wouldn't like an office job." He told me that there was "not too much pressure, except what you make yourself," and that he could not work like some people who were never out in the fresh air, as we were this morning. "Actually, this is two jobs. The garbage, and the [bill] collection in the evening. I don't like *that* part of it at all." (Ernie later said, "Collecting [bills] is okay once you get out, but it's hard to get out." Nick said, "Collecting's okay; it's getting up so early in the morning that's hard for me.") But Freddie was vehement: "I am sick and tired of dealing with the public. It makes you hate people. That's not my nature, but it's made me that way. They are all liars and what-have-you. They didn't used to be that way."

I had not had to ask Freddie what he did not like about the job. His vehemence was surprising. The worst thing apparently was trying to get the customers to pay for the service they had received, and yet what seemed to lie behind his unhappiness at the way people had "changed" was that his desire and willingness and actual attempts to do favors for those on his route in a friendly informal way *were not reciprocated*. That is, for him, the relationship of scavenger and customer was no longer an emotionally rewarding one in which each was important to the other.

I had noticed already, that day, that he was inexplicably strict about demanding advance payment from a new woman customer for taking some extra (and quite messy) stuff away. It was not her trash, she said. She had just moved in, and the trash had been left by the previous tenants. But he was adamant. So she paid him cash then and there. Then he asked her where she was going to keep her can, because no one else in the house was now paying for service and he wanted to pick up hers only and make sure he gave *her* the service. He told me a couple of hours later: "You know that woman I talked to about the service? Now, she may be a wonderful person, and I hated to say, 'Pay me,' just like that. But if I don't— agh, she'll be like all the rest: She may start out trying to keep her place clean, but she'll change too." It was true that some of this area near the university was pretty slummy and the refuse was often in a sloppy state.

The scavenger struggles with a conflict over the problem of pricing for the customer as part of a personal service or as part of a commercial business. I learned this when I listened to a discussion between two of the crew about new service instituted at a large house of flats. Nick had taken out three cansful the day before. Freddie told him that there should be only one can there. I asked Nick how come he had taken out three cans, when it appeared he knew that only one was going to be paid for. He told me, "I hate to have complaints from the customers. So I try to do something. I guess, though, what's right is right—they *should* be paying." The scavenger, in this district anyway, is torn. How can he satisfy the good customers in a building with bad ones? The good customers' view of the garbage service is lowered by actions of the bad customer or, worse yet, by those who do not have service at all but live in the same building and pile their garbage ever higher, near the paying customer's can.

Frequently the directions that the crew shouted at each other were aimed at limiting the amount of work (if any) to do at a particular address: "Hey, Ray, get outta there!" The

concern of the crew here was often to *avoid* service, rather
than to provide it—clearly a conflictful prospect to face every
day. Toward the end of the morning on this day, I noted
another ambivalent situation as one scavenger told another
to go easy on a customer: "Give 'em a little more chance
[to pay the bill]. Leave another [warning] ticket, the other
might have blown away." I got caught up in the business
of pleasing customers myself. We were moving the truck
ahead a few houses, and I was walking up toward the truck,
when a little Negro boy called from his front door to me,
"You haven't got ours out yet." (The access door was locked.)
"My mother says she'll be able to unlock the door after a
while [when the man with the key returned]. Can you come
back?" "We will if we can," I said. And I told Nick about it,
who said he would get it on his own truck during the next
break.

In another instance, Freddie was very cagey discussing
terms with an apartment house manager—an attractive young
woman who stood in ragged, toeless, almost footless nylons
in the basement-courtyard area. "My husband and I are sort
of taking care of this place now for the owner. He's had a lot
of trouble and is just getting on his feet again," she explained, to justify the fact that quite inadequate arrangements had been made for the amount of refuse. Bags and
bags and boxes and boxes, full and overflowing, were piled
in a corner next to a single can; and the whole place reeked
worse than anywhere else I had been. Yet, the order placed
by the owner was for only one can a week, which Freddie was
in the process of emptying into his blanket when the woman
appeared. She wanted to know how much it would cost to
take care of all the garbage, but Freddie hedged. He would
tell her how much it would cost to clear up the mess there
now, but he would not give her the rate for the house, saying
he would check on it. (He told me later that the problem
was how many people would be living in the apartments—
not how many apartments there were.)

Freddie tried to ascertain the number of people, but the woman did not catch on to the problem, and he did not press the issue. She told him the number of apartments and families, and he remarked that he thought there were more than that; for example, someone also lived in the basement. She denied that anyone lived in the open basement room, although we saw an old mattress in there. She was only newly moved into the building and admitted she did not really know, but she contended that maybe someone had slept there once, but no one lived there now; for, of course, there was no bathroom for it. "Well," said Freddie, "I know they go to the bathroom right here in the areaway [where we were standing]." "Oh, no!" the woman shook her head, "that must be just dogs that wander in." "Lady, do dogs use toilet paper?" That stopped her, and, indeed, perhaps it explained why the place smelled so. Each promised to check with his or her own authorities and to confer again about increasing the service. The woman said that they just must have more service, and she would try to do something about it; then she turned and wandered back upstairs.

Despite the fact that no real arrangements were made (or were possible without more information on the likely number of cans), Freddie agreed to take for free one or two cans' worth of the extra garbage that filled the corners of the areaway. He proceeded to place the dripping and breaking bags and boxes into a blanket. The stench got so great that I, for the first time, felt that I could not take it any longer. I tried to move casually out toward the street, but Freddie caught on: "You'd better get out; this is pretty bad, even for me." He tied the blanket corners together for one load, but he left it there and joined me on the street. "It's so wet, I'll leave it there till tomorrow." That way it would drain a bit and not run down his back when he carried it, he explained. But then he did go back and dragged out one blanketful.

Freddie had a special problem because he was the crew boss. He was not at all sure that it was worth it: "Why take responsibility? Nick's young yet, but Ernie could be a crew boss on another route. But what for? You get wakened in the afternoon by a telephone call, customer complaining, or some question. You have all the headaches, yet from the president on down, everybody makes the same money.''

This was before Lenny Stefanelli instituted pay distinctions for different kinds of work, and Freddie wondered how Stefanelli could take it. ''You don't get anything out of it. When everything goes good, he's a prince; but something's wrong, he's a bum. Sure, I agree with you, everyone paid the same has its advantages for the company, but why be president? I wouldn't want it.''

Nick's view was entirely different: Nick told me privately that he did not really mind getting up early, as he had told me earlier; he had just said that for Freddie's benefit. However, he confided, ''I'm getting out of this work. I'm no twenty-year garbageman. In ten years I'm going back to the country. Back to Wyoming. I was a carpenter there for a while; then went in the Army. When I came back, I took up carpentry again, but one day the weather was so bad, the wind blew off this big plywood piece I was working on, and I decided to come to San Francisco.'' He pointed out that carpentry pays a lot more than being a scavenger (perhaps $900 a month), but it is seasonal work, so in the end the pay is about the same. Still, he really likes the country and dislikes city life. And he will return there with his new wife and family, once they have saved up enough money. (Indeed, when I returned to go out on the route again in 1972, Nick had gone back.)

His wife was currently working as a waitress ''down the Peninsula,'' where they lived, he said. At first they had lived in San Francisco proper, but didn't like it. Too many different types of people in the city, he said. They are strange to each other and do not know how to understand each other. Of course, some people, born and raised in one place, do not know what life is like outside. He volunteered that as far as his own standing as a scavenger was concerned—how people thought of him—there was no real problem. On his street, it was all pretty high-income people: bankers, chief of police, head mechanic at Greyhound. No one really knew what his own work was, aside from one or two neighbors. His wife said once that she got the idea that another lady might look down on them, but no one ever said anything to him. He got into this work, he said, because when you have family responsibilities you have to do something you might not want to do otherwise. But any American kid who had finished high school could do better than be a scavenger.

Nick spoke very seriously but at the same time lightly. His human insights and the capacity to put them into words matched Freddie's; yet he was less outspoken. The previous time I was out with them, I had kidded Nick about his habit of picking up a stray magazine or book for a moment's reading. He was doing that this time too; but it was he now who said, ''You know how I am always reading,'' when he picked up a tattered leaflet for an idle glance or two. He did not take the work seriously, and yet he did not shirk. He was a valued partner. There were little things that gave Freddie the chance to pick on him affectionately: ''This is ridiculous. I ought to punch that Nick in the nose,'' he said, referring to something Nick had worked out so Freddie would have to do a slightly irksome task. Although it was Ernie's turn today, Nick might suddenly jump in the truck to redistribute the refuse, and Ernie would then playfully insist that Nick stay in the truck to do more of the distributing work; to which Nick's reply was a mock hurt rebuke, ''I always *do*, Ernie.'' And he *would* stay for a while longer.

Because I knew everyone better, perhaps, than before, the whiskey break was a little different today. They seemed to try to move the conversation to topics that I would have outside interest in. Of course, in a sense, I was the host. Freddie told everyone that I had bought the beer and whiskey today. Ernie joked: ''You can come with us *any* time.'' We talked about welfare and the poor, getting on to the topic from a consideration of the residents of the area we were working in. Ray felt that too many people were depending too much on welfare. Freddie insisted that any man can find work if he wants it. I objected to this, but my arguments were not well accepted. Some time later, though, Freddie said to me, "What do you do about the poor? They gotta eat too. I sure wouldn't want to be President and have to do something about the problem."

I had a hard time trying to understand the ebb and flow of their attitudes. Late in the day, Freddie had a see-saw conversation, hostility and friendliness alternating, with a large, sloppy woman customer who had an Italian accent. She was trying to get him to take more garbage for the same amount, but when he was adamant she said that she would get permission for more money from the owner of the run-down apartment house she ran. Freddie and the woman commiserated with each other about the animal-like living conditions of "you know who I mean," she said. (I never determined what part of mankind Freddie was supposed to despise.) She marvelled, "It's a wonder. In one apartment, I heard, the only furniture was straw on the floor. Real country people." And again: "I wouldn't rent to them in *my* house." Consensus on whom they despised led to the woman's asking for praise for the fence-like gate she had erected across the alcove in which the garbage cans were kept, just off the sidewalk. "I built that fence just for you," she said, "so no one will mess up the cans and dump them before you get here." Freddie was not impressed; as we left, he shook his head, "There you have a typical Dago."

Since Freddie was of course Italian and confidently content with his own ethnic extraction, his comment was a surprise. Perhaps it grew out of the woman's heavy attempts to establish a category of man that was below the two of them. However, there was, as I came to recognize, a stable pattern of ethnic commentary and sometimes derogation. Once, a couple of years later, on a beer break, resting in Ernie's pick-up with Freddie, we were talking and I asked Ernie if he were Italian too. He said, "No, the company *is* almost all Italians, but there's a few of us who managed to slip in somehow," he grinned. They had been talking about a customer who complained about a rate increase, and Freddie had claimed the customer was a "Dago," to which Ernie had replied slyly, "That's for sure. They are the worst." And then Freddie said, as slyly, "But I tell you what, the English are the worst." I was naive: "Oh, are you English, Ernie?" He was not, and it turned out that *I* was supposed to have been ribbed by the remark. They were both surprised that I did not think of myself as English (or anything in particular). To them, ethnicity was a fundamental fact of identification. It might, on occasion, imply prejudice, I was sure, but it was not that simple.

"You know how to make a Wop?" I heard Lenny Stefanelli ask once. "Take a piece of shit in each hand, and bring them together fast, wop!" That was over the telephone to one of his buddies, while I was in his office one day. And in an interview later, he tried to communicate to me the good relationships one of the scavengers had with customers in his district: "These people really love the guy out there. He stops and talks to them in the street, whereas most of the guys won't take the time to do that anymore, you know, unless they know someone who's been on the route a long time. But then, again," he corrected himself, "I can't say that's not true about a lot of trucks: The other day when I went out, . . . I'd see them: 'Hello, you old bugger, you,' he is talking to this guy. 'You god darn Wop,' he says. 'If you were a Greek, I'd kick the hell out of you,' you know, and this type of stuff. He'd say, 'There's nothing to beat up in a Dago,' you know—it's just a *good* relationship. In the majority of cases, the garbagemen are pretty happy people. . . ."

The work was harder than the language. Sometimes it seemed to me that the crew worked themselves harder than they needed to, but perhaps it is occasionally easier to work harder in a physical sense than to worry about ways to do it easier. For example, it was fairly often that a scavenger would come through a narrow passageway with a blanketful on his back; the blanket would bulge too much to take through the passageway and would require straining and jerking to pull the load through—scraping, dirtying, and scratching the sides of the passage. In houses where the customer had objected to marking the walls, the crew were careful, but careful for the customer, not themselves. Also, more than once I noticed that even Ray (the smallest of all) would do the same incredible feat the others sometimes did—that is, run up the steps of the truck with a heavily loaded barrel hooked over the shoulder with one hand and a large bundle of newspapers in the other hand.

Each man did have some little way that was his own for making the work easier. For example, Nick had a little leather strap on the hook-handle of his barrel, and this he used to hold on to the barrel while it hung from his shoulder—a more comfortable way for him to steady the barrel than to grab the hook. Then there was the crew's trick of shaking the truck to redistribute the refuse, instead of getting in and tromping around in it. This "trick of the trade" helped to avoid what was probably the most distasteful of all their tasks.

I had wondered what was going to happen when the garbage piled up to the top of the front wall, as it naturally would, before it filled up in the rear half of the truck. Would they get in and push it around? (They did, later, but not to deal with first pile-up.) Instead, suddenly there was a flurry of activity. One got in the driver's seat. Another, with help from a third, broke down a refrigerator-sized cardboard box. "Get the sticks, Ernie." The next thing I knew, the truck was tipping back slightly as if to dump its load, and as soon as the top of the rear wall got within reach, two men swiftly inserted the cardboard in such a way as to heighten the rear wall of the truck; two long staves were inserted between the cardboard and the truck wall to support the cardboard.

Since the truck bed was tipped, and since the truck was on a steep hill anyway, some of the refuse slid towards the rear. But not very much. Then the men got out of the way; the truck, with its body still tipped backward, moved up a bit; and then, to great shouts of "let her go" and "give her a good one," it was backed swiftly down the hill a few yards, and then abruptly braked. The whole load shifted in one great, clattering movement from the front of the truck to the back, piling up to near the rim of the cardboard. Now there was all the necessary space just where the men would go on dumping their barrels!

"Don't tell Lenny about this," they said to me seriously. "We are not supposed to do it." "Well," Freddie admitted, "he really does know about it, but. . . ." "We would have to get in there more often with a pitchfork, if we didn't do it," said one. "It's against the rules, though," another said nervously. I asked, "How come?" Freddie's answer did not satisfy me—something about its being related to salvaging materials, presumably because it would interfere with segregating the salvageable stuff from what would be dumped. "A leftover from the old days," he said.

I could not understand what this was all about, so I asked, "Is it bad for the truck?" This was denied unconvincingly, but I merely said, "I can't see, if it's not bad for the truck, why it matters." I was told that really there wasn't any good reason for not doing it, but later in the day I got a further view of the whole thing.

The truck had gone to the dump and unloaded, and there came the time in the second load for the crew's informal redistribution process. Everything was done the same way the second time. But when it came to the point of the truck righting its body, after shifting the load to the rear, the engine apparently would not lift the body to level again, the body being over-balanced to the rear, of course, by the shifted refuse. Before I quite realized it, Ernie and Freddie were shouting and heaving with their shoulders against the rear wall, to help the engine! I put my shoulder to it also, and finally the truck was level again. "Well, that's probably the reason," I said, unnecessarily. There was no comment.

I learned of other tricks of the trade to make things simpler or easier. For example, they might leave a couple of full bulging blankets on the sidewalk somewhere, waiting all morning until, at the end of the route, they would routinely be driving on that block. That would save a special trip out of the way to pick them up. Freddie pointed this out to me, saying, "We shouldn't have left these here so long." "A little dividend," Nick laughed. Freddie laughed too, but said, "It looks *bad*."

Some of the especially hard work was, of course, inevitable. The main problem, naturally, was the extraction of the refuse from almost-inaccessible places. A sign on one garage door read, for tenants who might park in the driveway, "Do not block this door on Tuesdays." On this Tuesday, just like every other Tuesday, according to Freddie, the door was blocked by a parked car. The garage door thus would not open far enough to let a man in and out easily if he were carrying the can.

At one house there was a low-ceilinged entrance which Nick had to go down to by steps that required bending double in order to sidle in. Once in the hole, Nick reached out and grabbed his barrel and pulled it in, disappearing down a passageway that was scarcely more than a 5-foot high tunnel. I was staring at this process, when Freddie came by. I said, "Surely they pay extra for *that*?" "Yeah, ten or fifteen cents more a month; but it's not worth it. When he comes back, he'll have to kneel down in order to get the barrel out—or else he'll have to put the barrel up first. The people should put their can out here instead. We shouldn't have to do that, really, not with a load on our back. That's how you

If the customer doesn't want to bring his garbage down a long steep flight of stairs, Ernie Samietz will run up and get it "for a fair price."

screw up your back—things like that.'' And, in fact, Nick
came up the first couple of steps virtually on his knees,
managed to turn and set the can down outside the hole, and
then came out himself. He seemed unfazed, shook himself
momentarily—like a dog who has plowed through dense
foliage and finally reaches the open—and then he launched
the partly filled barrel onto his shoulder and was off to the
next house.

Yet, as I have already reported, the difficult aspects of
the work were not always physical ones. The money problems
especially wearied Freddie. A customer said, ''Be sure and see
me next week. Knock on the door for me, so I can pay you.''
And when we left her, Freddie interpreted, ''That means 'I
want credit, and next week I'll be out when you come.' ''

Even when money was coming in, the relationship between Freddie and the customer was apt to be wary. A lady
came out and gestured to her neighbor's cans, ''I want to pay
for her. How much she owe?'' Perhaps Freddie's wariness
came from the possibility of misunderstandings, due to the
interpolation of a third party; but it was there; he almost
seemed unwilling to take the money. Or I would hear Freddie
say to a crew member, ''They say they ordered twice a week
service, but before we start that, I'm going to have the office
verify it.''

The truck that I first saw Freddie and his crew working
on remained their lot for a few more months. When I was
first going out with them, the next route already had a
packer, and they got some assistance from it. On the hardest
day of the week, they usually loaded some of the refuse from
the early morning blanket work into the packer. That would
mean that they could still make their own whole route that
day on two open-truck loads. This kind of cooperation between crews was common. Indeed, one time when Ernie had
to quit early because he hurt his back, a nearby crew took over
a few blocks of collection so that Freddie and his men would
get through sooner. That crew was Freddie's brother's and

included the brother's son who was working with him that day. They pitched in with energy and cheer to help out.

Relations between crews were not always rosy. On that hardest day when I was out with Freddie, he and his crew were feuding with the packer crew that ordinarily took the extra refuse for them. There was some problem about Nick taking some of their blankets while they were having coffee the previous day. "It was only ten blankets, and they weren't going to be using them," Nick said. Freddie was sympathetic, because they had needed some extra blankets that morning before Ray had arrived with the usual supply when he brought the truck. The feud meant that Nick and the others would not accept the packer's favor that morning, though it was available as usual. But: "To heck with them. We'll make it in two loads anyway today," Freddie said. Nick told me, "We'll be getting our own packer in a couple of weeks or so."

Nick was overly optimistic, and even when they did get a packer some months later, it was as balky as Molini's, even though it was not the same model. Finally, in 1974, when I was on a visit to San Francisco and went out with them again, they had equipment that worked efficiently and very satisfactorily. As I watched them tip their barrels in the compacter's hopper, it was hard to remember that such a short time before each man had used to run up the steps into an open truck, and that periodically they had to jump inside the truck to redistribute the refuse. The new compacter trucks saved all that, but the work of carrying the stuff out for every San Francisco householder still goes on. From fourth-floor walkups or below-ground garages, from backyards or basements, courtyards or curbs, thousands of tons of daily refuse are still being collected.

Six

Discontents

THERE are some parts to the work of the garbageman that are simply inherently disagreeable, and although technologically more of the disagreeableness may be evaded in the future, a residual unpleasantness will continue to bedevil refuse collectors. Even with the innovations of packers and plastic bags, plenty of dirty work remains. The scavengers at Sunset were certainly not immune to its discontents.

First and foremost, of course, they had to handle filthy materials—without much protection. Of course, a man can take precautions, and the more skilled he is, the less he will have to immerse himself in the filth. Some contact, however, is inevitable, especially under the contemporary circumstances of refuse collection in any older section of a city—where containerization, for instance, is not feasible.

For example, Freddie and his crew have to use blankets to bring out the wet refuse and garbage from some of the houses; there is just no way to carry it out except on your back, juicy from the rains or from more noxious liquids hidden in it. Even if there were not something like old paint or sour milk in the garbage, and even if the men had used their punching tool on the householder's can, after a rainy day

there was always a lot of water in the refuse that would perco-
late through the mess, distilling the essence of it to course
down your back or arms.

Handling such materials poses a clear, if sometimes indirect, health hazard. The worker may joke about it, but he
knows it is there. Lenny recounted shrugging off a customer's
concern. " 'Lady,' I told her, 'I have so *many* germs on me
that they are too busy fighting each other to get me.' " But
the work is also just plain hard and heavy; it wears a man
out. I could see this so clearly one day in the Haight-Ashbury
district. My notes read:

As the end of the route was drawing near, the crew seemed more
lighthearted. Ernie and Nick amused themselves throwing empty
cartons at a store-owner customer, who tossed back many dire
threats, unable to throw the boxes back up at the two who stood
high up on top of the refuse in the truck body. But the same a-
mount of humor towards the end of the route was not accompanied
by the same torrent of mutual urgings, directions, explanations,
and so on, that had kept them all going at a fast rate throughout the morning. I was struck by the change that had come over
Freddie's face as the day wore on. He showed the strain in a certain
intensity or inwardness of expression, as if, as the oldest man on
the crew, he needed to concentrate more in order to keep going.
His face was transformed from its early-morning warmth into a
rigid mask, creased and reddened.

Take a look at them, Stefanelli said once, the men may
be fifty but they can look seventy. Of course, this stress shows
up in the statistics. About fifty-one percent of the days lost
from work for U.S. refuse workers is due to sprains and strains;
and the highest number of all days lost is due to the single
cause of back sprain from lifting a container. Indeed, one day
in 1974 when the crew had a fine compaction truck, I had to
watch Ernie hobble and grimace for twenty minutes or so
with his full can or with blankets after he had strained himself
badly; and then he finally called it quits, feeling guilty that
he was leaving Freddie and the others to do the rest of the

route without him. Freddie was muttering to himself after Ernie left:

"He'll be off two weeks," Freddie told me, but really talking to himself. . . . "Well," Freddie turned to me, "you're on the payroll now." I said that I would be glad to help what I could. (I had begun, eight years before, trying to do what the men did—just for a moment or two—and knew I could not give more than token assistance, swinging a bundle of magazines in the hopper, or carrying a stray small cardboard carton of something, or pulling a light can from the curb up to the truck, and so on.) Freddie sighed, "Shit." I sympathized: "It will make you late, I guess." "It's not that. It's *him.*" He was worried about Ernie.

So, although in 1974 the crew had a compaction truck, there was still plenty of dangerous hard work. They no longer had to climb up the steps to dump into the open truck, but the scavenger was still hunching over and practically crawling through the grim little passageways between some of the houses of San Francisco. There is no way that modern containerization can change that, short of rebuilding the city.

In 1966, I saw what must be the most unusual route that any scavenger would have to take to get to a refuse can and bring out its contents. First, as usual, we entered a little side door into a narrow basement-like low hallway, traversed it for three or four yards, then down steps and again along a hallway with more headroom, until finally we emerged into the backyard. "Wait," Freddie had warned; that is, there was still more.

Passing an outside staircase leading up to the rear entrances to the first stack of apartments, we walked by a muddy path through the backyard parallel to the street into another backyard area uphill from the previous one. There we found another wooden open staircase for the next multi-family house. We climbed those stairs, too narrow for more than one person at a time, to the cans on the third floor—four flights from where we started at the back basement level of the house. In and out, it counts to 204 steps (Ernie said he had counted them, correcting Freddie's estimate of 220), not including walking the passageway or the backyards. It was like a roller coaster up and down; and for a 32-gallon can the Board of Health in 1966 allowed the company to charge $2 a month—the regular price being then $1.60.

By 1972, the scavenger no longer wound his way into that particular pick-up location. The householder apparently was bringing it down the steps and outside to the public sidewalk. But Fred Fontana and his crew are still climbing the same kind of narrow back stairs that barely permitted the passage of their aluminum carrying barrels—or ultimately required using a blanket.

Ernie once pointed out at one apartment house that a window on a turn in the staircase had been broken too often as the barrel was maneuvered up or down; and the resident had finally replaced the glass pane with metal, for which the scavengers were grateful because they did not have to pay for repeated replacements. But that particular resident's solution was definitely not to carry his own trash down. My notes on that day in 1974 read:

Regular extra charges are made for each flight that must be climbed—50 cents. Once when I followed Freddie up a staircase, he asked me, "Would you pay $1.50 a month extra for this, or would you carry it down?" I said that I thought I'd rather carry it down. "Well, it's not the normal way."

It often seemed to me that the crew did not really mind the heavy part of the work (so long as they felt sure that the customer would pay for extra barrels or for difficult access to the trash). That is, it was all part of the job, although there would be an occasional gripe at some extra-heavy can.

But the stresses posed by the heavy work were not the only physical dangers. You can corner a rat without realizing it. And broken glass inside a plastic bag cuts through pretty easily when you are stuffing it into your carrying can. Freddie would not wear gloves, at first explaining or excusing himself by telling me he was "of the old school," but then admitting that really it was because it was too much trouble when he smoked his cigars. So he was regularly cut, but worked on oblivious to minor bleeding. (Two percent of injury days lost nationally in this occupation are due to cuts, lacerations, or punctures.)

On some routes, physical injury is threatened by the residents themselves, who for one reason or another take out after a garbageman. In the six-month period just before I began studying Sunset, four men on a slum area route had been either cut or beaten up, presumably by residents of the area. That was an unusual concentration, but it is not a rare thing for a scavenger to be endangered personally while he works.

Yet, what is probably the most disconcerting of all dangers is that posed by traffic. (Traffic-induced accidents are nationally the third highest of known causes for days lost by garbagemen.) The passing truck or car may be a mortal threat, but in my own experience buses seem to be the worst. At least, I have all too often almost been clipped by one. And both in San Francisco and elsewhere, my feeling has been shared by refusemen. Indeed, the first day I ever went out on the trucks, as I have mentioned, there was a substitute on the crew for a man who had been hit by a bus the day before.

Traffic is a hazard partly because you are apt to be careless: early in the dark mornings, you seem to be the only ones out on the street, and you forget, as the morning wears on, that the number of cars, trucks, and buses zooms up, so as to make your back-and-forth trips to the truck fundamentally dangerous. But it may not, definitely may not, be your own behavior. In the broad daylight, in the going-to-work hour, on a narrow street, the garbage truck seems to make automobile drivers crazy, when they must wait to be unblocked.

Some inside back staircases are so narrow that the barrel will barely pass through.

It is amazing how a passenger car will try to squeeze by, and to hell with the man who is carrying the can. I have watched while an impatient driver maneuvered his car between the packer and a parked car, while the garbageman, burdened with a load, flattened himself against the packer, trying to hold still while the car intently eased by him, inch by inch. (It is true that, in the days before I ever went out on the trucks, I have also been irritably impatient waiting for a crew to move their truck so I could get by. Today, I can sit calmly—and watch the work with interest!)

The dangers, the hard work, the filthy materials—all these occasionally pale before the experience of a really revolting stench. Some workers will explain that they have a "garbageman's nose" and can take it, but that is an exaggeration. No one can take it all the time. Lenny claimed he had "a trained nose," but when I asked him what he most disliked about the work, part of his reply was as follows:

People would get a lot of crab meat or get fish, and they won't bother to wrap it up—they just throw it in the garbage can. Then you get a hot day, and the stink would knock a seasoned garbageman over; and you get these maggots inside there—and, like I say, [although] I've been in the business a long time, I'd like to have brought my breakfast up several times; [you do,] when you see something like that. If they wrapped it up in paper, the stuff would still be there, but you wouldn't see it. But people come along and, you know, they just scrape it right in the can.

I am relatively impervious myself, but there were times when I could not take it. However, what is more problematical is the way the physical traces of the work linger on. It may not be as hard to get your hands clean afterwards as it is, say, for a coal miner, but the odors can intrude into your off hours. I once listened while Rod and Johnnie, two co-workers in a municipal department in another city, discussed the problem. They both worked a "garbage only" route— that is, they picked up garbage that was sold for swill for pig farms. The crew picked up in residential areas, from backyard sunken wells, from which they extracted successive garbage buckets, emptying their contents into their own carrying pail, until it was full enough to warrant a return to the truck. In warm weather, this garbage was pretty ripe, and Rod insisted to Johnnie that your clothes can't help but smell and the smell gets on you personally. Johnnie disagreed, and Rod suggested he ask his own wife, "She'll tell you." (Indeed, my own wife had complained mildly to me in the past about the same thing.)

There were, of course, ways in which one might protect oneself a bit. Rod, who had been with that municipal department for twelve years, was perhaps the neatest of all in dress. He carried a rag with him, and I asked why. "Don't like to wear an apron." (Others sometimes wore an apron or a kind of chaps to protect their clothes.) And he demonstrated for me what I had not before noticed: after emptying a householder's bucket, he wiped his garbage pail clean each time along the rim where it might, when carried, rub against his pants. He said he intended to keep clean despite the work. Yet, it was Rod who insisted that one's clothes would smell anyway.

All these unpleasant characteristics of the job are shared more or less by refuse workers everywhere, but for years the Sunset scavengers had a specially irksome task that distinguished them from just about any other garbageman in the country. That is, they not only personally collected refuse from their customers, but they also personally collected money. It seemed to me that they disliked the second task more than the first.

Ernie and Freddie complained: "When I get home, I just don't want to go out again." The scavengers, just like survey researchers, for instance, who want to catch people at home, would generally go around at suppertime or a little later; so the work day would be very much a split shift for them, so to speak. And also there was a certain self-stressed as well as company pressure to appear in clean clothes. Paradoxically, appearing at their customers' front doors dressed in a nice suit was not always productive. Some of those customers (including professional people I knew) would comment on "Cadillacs" and "silk suits" and seriously aver that these were Mafia-types, wealthy beyond us all. The Mafia image for Italians, even garbagemen, appears hard to live down.

In any case, Freddie used to go out each month to collect from 300 customers. He had a personal overall total of about 600, and Ernie about the same. The rest of approximately 1,700 customers on that route paid by mail then—usually businesses or apartment house owners. All in all, it required a different kind of energy, compared to working the trucks—and definitely a lot of it.

Collecting was overloaded, so to speak, with special significance. Even though each crew was independent on its own route, the amount collected by someone on another crew would affect them one way or another. If a man collected less than what the route was really worth, that meant less income into the pot for all the partners. Freddie had implied this when he told me of a route on which he thought he could make several hundred dollars more than the current boss scavenger who was not very businesslike. If, however, the collector was hardnosed about taking a little more waste from a customer—an extra carton lying beside the full garbage can, say—and insisted on charging the customer for it (or even charged regularly more than was really allowable), then he might compare better than another who was more generous of his energy or fairer in assessing costs (or even more honest in his charges). In any case, there was always a possibility for true differences of opinion. I witnessed a serious discussion between Freddie and his brother Pasquale, who urged Freddie to charge one of his customers more than Freddie would have.

Moreover, for all regular weekday (residential) routes, the length of the route was traditionally based upon the amount of revenue it signified. Each route was supposed to bring in about $10,000 a month (in 1972). So the more you collected, the more likely your total route might be reduced and the less picking up your crew would be assigned. You might end up doing less work than another crew who did not collect as much money each month. Also, clearly, some stable middle-class routes were more productive—that is, easier to collect on—than others where the customers were poorer and where they might change addresses more often, leaving unpaid bills behind.

For the scavengers, the IBM billing system was a first step away from these irritations. About 25,000 of their 160,000 accounts in 1966 were mailed their bills. Eventually almost everyone was billed by mail. Moreover, by 1973, San Francisco passed an ordinance that made property owners liable for refuse collection charges, as billed by the scavenger companies. Thus, if the bills were left unpaid by the person living in the residence, Sunset could ask the city to collect from the owner. I was told, however, that this provision was only rarely invoked. In any case, headaches in the responsibility for charging the customers were considerably reduced. Now, the scavenger must merely keep track of any extras and report them to the company billing department. Nevertheless, the boss scavenger may still be called at home (or perhaps, worse yet, stopped on the route) by an irate customer who does not understand a high bill. Thus, many interpersonal burdens of the billing procedures are still not ultimately lifted from the man who carries the can.

Fundamentally, one might suppose that the most onerous interpersonal burden for the garbageman is his general public image. National surveys have successively demonstrated that the refuse worker is probably second only to the shoeshiner for the lowest occupational rating by the general public. It is true that another type of survey has also indicated that the public has more confidence in refuse collection service than in any other public institution, except medicine. Nevertheless, being a garbageman remains at a very low occupational level.

In my contacts with the scavengers, it was rare for someone to spontaneously offer comments directly about the public standing of his occupation or his own reaction to it. One exception to this was Lenny's comment that "in the old days" Italians would do the work because Italians had no choice. Also, Ron mused about it one day completely spontaneously, a few minutes after I had asked him what he disliked about the job. "People don't want to have anything to do with you. They ask you what you do. You tell them, and they right away think you make so much money. It's [the money is] okay, but it's not more than they get." And a bit later, he returned to the topic. He felt that people he knew did not want to have anything to do with him because he was a garbageman. "Maybe it is all in my head, but it seems like they go to the other side of the street if they see you coming." He was obviously troubled by what he saw as the public view of his occupation.

I have reported how Freddie and his co-workers responded to a direct question on the subject, and it bears repeating. The topic was not an easy one to deal with. Freddie had met it head-on, noting that he had been ashamed as a kid that his father was a scavenger; and he later went on to observe that as an adult he himself did not feel that way about it anymore. Yet, he explicitly recognized that there was a public status issue at stake, pointing out that the scavengers provided a service for a category of people (blacks) who were among the lowest status of all in our country. The topic was unsettling enough for me and the rest of the crew that we did not go on to further productive discussion. So I believe that it remains a potentially anxiety-provoking subject, even for these men who certainly are much appreciated by the people of San Francisco and are well-paid for their work.

Even in San Francisco, it has not always been possible for the scavengers to get credit for what they know about the overall field of solid waste management. For example, it was once necessary for Sunset and Golden Gate to call in a prestigious engineering firm to say in a report to them what the cooperatives would have said themselves. Stefanelli complained that he had had to educate the firm so that they would be able to write the report. "The average person thinks, 'You stupid garbageman, you don't know your ass from a hole in the ground.' So we had to go out and pay $25,000 for that report. . . . But if *we* say it, it doesn't mean a hill of beans."

Seven

What's Good about This Job?

WITH all the problems and discontents in the work of the garbage collector, there are plenty of scavengers who will answer positively when you ask them, "What's good about this job?" They do not necessarily start off with the pay, although by San Francisco standards and even nationally the pay is good. In the West generally, skilled refuse workers are paid more, on the average, than anywhere else in the country—although the difference in pay from that of workers in the Northeast is not very great. And it was not until 1969 that the national average gross weekly pay of skilled workers in private companies (which almost always pay higher wages than public agencies, probably because of overtime) reached $190 per week, about what the Sunset partners were making in 1966. By 1974, Sunset pay had gone up considerably to about $18,000 a year, as compared to $10,000 in 1966. And in 1976, with regular overtime, a scavenger partner could make about $24,000, although without overtime it was perhaps about $21,000.

Yet, the pay is not necessarily what attracts a man into this work. Al Macari, a friendly guy I met working on a route in an upper-class neighborhood, who is himself the son of a scavenger, told me that his own son became a scavenger even though Al had pointed out that the pay was not as high as the son might make elsewhere. In one of my earliest interviews with Stefanelli, he agreed that the pay was not the main thing, although he told me he was trying to raise the pay so as to attract the best men possible. He knew that he himself, in his previous extra job as a life insurance salesman, could make more working full-time than the $10,000 he was getting then from Sunset and probably more than any raise that the men would be likely to vote him in the future. It was true that, for a working man, $10,000 in 1966 and $21,000 in 1976 was good pay, especially when so many people were out of work. But the pay was not the chief attraction, apparently. ''I guess you have to go into the psychology of it,'' Lenny had said.

''The psychology of it'' had a great many different aspects. One of these was what might be called the variety of the work, as unlikely as that may seem to the uninitiated. Ron told me: ''Thing about this job is that you do different things.'' If he had taken the somewhat comparable job of pick-up man on a city street-cleaning crew, Ron said, he would ''go crazy. That would be monotonous.'' The tasks on his route were varied enough to break the monotony of the work's routine—operating the blade, solving problems with customers, blanket work and can work, driving the truck, and so forth. But there was also a different kind of variety, the unexpected in the human events of the work day—like the burglar on that day with Freddie and his crew. When I met Freddie's young son working with his father in 1972, he told me that he had refused a nine-to-five job that paid more: ''Staying in one place all day? Naw!''

Each route has its own possibilities; the early morning life varies from district to district. Yet, whatever the district, the scavenger comes to know a lot about the neighborhood. Life along his route takes on the quality of a continued story. You watch children growing up, older folks getting more

Like all the scavengers before and after him, Al Macari took away your old Christmas tree for free. Note trees in old open truck.

timid, a house deteriorating, another being rehabilitated; and there is a certain stability to witnessing that sort of continuity and evolution. The garbageman can develop the same appreciation for his route that others develop for a soap opera or the familiar characters of a television sit-com. That kind of continuity can be reassuring in a world of change.

Also, as Everett Hughes has pointed out, alluding to Ray Gold's study of janitors, dirty work gives entry to the underside of life. One has access to special information that others do not. Even a respectable-looking house in a fine neighborhood does not hide the alcoholism that a garbageman can read into the number of liquor bottles he takes out. ''*I* like to drink, but *still*!'' And one morning in a nice neighborhood, a scavenger showed me a garage full of motorcycles —stolen. ''You can buy 'em, if you want to. Other stuff too,'' he explained.

Of course, some routes are even more absorbing than others. Lenny told me about the route he had worked on for many years:

We had houses of prostitution; we had Lesbians; we had homosexuals, prostitutes, and streetwalkers. They just got all the publicity in the papers a while back, but that's been going on in that district for *years*. If the girls couldn't get a hotel room, they'd go right up in the park underneath a streetlight with some guy, and it's usually a Caucasian with a colored girl up there. You see these things going on in the morning.

I've seen people get shot; I've seen people get knifed. You don't see that in other neighborhoods. The garbageman is apt to see these things early in the morning.

I saved an apartment house from burning down; as a garbageman going down in the morning, I spotted a fire underneath the stairs. I went out and I called the fire department. I came back and put the fire out and got the people out of the house, and the irony of the whole thing was that the police and fire department chewed me out for not staying next to the fire box. It was right up at the corner, but I went back and put the fire out and got people out of bed in case they couldn't, and got a hose from the house next door and hooked it onto a place that I know where a faucet is because I always drank the water out of it, hooked it on and put the fire out. I got chewed out. I didn't expect a reward, but, Jeez, a "nice job" or something like that.

But I mean, these are the things you run into in the early hours. The prostitution, the murders, the knifing, and the stuff like that, you're more apt to find it in the lower-class neighborhoods than you are in the areas out there in the Sunset district or places like that. I mean, you could write a book on the things I've seen: naked women laying in the alleyways; guys with their head knocked off and laying in the street; stumbling over drunks in the early morning hours; finding dead babies in the garbage.

My godfather went in looking for the light switch in one of these dark places, and there was a guy hanging himself right on the rafter next to the light cord. Things like this that you don't even read about in the paper are an everyday experience for the garbageman. . . . That's what makes the job enjoyable—but not so much with my job now [as president]. Suppose you're running an IBM machine; it's monotonous. It's the same thing every day, with very few exceptions. It's a monotonous job. Well, this job that I have now—I thought I'd never want to work in an office. I thought I'd be a garbageman all my life because every day there was something different; and I enjoy that differential. I mean you go to a job, and you never know what you're going to get. Basically, you're still picking up garbage, but you're finding things in the garbage. You find nudist books or something, you know? You see *all* that stuff there—there's always something doing.

A garbage worker once told me that at one particularly nice house where we picked up, he had been asked to save all the rubbish and turn it over to the FBI. Indeed, during a period of my own life when the FBI was paying a rather unnatural amount of attention to my own doings, because I happened to be a downstairs neighbor of Daniel Ellsberg, I discovered someone going through the trash at the house we both lived in. The stranger said he was a newspaperman, and maybe he was. In that same period, another stranger asked me for permission to take a sample of the refuse "for a study of ecology.'' The point is that garbage can have considerable interest under some circumstances.

Another part of ''the psychology of it'' was being able to set one's own pace. Freddie had said: ''You are your own boss.'' A crew could work as fast or as leisurely as they wished. As I observed, they usually worked as swiftly as humanly possible—if only to go home early or, as Lenny told me from his own experience, to be in a bar waiting for another crew to come in and be able to say, ''What's been keeping *you*?''

They scheduled their own breaks and as many different kinds of breaks as suited them and the strenuous pace of their work. Indeed, even the breaks might be used to save some time, as I recorded in an observation in 1972:

On the second beer break, Ernie and Freddie exchange and sort out the service complaint or request slips [that the driver brings from the office each morning] and decide what to do about them. Freddie explains to me, ''They say, 'Oh, those garbagemen have it easy, stopping for a beer,' but we actually do some work while we stop, talking about customers, and things.'' I am sympathetic: ''Of course.'' But Ernie raises his eyebrows, laughing. ''Yeah, we work all right,'' he mocks.

Ernie refused to be too self-important about it, but they would have had to stop anyway to review the service slips, a chore that takes about five or ten minutes a day—which, incidentally, was another example of the variety in the work, the kind of thing that Ron was talking about.

Another special attraction of the work is what you can personally salvage for yourself. I was never out on a truck when one of the men did not at least pause to examine an item to consider whether it might be worth saving. Often it might be a good book, or perhaps a girly magazine, or a child's toy, or a busted radio (''Agh, no,'' said one man, reluctantly tossing a radio back into the hopper, ''I've got too many of those things as it is''). Lenny remarked once:

Another thing I enjoyed: you always found that if you want something, you'll find it in the garbage, eventually. It's hard to believe; but I mean, if it's something within reason. I wanted a brass rail from a bar one time, and I found one in [the trash from] a bar. I wanted a rubber life raft to go skin diving, and I found one. People throw away the damnedest things in the garbage. Maybe you've got no use for them, but you end up being a collector; you're bringing things home all the time.

A young scavenger, solicitous either of my moral well-being or perhaps my intellectual interests, once saved a seventeenth-century book of sermons for me. And I still prize a sheepskin rug that I retrieved in another city while out on the trucks one morning early. (As Lenny had predicted, since I had always wanted one, there it was!)

Incidentally, I found that my own pleasure in the deserted early mornings of a big city was no different from that of the scavengers. Being outdoors is a big advantage that even workers in less clement climates emphasized in our study of garbage collection in other cities. To be indoors all the time is a drag. In San Francisco, one scavenger who was "a real P.R. man," according to Lenny, was put in the new customer service office in the Sunset district; he could not stand it for long and asked to be put back on the trucks. Freddie felt the same way. "You're out in the open," he said. "Of course, this is all I *can* do now; but I would not like an office job." Yet, he himself was head of the Sunset customer relations committee because he was good on things like that, too. Of course, not all garbagemen are as fortunate as Sunset workers in the matter of outdoors work—and not only because of cold, rain, snow, or summer heat in other climates. Even the workers at the other San Francisco cooperative did not have it as easy as Sunset workers. Golden Gate Disposal Company scavengers have to do most of their work at night, when the traffic is lightest, because their districts are mostly commercial and downtown areas. So they do not have the pleasure of as much daylight work.

Any job is also made better by the relationships you have with your co-workers, the friendships you establish on the job. Garbage collection is no exception to this. But Sunset may have had an extra advantage here, too, in that many of the workers shared a common ethnic background and tradition. By historical accident and social oppression, other cities have also sequestered an ethnic group into the occupation; in such cases, it would seem that good morale and solidarity among the workers were engendered inadvertently, much like that among the Sunset scavengers. That was perhaps what was happening in the Memphis garbage workers' strike that Martin Luther King had come to encourage when he was assassinated. In San Francisco, certainly, the old country ties, transported there in a variety of forms, were singularly important. The Sunset company newsletter printed some of its articles both in English and Italian, and the articles often dealt with culturally specific matters—the mushroom-gathering exploits of a senior member, for example. And surely the values they shared—and the common fate of a disparaged social group—had made it possible ''in the old days'' to forego the intense competition in favor of cooperative sharing of the city routes.

The ethnic ties implied familial ties, and vice versa. In 1966, about half of the Sunset scavengers were somehow related to one another, according to Lenny's estimate. During the period of my study, the third generation (such as Al Macari's son or Freddie's son) was beginning to enter the company. In general, family relations are an important and rewarding part of life in the local working-class Italian-American community.

I have left until last what may be the most important reward of the job for the partners of the Sunset Scavenger Company: owning a share of the business. Their ownership is inextricably associated with a number of other things, including, of course, the ethnic and familial ties that so many of the men share. In the period that I have observed the company, the dollar value of stock in the company has appreciated considerably, but ownership had never before been particularly significant so far as monetary return is concerned. That is, the dividends on a partner's share have generally been modest (never as much as $900 in recent decades). In 1966, it was about $200; in 1973, it was $848; and in 1976, $500.

The dividends have always been welcome, especially as they are distributed at Christmas time, but the basic significance of owning a share is that, as Al Macari told his son, it is a permanent job. It is security.

If one only wanted security, however, that would be possible in a municipal job. In public refuse agencies, annual turnover, for whatever reason, is about 8.5 percent for skilled workers, as compared to 21.4 percent in private refuse companies. But, of course, the gross weekly wages of a public refuse worker are ordinarily lower than those of his counterpart in a private company. So the Sunset partner's job combines security with good pay, as compared to other refuse workers.

Again, however, what makes the job good is not merely the fact of ownership in these concrete ways, but, as Lenny told me in a tape-recorded interview, as we sat in his car outside his office one day to get away from the telephones:

A man always works for something. . . . I guess—again, I'm not an expert—but in my own opinion, I feel that . . . a man walks through this yard here [at Sunset] and says, "I own a piece of this; this is mine." And it's pride of ownership, number one, that's really the governing factor. Of course, there's a lot of them like a bunch of old ladies, but on the other hand, thank God, the majority of the stockholders take pride in their company. It's theirs. *E cosa nostra*—it's our thing, it's ours. . . .

But this [pride of ownership] is carried on through the family, basically, like you say. His father [*pointing to a man going by*] just retired at sixty-one, and he's got another brother that works for the company. I've been raised in the company. That guy there who's going by now, his father works over in the salvage department. I mean, you could just point these things out here all the way around the place, that they've been here [by families]. Myself, I was raised in the business. I'm speaking for myself now. I loved it from—when I was old enough to count money, I collected garbage bills. Fred Fontana, the same thing. He was raised here.

I guess we all have a piece of it in our blood in one form or another. It's the people who have never had any connection with the garbage company that are the biggest problems in this company; they come in and they want the buck today and the hell with tomorrow. [But] some of us look for a future in the company

and look back on their accomplishments. The old timers talk about
"Gee, I remember when we had a horse and wagon," and "I
remember when. . . ." I guess it's pride. I guess, just to summar-
ize in one word—pride of ownership. It's an odd thing.

Lenny felt that times were changing, to the extent that
it was necessary to provide much better pay. This was required just in order to attract outside people who would
have the capacity to move into the more complicated administrative and technical tasks, but also to get those who might,
because of family, have more of a reason to join Sunset.
"How can you encourage them?" I asked.

Well, I can encourage them now. But we've got the problem of
the dollar again. Most of the garbagemen want their sons to be
something better than they were. That's just a normal way of life.
They want them to be better than their father. They'll provide
everything for them; they'll give them education. But I know that
down deep in their hearts, they would like their sons to carry on
the tradition of the company. There's no question about that. But
I don't think they really get out and *push* it, because they say,
"Well, Jeez, I broke *my* back all my life." But now, since they see
the company starting to progress, and they see these new trucks
[they have more pride in the business for their sons].

For example, we gave a new truck to this new guy, Tony Lucaro,
the other day, [to try out], and if you took his *wife* away, he
wouldn't feel so bad if you took that truck away! I'm going to have
to buy it for 13,000 bucks, and the guy's going to crack up if we
take that truck away from him. I mean we need it—it's not just a
question of making him happy—it's a good buy, $13,000 for an
$18,000 truck regularly. So we pick it up for $13,000, and the guy's
just *so* happy about it. And [so] there's a situation where maybe
the guy would want his son to come and take part in this. . . .

To recruit the younger guys, we have to show their fathers,
because the fathers are the ones who are going to tell them to go
[into the company] or not to go. And the ones that we are getting
now, their sons, are out for the dollar, to make a buck. Maybe they
want to get married or they want some security for the future, and
to do that, they buy a share, and they *do* acquire the security.

Good God, how much security you've got in here once you've got a share in the company, if you do your job! Right now, what I feel is that it's been traditionally going along that the guys have had the pride that you're referring to, but I think it's going to get a lot better [with financial benefits as well]. Like today—three guys want to bring their sons down, they want to put them to work. [So even now] we have no trouble recruiting help. I just don't want to go overboard on it [by hiring too many people]. Because it's a question of economics now.

Five years later, I got firsthand knowledge of what Lenny meant, when I went out on the trucks again with Freddie and discovered that his 16-year-old son Danny was working along-side him. At the doughnut shop that morning, another crew, including Freddie's brother Pasquale, came in. For a while, Freddie and Pasquale kidded Danny about which boss scavenger he would work for, each pretending to top the other with hourly rate bids between $1.35 and $1.85 an hour. Then, according to my notes:

Freddie told me, while Danny lounged listening, that he had told Danny, "If you don't want to go to school, work on the truck." He said, "I thought he'd want to go back to school, but no." I turned to Danny: "How long have you been on the truck?" "Since April [eleven months]. My birthday I worked." Freddie couldn't believe it had been that long.

(Later:) In the cab of the truck, Freddie said to me: "I did not want to say it in front of him [Danny]: I'd rather he go to college, but what the hell, what else is he going to do? His father is a garbageman; his uncle; my father. What else is he going to do?"

On a break, waiting for the packer to return, I learned from Freddie that there were still four men on this packer because one was Danny, doing his apprenticeship. Freddie said: "The apprenticeship does not require a year, or maybe even six months, but being as he's pretty young, it's longer for him." It was then that I discovered from Freddie that Danny has been working for nothing! Since April, Freddie repeated. We were sitting in Ernie's pick-up truck, having a beer, waiting for Henry Ramirez (the new driver) to return. Danny was on the truck bed, eating and drinking something else. Freddie told me that he had suggested that Danny work for a relative who operates a dental laboratory. Then he called Danny, who came around to the truck door. "Are you sure you don't want to work with [name]? You know he'd take you in. It's a good job, making false teeth. Good pay." Danny shook his head. "Naw, I don't want those nine-to-five hours. Staying in one place all day? Naw!" He went back to the truck bed. Freddie had tested it out again, and it was still true: his son wanted to be a garbage-man. "What do you expect from someone who's sixteen?" he grinned at me. But he was thoughtful.

Later, I expressed my respect to Danny for his work and asked him when he thought he would be going on the payroll. "Pretty soon now. Couple weeks, anyway." He was very satisfied with his progress. Still later, I asked Freddie the same question. He answered, "Any day now. Whaddaya going to do? A baby. But now. . . ." He shrugged his shoulders.

At one time in 1974, there were, according to Freddie's estimate, thirty or forty sons of shareholders working as help-ers—that is, as non-partner workers. This family tradition would undoubtedly continue to be one of the strongest ele-ments in the stability and service that Sunset represents for the city. People continue to pull out the garbage because their fathers did it before them; because their friends and other relatives make the company a familiar and welcoming place; because they develop significant personal relations with new co-workers over the years; because of the specific rewards of this kind of job (the open air, the self-determined pace, the salvageable items, the change and variety and human excitement of the customers and their environment); because the pay is as good as their neighbors are getting and thus fulfills financial aspirations effectively; and, finally, because they own a part of the company, which means that they are more than workers and yet their jobs, as workers, are secure. It is no wonder, then, that the San Francisco scavengers ordinarily feel good about their work as garbage collectors and that that work is done superlatively most of the time. Their tasks, the dirty work as a whole, have been transformed by the social and economic relationships that make men proud of what they do for a living.

But by 1976 and for a long time before, those relationships had been subjected to a process of change that is undermining the old rewards. That process of change will be considered in the next chapters.

Eight

Challenges to a
Way of Work

LENNY Stefanelli already anticipated a major transformation for Sunset in 1966. "I am trying to educate these
guys to *understand* this," he said. "Years ago, when the company was formed—you can look at the minutes—and a very
simple set of bylaws drawn up, there weren't the problems
we have now. The goddarn business is becoming more and
more politically and technically complicated." The urgency
in his words matched the challenge that faced him as the
new leader of a group of men whose way of work was changing
under the pressures of the changing world around them. But
probably even he could not foresee in any detail what lay
ahead for Sunset, or what were the specific larger issues that
would undermine the traditions of the cooperative.

Almost symbolically, Lenny was elected to the presidency of the company in the same year as the passage of the
pathbreaking federal Solid Waste Disposal Act of 1965. That
legislation marked a departure from the public's common
practice of averting its eyes from a problem that was insis-
tently enveloping it. That same year, too, a trade group, the

National Solid Wastes Management Association, was formed to help refuse companies and others deal nationally with the issues that confronted them. Change was in the air.

In San Francisco during the same general period, the downtown refuse cooperative, on the advice of a public relations firm, changed its name from the Scavengers' Protective Association to the Golden Gate Disposal Company. Very shortly thereafter, the president of Golden Gate told me that it had been a mistake to jettison the scavenger name and the local image associated with it. (A local newspaper columnist had jeered that the public relations firm was the same that had just managed Barry Goldwater's ill-fated presidential campaign.) Yet, Golden Gate's action on its name was only a response (if perhaps a bit off the mark) to a growing recognition that the old ways would not suffice. Exactly what was happening was not clear, but the outlines began slowly to emerge as San Francisco itself does from a lifting fog.

Vaguely, several influences might have been discerned. Something that was to become The Ecology Movement was stirring, a response in part to the effects of the country's growth in population and in consumption. Moreover, that two-edged growth was independently affecting the future of the scavengers directly in an increased demand for refuse collection and disposal services. The incipient ecology movement thus was just a variation on a more profound economic theme. In addition, in politics a different drum was sounding out from the civil rights movement, and both the action and the rhetoric of the Johnson Administration in Washington seemed to support a gathering mood for a positive forward thrust towards equity for all sorts of groups who had been left out of America's affluent advance. Of course, that mood was to come rudely up against the Vietnam disaster, but it could not be denied, and before it curdled into anger, it brought gentle revolutionaries to San Francisco, with flowers in their hair.

Three major influences, then, were pressing the scavengers as they elected Stefanelli. Nationwide there was a growing recognition of the ecological significance of wastes and their disposal. An increasing demand for refuse services was stimulating technological and organizational innovations as the nation's garbage collectors, now "solid waste managers," struggled to meet the growing needs. And rising aspirations among those who had not participated fully in the affluent society were exciting others to seek denied rights. I want to assay how each of these influences was expressed in what happened to the Sunset Scavenger Company.

The scavengers had always been respectful of the value of things that other people threw away. For years they had maintained a repair shop where some of the partners worked to put to rights appliances or furniture that San Francisco citizens had tossed out. The great open trucks had been a miniature sorting arena, where the scavenger would segregate into a corner the rags or other articles that had not already been selected for carrying on the racks on the outside of the truck. Partially sorted on the route, the potentially valuable materials would be left at the salvage shop before the trucks went on to the landfill area. In the salvage shop, pickers and sorters would do the final work of distinguishing what could be used for which purpose and how it could be sold. Wiping rags were merchandized. Newspapers were baled for shipment by a special machine. Bottles that were whole could sometimes be sold for re-use; or broken colored or clear glass could be melted down by the glass companies if they had been separated, and so a shipment of either type was valuable. And, of course, scrap metal was particularly saleable.

Scavengers salvaged not as an ideology but because it meant dollars. World War II was a stimulant to the scavengers' propensity for finding and keeping anything salvageable, but actually it was in 1956 that the total salvage operation grossed its high of two million dollars. After that, it seemed that increasingly it did not pay to be economical. In 1966, for example, Sunset handled its last load of "white glass." At about that time, when I wandered through the Sunset yards in back of the offices, I saw an enormous pile of crates, caging sound old champagne bottles, forlornly waiting outside a building also no longer used, the home of the wiping rag business. The champagne bottles (of various makers) had suddenly lost their value, victims of the cheaper new plastic corks that required exact single-sized necks.

Thus, within a year after Lenny became president, the economic forces of a consuming society were edging Sunset almost completely out of the salvage business, while at the same time people were throwing more away. Newspaper and cardboard were usually still marketable, but even that had its ups and downs. With its large districts of residential customers, Sunset could always count on collecting a huge amount of newspapers, but it could not always count on selling them. For its part, Golden Gate Disposal Company, working the downtown office buildings, might have tons of paper and cardboard, but even one sheet of carbon paper mixed in it would disqualify a bale. Thus, the standards for sale rose as the market fell.

So, ironically, just at the time that the middle-class ecology buffs were beginning their emphasis on composting and returnable soft drink bottles, Sunset was finding it harder and harder to maintain an established salvage tradition. By 1972, things had again changed somewhat, partly in response to the increased attention focused by the ecology movement on the long-term diseconomies of a profligate society. It seemed to the great multinational aluminum corporations, for example, that eventually reclaiming beer cans could be profitable; and even if that were not yet true, there were some public relations rewards to be garnered if a corporation showed concern. In any case, Reynolds Aluminum built a reclamation station in association with Sunset and Golden Gate on the fill land near the old salvage shop. But the station was not really paying for itself. Later, as part of a major effort, the scavengers themselves established a sophisticated recovery system in which refuse could be moved along a path of magnets to extract all ferrous metals. Again, this massive equipment operated only periodically, because the ecology movement was far ahead of the economic forces that would make a fully active resource recovery system financially feasible.

Of course, in the 1960s two major technological advances had already begun to break the scavengers' habit of salvaging. The compacter trucks did not permit the same flexibility for saving potentially valuable items as the old open trucks did. And plastic bags usually hid the salvageable materials that the process of emptying a can into a barrel had revealed. The more householders used the convenience of the plastic bag, the fewer articles could be retrieved. The packers' mechanism smashed everything anyway, and if a packer truck dumped its load into the sluiceway of a futuristic pulverizing and sorting mechanism, the metals might be magnetically extracted, or wood might float to the top, but a walnut cabinet record player would be no more.

In those years from 1965 on, Sunset was whipsawed by impersonal outside economic and political forces away from and toward the practice of salvaging. The very terminology of the activity changed. "Resource recovery," "recycling," "solid waste management," and the like, came into the language along with the names of new government agencies and programs to encourage the scavengers to do what had come naturally before. Professional consultant firms studied the changing contents of the garbage can and plastic bag to tell the refuse workers what they were hoisting in their barrels. With federal subsidies, "the solid waste management industry" stepped into prominence.

With its concern for the environment, the ecology movement affected Sunset in still another way—in the local practice of disposal by the landfill method. Perhaps California, with its influential Sierra Club, was more swiftly mobilized on ''save-the-environment'' issues. Perhaps the state was more sensitive since it was experiencing an enormous population growth that finally made it number one. And perhaps the sheer increase in numbers of people made California cities suddenly more aware of the brute fact of competing land uses.

In any case, Sunset and Golden Gate got caught in the squeeze. Their subsidiary (the Sanitary Landfill Company) had contracted with the little town of Brisbane, just south of San Francisco, to use an inner-bay tidelands and swamp area next to the old fill area that was rapidly being exhausted. Brisbane was poor in services and virtually without new tax resources, and its officials had looked favorably upon the per-ton royalty that would add as much as ten percent to the total town income.

Then, a few months away from a partial shift into the new tidelands area, Brisbane suddenly passed an anti-dumping ordinance and cancelled its contract, on the grounds that it would be improper use of the land. This was Leonard Stefanelli's first major crisis in office. Although he and John Moscone, president of Golden Gate, had thought they had planned ahead adequately to handle the disposal problem, suddenly their solution had evaporated. Now, indeed, the people of San Francisco had to consider that it was *their* garbage that the scavengers were collecting, not the scavengers' garbage! The city was up against the prospect of being absolutely without any place to put its refuse. The scavengers were still prepared to collect it, but what were they supposed to do with it?

The city fathers had no solution. They had always depended upon the two cooperatives to handle everything. There was still some lead time, but not much—not enough to look to definitive alternatives. There were only a few more months of space left in the old area. That gave the scavenger corporations time to contest the Brisbane action as an unfair cancellation of a valid agreement. But it certainly gave no time, for example, to construct an incinerator. Nevertheless, Stefanelli and Moscone carried on exasperating and long negotiations with a secretive inventor who claimed to have a means to incinerate under extra-high temperature without excessive smoke or noxious fumes.

For months, as the case of the broken contract was fought in court, environmentalists latched on to the value of unspoiled tidelands and accused the city and the scavengers of ruining the San Francisco Bay. There was, however, no evidence presented that the previous fill operations had been destructive, and Lenny snorted contemptuously at stories about the gulls and the horrors of "rats as big as pups" at the landfill site. Caspar Weinberger, then counsel for Brisbane, showed movies of seagulls making a big ruckus. So Lenny planned to use cherry bombs or the like to frighten the seagulls away. He told me:

If we get the seagulls out, I don't think there'll be absolutely *any* objection, because there's absolutely no odor over there now. If there is any, it blows out over the Bay and nobody can even smell it. Of course, I've got a trained nose! When I go out there, it doesn't smell bad to me at all, but to someone like yourself, who has been working in hospitals, it may be a little obnoxious. But the smell doesn't blow on the freeway. The only thing there that is really a problem now is the seagulls. And this time of the year, when the sea gets rough, they all come inland and they come over here for their buffet lunch.

Lenny's plan for scaring the gulls never did get used, although he soon had his own photographs to show in court, demonstrating that the gulls could in fact be frightened away. However, all this was quite beside the basic issue of what was the best way to dispose of the great city's refuse. There was a great flurry of talk and news articles about all sorts of solutions—including trucking everything to the Nevada deserts (Nevada declined the honor), a Japanese businessman's process for making compressed garbage into construction blocks (they had an unfortunate tendency to crack and ooze odors and methane gas), and so on. The city considered many alternatives—futuristic schemes of some attractiveness but great expense, and crackpot schemes of little cost and no real prospect of success. One great plan envisaged landfill dikes and a canal a mile wide around the entire circumference of the San Francisco Bay; it would cost three billion dollars. Another idea was to compress the refuse in bales, wrap it in concrete, and dump it out in the ocean.

While all this palaver was going on, the courts agreed that the scavengers' investment of $1 million in the Brisbane fill area after the contract had been signed gave them some rights to continue in part of the site in spite of the new Brisbane ordinance that prohibited the dumping. But the permissible site was smaller than the scavengers had planned on, of course, and it would last only a short time. Then, just as the last square inch of approved dumping space was used up, the scavengers obtained another franchise from another little community. Mountain View, down the peninsula about thirty-two miles away, asked the companies in July, 1969, to fill an area of 544 acres in order to make a park and a golf course. That would handle San Francisco's refuse for at least five years more and give more lead time for other plans. To date, the landfill method is still the leading solution, and Lenny told me once that he was working on getting a site that would handle the refuse of all nine Bay Area counties until the year 2010. He pointed out that there will always be some residue (even with pyrolysis) from any disposal or recovery process, and so San Francisco will always require a dumping or storage area.

The new Mountain View site, however, had its own problems. It called for the kind of long haul that collection trucks are not built to make. To deal with this, the two scavenger companies organized another subsidiary—in partnership with the small engineering firm (Easley and Brassy) that had traditionally carried out the cover part of the fill

Curving roads lead into SWETS, reputed to be the largest resource recovery station in the world. On right are sheds for Sunset trucks (white noses sticking out from under the roofs); below sheds are Sunset headquarters and mechanics shops.

and cover operations at the tidelands location. Together they set up Solid Waste Engineering and Transfer Systems (SWETS), which now hauls the refuse to Mountain View in huge gleaming aluminum transfer trucks. (Lenny told me that the gleam is part of the image they are trying to create—to take people's minds off the fact that inside is the refuse of ten thousand households.)

SWETS also holds title to a new facility, a transfer station, built on the landfill a few hundred yards from Sunset's headquarters. Each collection truck still brings the refuse to the old tidelands area, but once there the truck disappears into the transfer station and emerges empty to return again to the city streets and the waiting crews in the Richmond, Sunset, Haight-Ashbury, and the other districts.

Inside the transfer station, the garbage has been dumped into a concrete pit where a bulldozer pushes it toward another pit. Below the brink of the second pit stand the transfer trucks, their tops open, ready to receive whatever comes. Filled to the brim and closed over again, the gleaming trucks emerge importantly and move onto the freeway to Mountain View. Everything takes place indoors, out of sight, without pollution possibilities—even the seagulls are no more: "Il Palazzo della Immondizia," as Lenny calls it—a big million-dollar "palace for garbage."

The process is pretty dusty inside. Workers wear masks there, and periodically a spray of water plays over the refuse to dampen things down. Genially, Lenny will tell a visitor to the Palazzo, "When women's clubs come to see our innovation here, we generally put perfume in the spray." (Of course, they do not use perfume; besides it is the dust and the noise at Il Palazzo that is most objectionable, not the odors. But, I may have a "trained nose" by now.)

Another part of the transfer station is outfitted with the metals separator, which can remove ferrous metal, crush it, and dump it into trucks for sale to industrial customers. Ultimately, the transfer station will undoubtedly evolve into a massive, multi-faceted resource recovery operation. But its origins lay in the crisis of what to do when San Francisco's garbage was refused by the little town of Brisbane.

Naturally, all this was not free to the citizens of San Francisco. Disposal costs at Brisbane had been about $3.50 per ton; for the Mountain View site it rose immediately to $6.55, and later to $14.10. To accommodate the first increase, the scavenger companies got a 30 percent increase in collection rates from the householders of the city. The usual one-family, once-a-week house with a single 32-gallon can began to pay $2.40, instead of $1.85. However, the transfer facility also annually accepted for free 50,000 tons of city wastes from sewer sludge or street cleanings.

The expansion represented by SWETS and the Mountain View operation was only one sign of Sunset's general growth in response to increased demand for refuse services. Environmental or ecological concern, paradoxically, is accompanied in San Francisco and throughout the United States by a rise in volume and weight of refuse. While some kinds of refuse are decreasing, others more than make up for that. Garbage and ashes go down, but general rubbish goes up astronomically. In 1950, there were 3.5 pounds per day of solid waste collected per capita in the country, and by 1972 the estimate was 5.5 pounds. This statistic looms larger when one considers the absolute increase in population over the same quarter-century: 63 million. The result is that the burgeoning, throw-away society is demanding more and more refuse collection service, and the workforce grows to meet that increased demand.

So Sunset had continued to grow. Sheer size began to push the cooperative toward an uneasy evolution that fitted the conventional needs of expanding business but departed from the strong familiar interpersonal and social structures of an earlier time. There were four or five prominent signs of change and stress that appear to be directly related to Sunset's expansion.

In the beginning of my contacts with Sunset, I did not foresee what eventually happened. Yet, retrospectively, some things now seem predictable from my very first interview with the new company president when he proudly took me into the room next to his where their IBM computers were being installed. The technological economies of scale were becoming insistent. And then, a few months later, when I was visiting the headquarters again, on a Friday, payday, there were further signs of the complex juxtaposition of the new technology and the old ways of working. Lenny had been evicted from his own office room because of the expansion of the IBM equipment into it. A new addition was being constructed that would give him an office, but he was temporarily sharing a room with the dispatcher, John Armanini, who had also been displaced. My notes at the time read:

A tiny little room, with scarcely any space for walking around their desks, is crowded also by a little side table loaded with glasses and a couple of bottles of whiskey. These are on display temporarily because there is now no cabinet to keep them in—another casualty of the remodeling. The whiskey is there, John the dispatcher told me, to be doled out to partners who come in to see him and complain about this and that. After John has heard them out and tried to take care of their problems, they all help themselves to a slug of scotch or bourbon.

While I waited for Lenny to take care of several demands, in and out of the office, at least two partners came in and dealt with John and then poured themselves a drink and stood around chatting for a moment in the doorway, cheerfully surrounded by a couple of others who did not take a drink—presumably because they had not come to complain but just to say hello! The complaints had to do with needing an extra man, or needing a packer, or other special assistance.

Sometimes a partner would say to John that Lenny had okayed something, but the lines of duty were kept clear, and no matter what the man might report about Lenny, John would refuse to go along if he did not agree. Lenny would back him up when he returned—especially since it would appear that Lenny had said nothing of the kind that he was reported to have said! The entire air of the business going on was rather frantic—even more so than usual, I guess, because of the remodeling. Also, things were always especially hectic on Fridays, because of the special Saturday and Sunday assignments; and, John said, even more hectic on the Fridays that were the bi-weekly paydays—*every*body coming in then, since they had to come to the office buildings anyway to pick up their checks. But John's desk was a model of neatness, and he kept lining up his well-sharpened pencils in a level row.

The IBM machines next door were causing more than office dislocation. I noticed scavengers leaving the front office, from which they picked up their pay, with their new IBM paychecks in their hands. The stiff cardboard with the little holes punched in it was obviously a thing of wonderment and uneasy novelty to the stiff and soiled fingers that held it gingerly, turned it around for close inspection before pocketing it, and then checked the pocket to be sure it was still there.

In time, the IBM billing system was to take away the scavenger partner's major task of ringing the doorbells on his route to present and collect the bi-monthly bill for services performed. It eliminated the routine and regular interaction of the customer with the scavenger dressed in business suit and prepared to answer questions, consider problems, receive compliments, and otherwise elicit a more sustained recognition of his being. But perhaps "eliminating" is too absolute; "reducing the occasions" is more accurate. The computerized system is much too inflexible to handle the many changes in accounts, in service requests, and the like, that occur in some neighborhoods that are in transition (or have "transient trade," in Freddie's words). So it cannot do everything.

Nevertheless, Freddie Fontana and other partners find the change a relief, and the new city regulations, as I have mentioned, also reduced bill collection problems: the property owner (rather than the tenant or other service user) is legally responsible for charges; so if a tenant moves and leaves behind a mess to be carted away, the health department can order the service from the scavenger, and the property owner will find his tax bill commensurately increased.

Under these circumstances, the man on the route is relieved of much of his previous responsibility for maintaining the revenue flow into the company. More of this responsibility is placed on the people at company headquarters, who must program the machines, call the health department, fill out forms for city action, explain problems over the telephone, and answer questions. The division of labor has shifted in response to new technological and municipal conditions. One result has been that the customer-scavenger relationship has been taken out of the more personal context that it once had and molded into a more limited routine. This has relieved the scavenger of some problems, but it has also reduced his interaction with his customers.

Another result has been an increase in the office staff. Soon after he took office, Lenny upped the number of partners doing managerial duties from three to six—still a rather modest number. More was to come, and Lenny saw part of his job as "educating the membership" to the importance of the administrative tasks. He felt that unfortunately the partners usually only want to know how much the profit is and how much they are going to get, rather than to examine the critical issues of increased costs or increased efficiency measures that lead to profits or losses. They do not necessarily appreciate what must be done, he told me:

If they see a man that's working on a truck, he's okay, but they figure a man who is using his brains or something in the office, going through the mental strain of running the business, well, he's a loafer and he's not doing a damn thing to earn his bread and butter around here. Now, here, again, comes the question of educating the membership to a complete changeover. Where we ran into trouble before was when people saw a guy working in the office and said, "Well, he's not doing anything." Now, what I have done is periodically to take some of these younger guys off the truck, and bring them in the office down here, and let them work a week and understand the responsibilities and complexities of operating a business of this kind, so they can appreciate it a little bit more. So the next time the man comes into the office, they're not going to holler too much about it.

Lenny took other steps to make sure that information about company problems was diffused throughout the structure. For example, instead of the eleven-man board of directors handling everything, committees of the membership were set up to take on specific functions. Freddie was head of the customer-relations committee, for instance, and there were other committees, such as traffic and safety. Moreover, while the board had previously handled all disciplinary problems, Lenny's new procedure required that these be screened first by a members' committee which would recommend a disposition to the board. He gave me an example of the kind of thing that was taken care of this way:

The other day, one of the customers told the man not to take the sack out that way, that he'd knock all the cans off her shelf. I don't know, but apparently he was short-tempered: he told her to f-u-c-k herself. He told a *woman* that! Oh my God! But he was fired. . . . He was an extra man—but a stockholder's son, too. Nice looking kid—quiet when he was around me, but you can't tolerate that kind of stuff.

Lenny's managerial style clearly differed from his predecessor's, and he probably had a more difficult role to play. He had to balance, indeed combine, the old personal ways of dealing with problems with the more bureaucratized mechanisms that would respond to the expansion and improvement aims he had in mind. It was not enough to push a modernization program of buying new packer trucks, he had to manage the internal politics of the organization as well. He once said that as president he had "to deal with all kinds of crazy things, like rumors among the shareholders that the company is going broke. They pass rumors faster than you could think. They are a bunch of old ladies. That's just what I tell them in the meetings." He explained to me, "I give them a real talking to. I say, 'Petty jealousy is our main problem.'" The jealousy might have to do with whether one man had an easier route than another, or with even more tangible rewards.

Once, Lenny pointed out a partner, a route troubleshooter, driving into the Sunset compound in a new company car. He play-acted to describe some members' reaction to the purchase: " 'Jeez, a new Impala—how come they didn't buy the cheap one? You know! It's got a radio in it and a V-8. Why didn't they buy the 6-cylinder?' "

He told me that after the members got used to the new car "in their fashion," some of them thought that Lenny too ought to have a new company car instead of the one he was driving then, which was four years old. " 'You think I'd buy one?' I tell them. 'I'd be nuts. You guys would be picking the shit out of me. I'll drive around in an old *baracca* [any old thing], I don't care.' "

"If I have to go anyplace fancy," he told me, "I always have to use my wife's car." And some months later, when I noticed Lenny did have a brand new company car, he told me that the other one had broken down, was repaired, and turned over to another staff member; and he was using one that a Pontiac dealer loaned the company for promotional purposes. "I have to explain all the time that we did not buy it. They all think, 'Ahh, what you spending our money on?' "

He complained, but it was all affectionate; and he admitted it later: "Like I say, all these piddling things like the guy getting the car—*but* if anybody attacked the company, you'd see them together like *this*. You know what I mean? They may bicker among themselves, but let someone from outside criticize the car, and that's different."

Recognizing the attitudes of his co-workers, Lenny could make some of the internal changes relatively easily and receive broad support from the membership. But Lenny's job, at least as he viewed it, was by no means easy. "Educating the membership" was a long-term thing and required considerable sensitivity to the expectations, feelings, and fears of the partners generally. He said: "I mean, by getting into the position that I'm in now, I've become Big Daddy of the whole operation, and I listen to everybody's arguments, or their complaints—they don't like this and they don't like that. Like you say, what's keeping me here, with all the headaches and the work that is involved?"

Of course, he loved the work. He saw it as a challenge to build the organization into something bigger and better—

in the usual expectation of our society. Also, for him, there was the added dimension of a long, meaningful association with the company. He grew up with Pasquale and Freddie Fontana's family, and he married the granddaughter of one of the founders of the cooperative. Under Lenny, Sunset would continue, but it would change and grow.

Despite the fact that the number of Sunset accounts rose over the years, there were obvious limits to growth within the San Francisco County limits. By the original geographic allotments, Sunset Scavenger Company had the less populated outskirts of the city, compared to Golden Gate; but Sunset's area had increased in population in a way that downtown San Francisco could not. Eventually, then, Sunset was collecting 65 percent of the city's refuse, and yet it too was reaching absolute constraints on expansion, like Golden Gate. For instance, the number of residential accounts actually fell by about 5,000 from 1966 to 1973, though it remained fairly steady thereafter. The number of commercial accounts could rise, but stability or decline in the number of city residents was in the cards for San Francisco. However, it was clear that there were many other ways in which Sunset could increase its operations—for example, by buying out or absorbing other companies in neighboring counties.

In August, 1973, Sunset bought the family firm (husband-and-wife-operated) that had served the residents of Mountain View since 1941. Even before that, in 1969, Sunset had begun buying out a nine-man partnership, the Los Altos Garbage Company, at first purchasing four of the nine shares and then finally the last share in 1974. By 1976, Los Altos was serving perhaps 30,000 accounts (25,000 residential) in 250 square miles of scattered suburbia.

In addition, Sunset had organized a subsidiary that rented debris boxes—the huge truck-portable containers parked at a curb to hold demolition materials at a remodeling or construction site, or other commercial wastes. Integrating these new activities and the new companies within the simple structure of the cooperative partnership posed managerial and organizational tasks that the scavengers had never had to face before.

The modern business and managerial methods and technological advances that the company began to use under Lenny's leadership were accompanied by psychological and social pressures for further change. The new technology—the IBM machines, the new compacters, and so on—was not the impetus for change in management when Lenny was voted in. Nor was change due to some personal drive for power in the particular man who became the means for change. The new technology and the new leader were symbols of the potential in new ideas and methods responsive to the aspirations of the workers. The new president recognized that potential and responded to his partners' expectation that things could change inside Sunset as they were changing outside the company.

The decade of the 1960s had been a turbulent time of new expectations and new demands by many different people for different and more equitable rewards. Garbagemen could not be immune to the rising expectations that were occurring elsewhere. In Memphis, Tennessee, they had gone on strike against the city department for the simplest kind of equity—for the right to be paid for each day they reported for work, even if their bosses sent them home for the city's administrative convenience. Martin Luther King had led them in a march to achieve that right and had been killed while he was there.

Some new expectations of the 1960s were merely for access to what others already had (the civil rights movement), and some were for a different and presumably more rewarding style of life (the counter-culture movement). The scavengers of San Francisco rode through the streets and walked through the backyards of society's shifts and transformations, and they also were prepared explicitly and implicitly for change in their own situation.

Of course, what happened with and after Lenny's election was not just a single, long-overdue, board-room revolution, for in fact the company had always undergone and continues to undergo change. After all, without previous structural reorganization, the company had evolved over a period of fifty years from 92 to about 320 partners. That growth itself expressed a radical transformation of the city's population and of the organization of the work. Finally, the group simply had to shift managerial gears, and that shift required still other changes in organizational structure. Thus, the bylaws were amended in 1966 and formalized to omit almost all of the "advisedly diffuse" language. But the members were still liable for fines if they did not attend the monthly business meetings. In short, the strength of the company still rested on the commitment of the partners.

Surely, not all members were really interested in the details of the business, as Lenny pointed out. "You have to limit what you tell them" in the regular monthly meetings at which the president and other officers report to the shareholders. Yet, as Lenny knew quite well, there was a fierce expectation that what was done by the administrators had to be done for the good of all. In the beginning, he had had to avoid even the appearance of self-enhancement, driving "an old *barraca*" until they could accept his enjoying the Pontiac dealer's gift to the company.

The palace revolution that had put Stefanelli in the presidency and had engineered changes in the bylaws were especially visible signs of the partners' demands for a more open and more satisfying relationship with their own company. The self-determination that these events expressed, however, might be likened to that of the Magna Carta, in which the nobility extracted from the sovereign certain rights for themselves, but rights for others were not included.

Similarly, at Sunset the partners had wrested a new sense of participation from the traditions of the old regime, but it was not until later that their rights became an issue for others in the company (the helpers) who did not share the same access to benefits as the company partners.

In December, 1973, Sunset, Golden Gate, and the Sanitary Truck Drivers and Helpers Local 350 (as well as the Teamsters International) were named in a civil rights suit. Although the plaintiffs appeared to focus primarily on Golden Gate, Sunset was also cited as denying equal opportunity to black and Hispanic employees. One of the contentions was that members of these groups could not buy into the company. While Lenny had been bringing in the fresh air of increased participation to the partners, Sunset seemed to the plaintiffs to deny the opportunity of participation by share-holding to those who were hired on as helpers.

The plaintiffs noted that since 1968 the sales of shares at Sunset had been discontinued (to anyone). However, the real crux of the suit was probably the complaint against the difference in pay between helpers and partners, not the right to dividends. The hourly rate for non-partners was at that time $4.79 or, at most, $5.12, depending upon the job classification. The lowest hourly rate for a partner (for doing approximately the same kind of work as the highest-paid helper) was $6.20. In an interview for this study, a group of plaintiffs seemed to indicate that they were not so much interested in share-holding as in higher pay, although their legal counsel, present with them on that occasion, sought to correct that impression.

The complexity of the case and the fact that it still remains in litigation makes it very difficult to come to conclusions about it at this time. For example, one of the Hispanic plaintiffs was listed as a former Sunset employee, as well as a current Golden Gate employee. The fact, however, was later established that he was actually a Sunset shareholder for seven years, from 1952 to 1959, and had left for personal reasons. There had been and were several Hispanic partners, as well as helpers, at Sunset. However, at the time of the suit, only three Sunset employees were black, and these were in the helper slots. No black had ever bought in as a partner. Whatever the performance of Sunset in this arena, it was a matter of fact that no Sunset employee joined the original plaintiffs in the initial suit. The plaintiffs were all associated with Golden Gate. Six months later, after the case was filed, one former and one current Sunset employee (both black) joined as plaintiffs.

While Sunset had only three black employees at the time of the initial suit, Golden Gate had 24 (23 of whom were plaintiffs). Both companies had recruited an even larger number of Hispanic helpers (in addition to some Hispanic partners). This extraordinary mixture of acceptance and rejection in the informal recruitment practices of the two refuse cooperatives reflects the city as a whole. San Francisco has a polyglot, cosmopolitan, but still racially discriminatory social climate, in which, for example, one construction union local (mainly Irish) somehow never has admitted blacks but accepts Orientals, while the adjoining local (mainly Scandinavian or Finnish) has encouraged black but not Oriental members. In any case, Golden Gate thereafter sold one share to a black partner; and out of the last sixteen shares sold in the Sunset company, twelve had already gone to Hispanic partners before the 1968 share retirement policy went into effect, but no further shares had been sold.

"*You* know we are not prejudiced," Freddie told me, discussing the suit with me on a beer break in 1974, four or five months after it was filed. "We would have been glad to have them [blacks], but they never came. We'd take anybody." The fabric and pattern of social relationships is rarely as uncomplicated as Freddie would have it, but I have never adduced evidence of systematic or intentional discrimination. I once attended a business lunch with scavengers and others in which their own racial attitudes were explicitly discussed.

In the course of it, one scavenger was jeered by all the others for saying that he was not prejudiced; and yet, at the same time the whole lunch group indulged quite freely in slurs on a variety of ethnic groups, including their own. On the trucks (or at a business lunch), ethnic jokes or other slurs against any group, including one's own, are a commonplace of daily conversation, as I have already noted. However, in the usual confused pattern of our inequitable and equitable society, this did not prevent warm personal and mutually respectful relations between members of different groups who would regularly give each other the dozens.

The issue, of course, is not whether or not one is prejudiced or uses such ethnic gambits, but whether there is a patterned exclusion (formal or informal and unrecognized) from common opportunities. At Sunset, what may have been without intent was yet exclusionary by custom and reciprocal expectation. For the close family, friendship, and ethnic ties of the San Francisco Italian-Americans in the two refuse cooperatives clearly had operated to build a naturally bounded group that was hard for outsiders to penetrate. The suit, whatever its merits otherwise, highlighted that feature of the scavengers' companies. But new standards were being created. The process of freeing the workers at Sunset from the past—a process that had begun with Lenny's election to the presidency—was continuing in the demands of the black employees who wanted to collect the garbage on the basis of equal status and equal pay.

As Leonard Stefanelli was the means for the expression of the partners' aspirations, so too he figured, at first unaware, in the aspirations of other groups in the company. Initially, the plaintiffs in the discrimination suit probably were aroused into their legal action by their discovery of a letter from Lenny to his fellow shareholders, in which he urged them to turn out for a union meeting and reverse the action of a poorly attended earlier meeting.

The letter read:

August 6, 1973

Dear Shareholder,

I am writing you this letter, asking for a personal favor to make an extra effort to go to the Special Union Meeting called to ratify the San Francisco Labor Contract, THURSDAY EVENING, AUGUST 9, 1973 AT 7:00 P.M., AT THE FRANCISCAN HOTEL, 1231 Market Street, between 9th and 10th Streets.

At the last Union Meeting to accept this contract, only about 40 shareholders of this company appeared to vote on this contract, which was ultimately rejected by a scant 26 votes.

I, as your President, look not only to the future financial security of your company, but the political implications of an unfavorable response on a "wage contract" by the political bodies of this city, especially in view of the recent economic conditions of the Nation, and certain unfavorable articles in local "alternate" newspapers.

I am convinced, along with your Board of Directors, that the contract that will be submitted to you for your consideration is fair, reasonable and advantageous to each of you, and urge that you accept it.

I also remind you that, for the first time in the company's history, we are in a position to receive a "Rate" increase that will coincide exactly to the same time these "Wage" Increases will become effective; therefore, the company will not be faced with a deficit cash flow situation, as it has had in past years.

Plus the fact that the timing is such that the majority of the "blame" for the increase in rates, as far as the public is concerned, can be attributed to the extension of the landfill operation in Mountain View, thus minimizing the effect it will have directly towards the company and its *shareholders*.

I know that most of you were contacted by phone, from members of this company, urging that you attend the last Union Meeting, and even by personal contact; only a small and ineffective group took the time to attend; therefore, the purpose of this letter.

Time and space will not allow me to go into more detail on how important this contract is to all of us, and knowing personally how it will affect this company, I would not hesitate to "beg" each of you to go to this meeting if I thought it was necessary; however, I will respectfully remind each of you that as "SHAREHOLDERS" you have assumed the responsibility of that position; therefore, between my personal request that you attend this meeting and your capacity, it would be apparent to me that each of you will be there on THURSDAY EVENING, AUGUST 9, 1973, AT 7:00 P.M., 1231 Market Street, Franciscan Hotel, to accept the contract.

PLEASE HELP ME, TO HELP YOU.

> Sincerely yours,
> (Signed) Leonard Stefanelli

Since the shareholders were, of course, negotiating with themselves, their contract "offer" was virtually unassailable because, for one thing, the offer was naturally very generous. The main points of the offer, which was eventually accepted, were as follows:

August 9, 1973

To: All Members of Local 350
From: Companies: Golden Gate, Sunset, and Sanitary Fill
Subject: Last proposal from companies for new contract effective [January 1,] 1974

1. Wages: 50¢ per hr. per each year of new contract: $1.50 total.
2. Cost of Living: 1¢ for each full point, September to September index. First to be effective on 1975 and last one in 1976 of the contract.
3. Funeral Leave: 3 days off with pay on the death of any member of the immediate family. Wife, children, father, mother, father-in-law, and mother-in-law.
4. Holiday: Birthday to become a holiday. Companies will pay holiday pay on the first Tuesday of August of each individual year to all employees.
5. Packing Can: Companies will provide a can with wheels every 18 months. These cans will be supplied at the companies' manufacturer, any extras added to any can will be paid by the employees. Maintenance to be paid by employees. Any new member or employee with less than 90 days will not receive a new can. Upon completion of probationary period he will be eligible for this.

6. Shoes and Uniforms: 5 sets of uniforms per year to be provided
   by all companies. 2 pairs of shoes to be provided by all companies per year.
7. Vacation: 1 yr–1 wk, 2 yr–2 wks, 5 yr–3 wks, 10 yr–4 wks,
   20 yr–5 wks.

The points of this contract offer were finally accepted,
but it did not speak to the differential between helper and
partner wage rates. That was the main reason it had been
rejected in its first version by most of the helpers. When it
was voted on the second time, some of the helpers felt that
Lenny's letter had sidetracked their interests in favor of quick
action on an otherwise generally acceptable new contract.

It is possible to speculate that the contract dispute might
never have gone to the point of the suit and could have been
resolved by astute and sensitive attention to everyone's needs,
the kind of attention that Lenny was ordinarily capable of;
but at the time, his eyes were on a very different problem.
During this period, he was deep in the legal and organizational details of a project that was to fundamentally alter the
structure of the company. In a few weeks, Sunset was to
approve the incorporation of a holding company, Envirocal,
for the shares of which each partner would exchange his
Sunset stock. Organized as a conglomerate to handle the
burgeoning divisions and activities initiated under Lenny's
aggressive business leadership, Envirocal epitomized the
evolution of the cooperative from its relatively uncomplicated
beginnings to the complexities of the modern corporate
world.

New technology had played its part in all these events.
For example, when the new packers entered the picture, it
became apparent that the number of men needed for carrying the cans would be less. Also, the automated billing
system lowered the demands upon the partners for evening
work (ringing the doorbells of their customers). Both of these
technological changes suggested that the company could and
should reduce its membership in the face of reduced work

demands. But, of course, no partner could be eased out on such a basis, and Sunset came to rely upon the natural process of attrition. Beginning in 1968, as a matter of policy, the company bought back the share of everyone who quit, died, took his pension, or moved away. A man's share could no longer be sold to others, either by himself or his heirs, as it had in previous times.

It was certainly true that the new equipment required fewer men, but the share-retirement policy had some unintended consequences. A group is renewed by its new recruits, and it can gain new strengths or lose vitality in the process. The freeze on the sale of shares cut off the entry of any new partners and thereby symbolized an attitude of exclusivity and special importance for the current partners. In this manner, it served to reinforce identification of the partners with each other and the company. But it had certain very definite disadvantages too.

Restricting the entry of new partners suggested an ever-tightening circle in which the survivors would divvy up a pie that was bigger because there were fewer and fewer to share it with. That would not encourage generosity or cooperation. Furthermore, it certainly worked against one of the more solidary forces of the organization—the family ties that were maintained as a partner passed his share on to a working son or nephew or son-in-law. Family and friendship bonds had hitherto been important in recruiting people who would be identified with the overall good of the company, partly because of the reinforcement of personal relationships. But if the sons would have little prospect of attaining the status of their fathers in the company, then they would surely seek other occupations. And the company would increasingly depend upon helpers with little interest in the organization itself.

I brought up some of these points in a discussion with Freddie and Ernie in 1974. They joked with me about which one of them was going to live the longest and be the last shareholder and own the whole company. But they were also puzzled about the rights and wrongs when they tried to confront the issue as to whether it was fair for helpers to be frozen out. At the time of this conversation, Danny Fontana was working as an unpaid helper and Henry Ramirez, a Mexican-American, had become the regular driver-helper on Freddie and Ernie's crew. Under the share-retirement policy, neither would have a chance to become a partner. The civil rights suit forced upon the consciousness of all the partners not just the question of rights for blacks or Hispanics but the rights of all helpers in the company.

The share-retirement policy also was likely to have another profound effect. To the extent that Sunset expanded (and especially to the extent that it bought out other companies), the balance between the smaller number of helpers and the larger number of partners would shift, and the potential identification of helpers with partners as people with whom they would or could eventually aspire to join would disappear. The stock freeze eventually would result in the company having the same management-labor adversary relationship structure that is a part of the conventional business world. The company would then gain at the expense of its non-shareholding workers, and these of course would seek to cut into the company's (the partners') potential returns as much as possible. The adversary structure would naturally induce different relations among the partners and the helpers, who in my observations had been real team-workers, but who would no longer have the same motivation to team together.

Indeed, the partners found themselves involved for the first time in strikes or threats of strikes—at their subsidiaries. Now, it is true that management is not always averse to experiencing a strike and can even use it as a bargaining tool with third parties. In fact, in one case, Stefanelli had done just that in gaining a municipal rate increase for one of the smaller companies that Sunset had acquired in another community. The workers got a pay raise and the company actually made a better profit, all on a reasonable rate increase. But what had happened in that distant community might not be so fortunate if it were closer to home. The emotional complexities of the relationship between scavenger helpers and scavenger owners would be considerably greater in a strike if partners and helpers were working closely together on a daily basis, as in San Francisco itself. The distinction between partners and helpers might then become cruel.

The resolution of this fundamental issue of stock sales, which challenged the meaning of Sunset as a place to work, was not impossible. By 1974, chit-chat around Sunset turned toward the idea that shares should again be sold on the basis of some system of seniority among the helpers. That would be a first step, although there would still be an argument as to whether the companies had encouraged blacks and Hispanics enough so that they would stay to build up seniority. The point that is important, however, is that the construction and maintenance of high motivation and identification with the organization is threatened by any policy that draws unjustifiable distinctions between men working side-by-side doing the same kind of work.

Lenny Stefanelli had recognized this problem when he first came to the helm. One of his first actions was to develop a rational pay system of graduated rewards depending upon the kinds of work a man did. That system, however, was still vulnerable, especially on one count—whether helpers were paid the same as partners (excluding dividends) for the same work. There were some partners, for example, who simply were not able to handle books and money collections, and even some who were not responsible enough in the care of the trucks. These men were assigned only to carrying the can, and a helper (on their crew or another) might be doing that work *and* caring for the truck but not be eligible for the same hourly rate. A further rationalization of the pay system was required to erase that potential for conflict.

Equalizing work and pay scales (even between competent partners) is a complex task simply because the daily demands upon the individual worker vary so, depending upon the particular route he is on. Each district varies, of course. Some are hilly with narrow winding streets. Some are broad plateaus of row houses with easy access. Some include daily commercial accounts with vast quantities of refuse at the same location. Some multiple dwellings make the scavenger climb three stories to find an elderly widow's tiny paper bag of scraps. How do these differences get rationalized into expectations of a day's pay for a day's work?

Every year, a committee of the scavengers meet to consider the changes in the collection tasks presented by each route. To adjust the work required for each man, the committee tries to shift a block or set of blocks from one route to another, engaging in a Chinese puzzle of substituting blocks, half blocks, and whole streets among dozens of different routes. But what is the standard for comparison? It cannot be the amount of time a crew spends on its route, for some men work faster than others in order to get home earlier or to have more time for a second job or business. It cannot be the same number of accounts, because each account can vary widely in the amount of stops required. It cannot be the number of stops, because some have more cans at each pick-up. What then?

Sunset has always handled the equating of routes according to the amount of money they bring in. If a crew consistently handles a route that brings in considerably more money than another route, they get their work decreased. An underachieving crew is given more accounts to pick up. That standard fits the traditional idea of each man contributing his share of money to the pot, putting it out on the round table, so to speak, to be divided up. But it obviously has grave disadvantages as a measure of the effort a man and his crew have put out to bring in the same revenue as another crew.

I once tried to delicately raise this problem with Lenny and was greeted by a distressed, bewildered, and sometimes almost incoherent lecture:

We have strove—and Freddie's been [in the forefront]. . . . He has been a great proponent of, you know, equal work for equal pay. . . . I mean, here's a situation [where] everybody's equal in ownership and compensation. My compensation is the same and probably less than Freddie's because he's in the union and gets overtime. [Actually, Stefanelli then ranked 72nd among the partners in the amount of pay received.] And he [Freddie] looks across the street to his brother's route and says, "My brother's got an easier route than I do; I've got to carry these stairs [and Pasquale doesn't have as many stairs to climb]." The [main] reason his brother's got an easier route is because he [Pasquale] has nurtured the University of San Francisco [as a customer]. Where the city has become stagnated in growth, the University has grown, and he has containerized it. He has [nurtured them], and he's got a good rate out of it. So if he's got a $3,500 customer in one place out there . . . , Freddie's got to pick a thousand cans of garbage a month to equate to what that one customer's paying out there. So Freddie looks at that, and he gets pissed off.

But the question is, how do you equate the production of cans out there? If all the cans are in front of the house, against those that are all in back of the house, you could pick up the same amount of garbage but be doing twice the work.

I said, "Freddie, *you* give me the formula." I says, "I sat and pondered this question for *years*; *you* tell me how to do it." [And Freddie said,] "I don't know. That's *your* problem, but you ought to do it." And I says, "Well, I'm a garbageman like you." I said, "*I* can't find the answer. *You* tell me what it is; I'll believe it." So what is our only alternative? . . . [It] is to use money [that is, to use revenue as a measure].

Now, we are striving toward equality on the basis of this, and the people [scavengers] don't understand that. If you take all the gravy (which are your commercials) and containerize them and put them into a front-loader system [separate routes of one-man trucks hoisting and emptying the containers into the truck], then the balance is nothing . . . but apartments and residential income. And therefore everybody *is* starting to become equal in the loads out there. And that is a stride. [In addition, there is now something like $500 "allowances" for "hill trucks."]

But the guy like Pasquale, who's got the big customer, loses it. He says, "I am being screwed." The guy like Freddie that don't have any meaningful amount of commercials, he's not affected by it at all. . . . But Freddie still thinks he's working harder than his brother out there. But [anyway] by the time the route transition takes place, Pas will be retired, and that will be the end of the battle [between them].

All garbage companies, of course, have a similar problem, since it is important for various administrative purposes to more or less equalize the routes and each day's work for the men on the trucks. But in some communities it is very much easier to do this. For example, in Mountain View, Lou Pitto, the manager for Sunset's subsidiary there, does a rough time study each year, hiring senior high school students to ride the trucks with the men and record the work characteristics. But Mountain View is a very homogeneous (and flat) area, so the problems of variation are much less; and when there is a significant variation, it can be more easily handled. Pitto had worked as a partner on a truck in San Francisco before he went to Mountain View; he felt that the same kind of time study might be made there, but that it would be an enormous job.

Then there is the question of the comparative productivity of the whole set of Envirocal companies. How does the productivity of a route that is being collected under a different rate system (as in Mountain View or Los Altos) get compared to a San Francisco route? As of now, only tonnage comparisons can be made between the crews in those towns and the crews in San Francisco. But the same strictures can be raised. On the one hand, for the new companies the garbage is ordinarily set out on the sidewalk by the householder on collection day, and picking up a ton of that garbage is a lot easier than going into backyards. On the other hand, in the little suburban towns the streets and houses are more strung out, so it takes longer to get from one can to another. And there are differences in the time it takes to go to the central disposal area in different locations. Then there is the matter of equipment differences. For different types of collection tasks, different equipment can make things easier—as in the case of containerization and front-loading operations. And as time goes on, there will be further technological changes and improvements, proceeding not evenly across the board but jumping from one sort of collection task to another.

All around Sunset, social, technological, and economic transformations continue to unfold, and the scavengers, too, move in the midst of their own evolution. Things that looked somehow one way in the past seem different today. By 1974, Freddie's hair curled longer, like the young hippies he used to deride to me as we watched them padding by in the early Haight mornings in 1967. Americans who would glance away as a garbageman came by recognize now the increasing importance of what he does, and want more and more from him. For example, they may insist that he engage in a set of sophisticated resource recovery procedures that either may not be economically feasible or else will place a higher cost on the garbage company customer (or local taxpayer for the sanitation department). Or the public may insist on quieter trucks and no collections before 6 A.M., yet complain about the cost and about trucks blocking traffic for longer periods throughout the day.

"In the old days," there was a certain anonymity for the refuse collector; he could live in his own world and shape it as he wished—within certain limits, of course. Now the limelight of public attention brings new demands as well as new resources. The scavengers of Sunset have had to move in new ways to meet the challenges of their changing world. Those new ways have carried within them both danger and opportunity.

Nine

Envirocal: The Cooperative's Conglomerate

In the fall of 1973, each scavenger partner exchanged his share—block of 32 shares—of Sunset stock for a block of 1,000 shares of stock in Envirocal, Inc., the holding company organized to handle the different enterprises that Sunset was acquiring or starting. As a corporation, Sunset became thereby a wholly-owned subsidiary of Envirocal, taking its place alongside a number of smaller collection companies that Sunset had previously bought and a variety of other ventures that it had invested in.

In 1966, Stefanelli had said, "I believe in diversification. I always have. We have stayed in the garbage business; we should be in other lines, such as land company, investment company, or, you know, *something* like this—on the side, that would be owned by the stockholders. . . . Now you can't say, 'Today we're going to run it this way, and tomorrow that way.' It's a long-term program for a business of this size to go diversifying into separate business types."

With Envirocal established in 1973, the structure was in hand for diversification, although most of Envirocal's activities would still be mainly related to solid waste management for the foreseeable future. Besides Sunset and other garbage collection companies, the Envirocal umbrella sheltered two equipment leasing companies, a property development company, a computer service firm, a demolition company (which was quickly phased out as unprofitable), two debris box companies, and assorted partnerships or joint ventures, such as the Sanitary Fill Company, SWETS, and a manufacturing firm for the aluminum carrying cans. There was also a salvage company that the stockholders jointly owned. Most of these companies are clearly within the general field of solid waste management, but, because some are not, it is admissible to call Envirocal a conglomerate rather than an agglomerate, which would be a company made up principally of subsidiaries all in the same line.

During this same period (1966–1973), massive agglomeration had, in fact, come to the refuse industry. Refuse collection had been characterized by many small- or medium-sized companies. From these, huge national firms were built in a frenzy of acquisition of the local companies. In fact, the solid waste agglomerates had become "glamour" stocks, according to a *Business Week* article of the period. There seemed to be no limits to the growth of Browning-Ferris, Sanitas, SCA Services, Waste Management, and the other multi-million dollar agglomerates that ran around buying up every local refuse company with a good record and a willingness to be bought. Economies of scale in the purchase of expensive modern equipment, established relationships in the money market for capital loans, and computerized management techniques were touted as the inescapable reasons for the end of the small company and the future of the national agglomerates.

In the heyday of acquisitions, Sunset and Golden Gate had themselves been approached by more than one national firm to sell out. "You can't believe the salary I heard one of those East Coast people offering [a cooperative executive] in the bar at the convention, but he just turned it down like that,'' reported one awe-struck partner from another firm. Executive salaries were not the only possible inducement, of course, and the partners in one Bay Area cooperative were persuaded to sell out in an exchange of stock that instantly made each partner (on paper) a couple of hundred thousand dollars richer. But neither Golden Gate nor Sunset nor any other Bay Area cooperative succumbed to these blandishments. Instead, Sunset itself was soon listed among the top eight or nine largest waste managers in the country.

It might be thought that Sunset was merely following a national trend set by the national firms. But Stefanelli had made his own plans for growth and diversification and had sold his partners on them before the trend was apparent. Moreover, by the time the actual transformation of Sunset into a subsidiary of Envirocal took place, the glamour had left the agglomerate stocks. By the fall of 1973, when the partners approved Envirocal, the waste agglomerate stocks had plunged even more than the stock market generally. Then analysts began to raise questions about whether the economies of a national firm might be overbalanced by the loss of flexibility for each local company that had become a new division of an agglomerate. After all, some argued, the refuse business is a different matter in different localities, with varying climates, housing patterns, street and other geographic configurations, citizen expectations of service standards, and other cultural patterns. So when you have seen one garbage business, you have *not* seen them all. They may not be fully rationalizable under one system, or so some critics contended.

Whatever the pitfalls of acquisition, Sunset, in its new guise as Envirocal—and before that change—also pursued other companies successfully. By the time that Sunset incorporated Envirocal, both its revenues and its profits (before

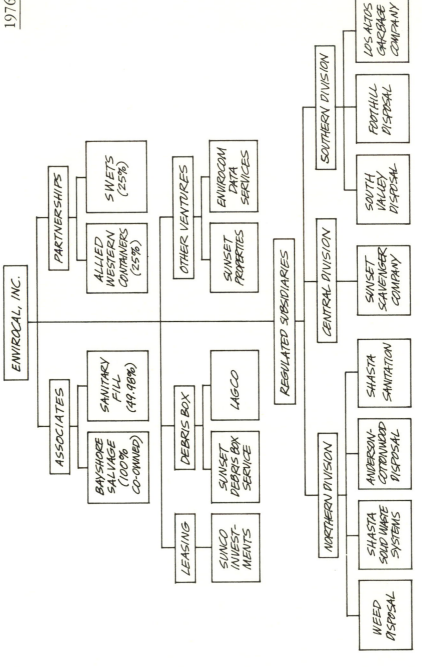

ENVIROCAL, INC.

PARTNERSHIPS
SWETS (25%)
ALLIED WESTERN CONTAINERS (25%)

OTHER VENTURES
ENVIROCOM DATA SERVICES
SUNSET PROPERTIES

ASSOCIATES
SANITARY FILL (49.98%)
BAYSHORE SALVAGE (100% CO-OWNED)

DEBRIS BOX
LAGCO
SUNSET DEBRIS BOX SERVICE

LEASING
SUNCO INVESTMENTS

REGULATED SUBSIDIARIES

CENTRAL DIVISION
SUNSET SCAVENGER COMPANY

NORTHERN DIVISION
SHASTA SANITATION
ANDERSON-COTTONWOOD DISPOSAL
SHASTA SOLID WASTE SYSTEMS
WEED DISPOSAL

SOUTHERN DIVISION
LOS ALTOS GARBAGE COMPANY
FOOTHILL DISPOSAL
SOUTH VALLEY DISPOSAL

Comparative Financial Data for Leading Refuse Collection Companies
(in thousands)

Firms Ranked by Sales	Sales and Profits (Losses)*							Assets	Number of Accounts: 1975	
	1969**	1970	1971	1972	1973	1974	1975	1975	Industrial/Commercial	Residential
Browning-Ferris	NA	$100,947	$125,928	$154,241	$199,812	$237,246	$256,331	$334,434	146	1,158
		12,620	16,770	22,259	26,795	29,658	29,433			
Waste Management	$47,749	60,334	75,786	97,730	132,110	158,482	158,691	211,056	119	1,100
	4,424	5,468	8,033	11,069	15,500	17,150	24,210			
SCA Services[a]	36,921	48,669	62,267	82,330	128,372	149,027	146,495	161,125	100	200
	2,921	2,773	4,197	6,818	8,297	(3,185)	2,142			
Brenner Industries[b]	13,363	16,003	17,484	19,546	24,866	35,414	27,195	7,959	NA	NA
	640	761	958	1,166	1,500	2,656	4,703			
Sunset/Envirocal[c]	8,173	8,854	11,831	12,772	16,000	24,000	25,000	8,500	23	175
	605	558	725	956	1,200	1,500	9,600			
Waste Resources[d]	—	5,894	5,041	8,259	13,546	16,550	20,886	23,027	14	116
		223	937	1,435	2,120	2,539	3,204			
Superior Sanitation	—	—	1,800	4,000	12,000	13,200	16,000	NA	7	275
			NA	NA	NA	NA	NA			

Source: Adapted from tables presented in *Waste Age* (August, 1975), pp. 12–13; and (August, 1976), pp. 14–15. Two companies, Theta and Sanitas, probably ranking seventh and ninth in the nation respectively, are not included because data from them are unavailable. NA = not available. I am indebted to *Waste Age* for permission to use the tables and to Michael Oberman, Editor of *Waste Age*, for discussions regarding the data.

* Generally, these figures are before taxes. However, the interpretation of yearly intra-company and inter-company comparisons are problematical because of differing accounting practices, especially including a refiguring of sales and profits due to acquisitions, liquidations, or divestments. In one case (Waste Resources for 1970), I chose to use an earlier report rather than the refigured reports which are otherwise used for that company.

** Calendar years are used throughout, except for Browning-Ferris, SCA Services, and Brenner Industries, which have varying fiscal years.

[a] Profits and losses after taxes for each of the years 1971–75.

[b] Profits and losses after taxes and extraordinary items for each of the years 1969–74.

[c] Assets for 1974.

[d] Profits and losses after taxes and extraordinary items, 1970 and 1971.

taxes) had doubled, according to a trade journal report. The new holding company made sense for reasons of tax laws and the complexities of service-rate computations.

For example, when Stefanelli first sought to undertake a massive up-grading of collection equipment from the open-bed trucks to compacters, he discovered a catch-22 in the way San Francisco computed costs for setting the rates Sunset could charge the householders. City accountants would not allow any equipment costs, not even the interest paid on money borrowed to pay for the equipment. However, charges for leased equipment could be figured into the base costs for computing a rate scale. So it was a natural step to set up a leasing company to buy the equipment to lease back to Sunset Scavenger Company. Financing such a purchase was easy since the leasing company was able to present to the equipment manufacturers and banks its long-term lease agreement with Sunset. Thus, the partners thereafter made their case for rate increases when and as necessary for updating equipment. Financially, then, the Envirocal concept seemed to make sense.

Another advantage of the acquisition and diversification policy was the opening up of managerial and other opportunities for promotion and skill development within the companies under the Envirocal umbrella. Not the mere paper structure, of course, but the development of new divisions or their acquisition made internal promotion easier and created meaningful new posts. (By 1976, with more than 600 workers, there were 11 partners in managerial jobs.)

To qualify for the management posts, Sunset stockholders could take tests to determine their aptitude and management skills. The names of those who successfully hurdled the tests went into a pool of those to be offered administrative posts as they became available in the new companies.

Actually, there was apparently some unwillingness among some of the qualified men to leave their outdoor jobs for an indoor desk. One man moved back to his route from a field office job. In particular, of course, taking an administrative post was a problem when it meant leaving the city. On one of my later field trips, Envirocal was in the process of bidding (unsuccessfully as it turned out) on a contract in the city of Little Falls, Montana, and if they got the job, someone would have to go out there to manage it. Freddie told me that maybe he or the others might not mind so much transferring to a desk job if it was nearby. "But who would want to go to Montana?" he complained. Yet, in fact, younger men probably still want that kind of opportunity, just as the older shareholders (like Freddie) had thrust the younger Stefanelli forward into the presidency. Maybe, if the chance had come earlier, Nick, who disliked the big city, might have spoken up for the Montana opportunity, just for the chance to return to a life in a smaller city more like his old home territory in Wyoming.

The new jobs were not necessarily easy to move into. The use of new equipment and technological advances (such as the computerized billing system) required skills that Sunset partners did not have. However, they were given a chance to take specialized training in order to supplant certain outside experts who were on a time-limited contract for their services. These sorts of opportunities could serve the organization well in recruiting new partners or helpers who wanted to become partners. The opportunities for promotion from the senior role of boss scavenger would otherwise be few and far between. Perhaps it was that, too, which suggested to Lenny Stefanelli the importance of diversification. How otherwise would the organization get the talent and skills it would need from its pool of partners for a "goddarn business becoming more and more complicated"?

Of course, the inescapable bureaucratization of an organization with increasing size and diversification of divisions and subsidiaries entails its own problems. One is the increasing distance of the managers from the field activities, such

Retired now, John Molini may still drop by and check out the computer facilities.

that they are out of touch with the tasks that make up the basic work of the company. For example, research on other refuse companies (including local divisions of national firms) turned up complaints from lower-level managers about "high-powered Harvard M.B.A.'s" in the central office who did not have the immediate knowledge and experience to make a local company profitable, once it had been absorbed by a major agglomerate. And, of course, those working on the trucks were also vociferous about inefficiencies and mean-ingless routines dictated by a far-off management.

In Envirocal, which carried out the tradition of Sunset, a company policy forestalled this problem. Any division manager had to have first spent a good long period on the trucks, carrying the can. Special sources of knowledge and judgment are tapped when the managers of an organization have intimate personal experience with the basic daily work on the lowest levels of the organization. Stefanelli could call upon that knowledge and judgment from his own experience as he took the leadership in 1966–67 to meet the city of San Francisco's garbage disposal crisis. City councillors, the mayor, and city administrators could intelligently assess and dismiss the crackpot schemes; but it took more than intelligence to evaluate the various serious alternatives that the city was considering, and Stefanelli (and his counterpart at Golden Gate) was a major resource.

When you collect the garbage, you can learn a lot of things. For example, the loads lighten considerably during a recession. Long before national figures in Washington were willing to use the word "recession," Fred Fontana was telling me that it had come. He knew because the rate at which people were throwing things out on his route had drastically changed. And down at the Sunset headquarters the daily figures on tonnage collected revealed the city-wide pattern of ten percent less refuse. Of course, there are more sophisticated economic indicators of a downturn in the nation's economy, but my point is that there is special knowledge held by the man on the truck that must be tapped if we are to understand our national refuse removal problems.

As Max Elden of the Work Research Institute at Oslo has shown, there is, generally speaking, important information held by those who are low on the totem pole of social status but high in access to experiences denied others. Those with this specialized knowledge (such as hospital attendants, bank tellers, and the like) are not always recognized for what they have to offer, and for that reason they themselves may in fact actually not make use of their opportunities for obtaining useful information. In the instance of refuse collection, the motivation to provide the information as well as the capacity to be open-minded enough to recognize it is enhanced by the Sunset policy that puts a premium on having carried the can. Thus, for example, in 1976 as in 1966, the board of directors was made up exclusively of men who had

spent many years on the trucks. With one temporary exception who was soon replaced by a former can-carrying
understudy for the more technical managerial duties on the
computer operation, all operating managers have formerly
worked the trucks.

Each solution, however, brings with it its own problems.
The obvious counter-argument to upgrading those who pull
out the garbage is the efficiency of directly recruiting trained
specialists who would not waste time and specialized abilities
sharing the line work. The costs and benefits of the Sunset
policy will doubtless continue to be argued from time to time
in the monthly meetings, where the partners may change
their minds and settle the issue variously at different times.

Will it be possible for the partners to maintain control
over their own corporation if they are out there every day
wrestling blankets and cans while the managers are develop-
ing more and more intimate knowledge of the office-based
details of the business? The history of Stefanelli's dramatic
rise to the presidency offers both encouragement and questions about whether the increasing sophistication of the
business will make this possible again. A year after Envirocal
was formed, I asked Ernie and Freddie how they thought the
new holding company would function. They were both en-
thusiastic. Freddie hastened to reassure me that basically
things were still the same; that the partners still controlled
their company at their meetings. "It's still the vote," he
explained. And he and Ernie felt, "It's the way to go—kind
of conglomerate, the way the big companies do. Of course,
we are small."

Certainly, Envirocal was still small then, compared to
the national solid waste firms—and even smaller, of course,
compared to America's international conglomerates. Even in
1976, Envirocal was still confined to operations in Northern
California; but in the absence of a specific policy to the contrary, it was due to grow larger, perhaps moving into the
other western states. All the personal relationships that meant
so much to the partners would be affected by that growth.

For example, one of Stefanelli's most excruciating personnel problems was what to do for and with disabled partners who did not want to retire. I was once introduced to one retirement-age partner who insisted on continuing work on the truck although by doing so he had automatically forfeited his company insurance rights. One senior manager, Gal Campi, had to retire from board membership by reason of age but continued his headquarters job as head of the southern division of collection companies.

Handicapped partners could legitimately receive assignments to easier and safer jobs, but that was also ticklish. I once heard Lenny try to persuade an older partner to make out a claim form to get state disability payments as a supplement for retirement pay. The man argued that he wanted to work, not get disability, but Lenny told him that there were two other disabled partners, both much younger than he, who still needed special jobs because they were a long way from retirement. When the man finally left, Lenny shook his head, "I have to take care of everybody."

That interchange took place in the first few months of Stefanelli's presidency. With the expansion of the company over the succeeding years, would he still be able to handle such problems on the same personal level? And would there still be the same feeling of being needed and wanted on the part of the aging partners? I met one partner, severely disabled and very far along in years, who continued to work (for minimal wages) by cleaning the grounds around the offices—although he was quite wealthy and would have been fully respected by everyone if he had retired from daily work. Would the impersonality of a larger and larger organization finally attenuate the relationships of the men to each other and to their group, so that Sunset could no longer give the same meaning to that kind of yard job?

Moreover, Sunset had traditionally depended only partly upon a system of formal rewards and punishments for maintaining a good performance level. I have described the various rewards and alluded to the punishments—usually fines or temporary layoffs for partners and, ultimately, dismissal for helpers. But, as any administrator knows (or should know), performance on the job is not merely a matter of such a formal system.

As Lenny told me, fining partners did not always work, and sometimes a man would be suspended from the job for a week or so in more serious cases. Lenny pointed out that suspension was an important disciplinary tool not just because the man lost pay but because he had to explain to his wife why he was not at work. In short, the informal means of social control were recognized as immensely important in engendering the highest level of performance. Indeed, there were many levers in the complex ties of informal relationships of friendship and of family that had insured the high quality of service to the community. As Envirocal moved into a larger sphere—for example, into out-of-state operations—it would not be able to count as easily upon those ties. And if Envirocal eventually evolves into a publicly held company—selling stock on the open market rather than just to worker-owners—still greater strains will be placed on the ties between the company and its stockholders who work within it, as managers or otherwise.

In those instances in which the workingman's identification with his organization changes and erodes from such expansion, the question must arise as to what quality of work he can maintain. If Sunset eventually becomes just another corporate employer, will the man on the truck work the same way as he does now? I have often seen scavengers pick up a little piece of paper that fluttered away from the hopper. I have even seen them pick up something that had been there in the middle of the street before they arrived. A crew did not want a stray bit of trash left so that someone would think, even erroneously, that they were messing up the neighborhood!

While customers were expected to pay more for the special demands they regularly made on the man who picked up their refuse, they often got extra-curricular free assistance. For example, at one particularly careless household on Lou

Pitto's route in the wealthy Forest Hills area, Pitto (who incidentally later headed up Sunset's Mountain View subsidiary) charged extra for "janitor service," regularly cleaning up the refuse that had been scattered around the cans helter-skelter during the previous week. But like any other scavenger, he might do a customer an occasional favor and clean up around a barrel he found accidentally tipped over.

The favors could be even more thoughtful. I once heard a lady ask Lou if he had thrown away a five-gallon can that she had by mistake put out the week before. Of course, the can had long since disappeared in the fill by then, but Lou merely told her that he would bring her a replacement next week. The lady was very grateful: "My husband uses it to mix paint in, and you'll make him a lot more friendly to me, because I shouldn't have put it out." The woman was not a special favorite on the route or well known to him, but Lou was very willing to help her out. Is this attentiveness to a customer likely to survive the evolution into a larger, more impersonal organization of paid employees?

The process of diversification and agglomeration of new subsidiaries also is relevant to the same general issue of maintaining one of the major strengths of the company—the minimization of management-labor distinctions. Since the new subsidiaries are run by partners but manned entirely by helpers, they increase the vulnerability of Sunset's own pattern of partners and helpers. Further, the union local (which includes most of the subsidiaries as well as Sunset) may gradually become increasingly populated by helpers, tipping the balance in the relationship of the union to the company. Instead of being merely another tool for the benefit of all of the workingmen, the union may become the conventional asset of the worker in his struggle against management—and justifiably so, especially if the partner members try to use the union to their own advantage vis-à-vis the helper members.

In short, the evolution of the Sunset Scavenger Company in response to the increasing growth of its market and the increasing complexity of its field is a case of buying solutions for one set of problems by a willingness to encounter another set. Yet, the newer problems are not inevitably recalcitrant. For example, meeting the issue of helpers who will not have a chance to buy in has its analogs in other institutions and communities. A cooperative like Sunset probably must always have a certain number of non-members, not just as early-stage apprentices but because fluctuations in the number of workers needed (caused by the loss of a contract, for example) might dictate layoffs and furloughs against which the partners, with their investments of time and money, would naturally seek protection. But helpers themselves could be protected from exploitation by rules that required a chance to buy in after a set period of time; and for others the helper slot could be designed as a short-term or at least delimited "appointment," at the end of which it would be up or out, and during which the company could encourage self-development through training opportunities, scholarships, and so on.

There is no formal company policy in this respect, but at the Foothill Disposal Company in Mountain View, Lou Pitto said, "It's always been my philosophy that a man shouldn't try to make a career out of the garbage business. I think it's a good job for a young man. You know, you do it ten or twelve years or so, but you should go for something else, either go to school or try to learn something else. Because that day comes, you know; it comes, and when it does, it usually starts with an injury. You'll either turn an ankle or wreck a back or something, and you just can't make it. Or a knee goes out on you or things of that sort, and you just don't come back to it. There's only so many other company positions that you can create for a man then." So he tells the younger fellows, "You're not going to do this job all your life. The next thing you know, you're going to be forty years old, and you are going to look behind you and most of it is behind you, and then where do you go?"

Ten years before, when Lou Pitto was pulling garbage out of the houses of San Francisco's swank Forest Hills section, he told me that he was stuck in the job and wished he had made another choice of occupation. He turned out to be wrong, but he was certainly one of the lucky ones. Not every scavenger at Envirocal can move into a physically less demanding job, and a challenging one at that, like Lou's managerial post. Shareholding is no solution to the crisis of age, physical disability, and retirement—particularly for those whose life has all along been in hard physical labor.

In a sense, the partner who stayed his whole life as a scavenger would be in more jeopardy than the helper who signed on knowing that most likely he would not buy in and had a set time within the company to prepare himself for other work. What had made some problems of dirty work somehow more manageable and reasonable in the past was the enduring community of shared work experience that the partners created in their cooperative endeavor. Perhaps in the future there could still be an informal or formal understanding that the routes should be shorter for those on the tougher ones and that the older scavengers and their crews could finish work earlier. Ten years after I first went out with Freddie, I saw him again, and he had just returned to work after a knee operation. He claimed he was all right, just a little overweight from convalescing at home too many months. The exercise would get him back into shape, he insisted. But he could not work the same long hours he had before, and, indeed, he and Ernie finished each day much earlier than the other crews. Had their route somehow been changed to fit their needs?

The renewal of the company will depend upon recruiting younger men to take Freddie's burden and to take responsibility for maintaining the productive traditions of Sunset in the Envirocal format. That human fact involves fundamental financial issues inherent in the role of worker shareholding—worker ownership. What Envirocal is actually doing today to confront the issue of new stockholders is somewhat ambivalent and ambiguous.

It seems likely that many non-shareholders in Sunset still have hopes of buying in. A conversation I had with two officers of the company, Julio Goggiano and Gal Campi, both of them with long-time ties to the company and its traditions, focused on the issue. Campi, by company rules, has retired because of age from the board of directors, but he still heads the southern division of collection companies. Julio Goggiano, a much younger man and a relatively new member of the board of directors, is secretary of the corporation.

Gal: . . . This company has always been very close. Not only the partners but the workingmen [non-shareholders], because the workingmen become partners. So it was a family. I started as a workingman . . . we all started as a workingman. That's a steppingstone. The relationship, so, was very close.

Stewart: That seems to me to be very important, . . . [but] nowadays the workingman who is on the truck does not have the same chance to buy in, to become a working partner, as you did, you know, years ago.

Gal: That's right, but we try to maintain those qualities by giving them as much as we possibly can as far as working conditions, benefits, and relationship between one or the other. We try, and I think we succeed in treating everybody, management, labor, as people.

Julio: I think most of them feel that eventually they will buy in, get a share.

Gal: They're going to buy a share [is their thought].

Julio: Now, how true that it's going to turn out, I don't know. I don't think anybody does, but I think the people that have been here, you know, anywhere from five years and over do harbor a feeling of eventually becoming stockholders, for whatever that's worth.

Stewart: Well, what do you think is the general feeling of the stockholders towards that possibility?

Julio: I really feel it's mixed.

Gal: I have to agree with Julio. There is a mixed feeling about selling additional shares. You know that we haven't sold any since 1968; we've been retiring every one of them, and again that's all dependent on the cash flow and all sorts of things and actually your needs in the company as far as what you consider supervisory personnel. . . . There's a mixed feeling. I think there's still hope in people that have been employed here for a while, particularly people that are here (we have quite a few of them) that their dads are in the company, that have a connection some way through a relative. They still have hopes, and I think everybody has hopes, how high I don't know, and again there's an uncertainty of what the future holds because of the changing structure of our company from 1973. It's changed dramatically, the whole concept has. We've adopted different policies as far as, you know, growth—buying companies this way and that way and stabilizing them. So there's a lot of uncertainty in those areas. There's a lot of uncertainties. You get an area where an individual says, "Well, heck, as the partners go," he says, "I'm the youngest as far as stockholders [are concerned]," and, you say, as each one retires, "I'll be the last one," you understand?

Julio: Yeah.

Gal: That philosophy in itself has gotten a lot of people thinking. They feel, "Well, less stockholders, more money." But then it could present other problems, but again the possibility that it's not certain, there hasn't been a definite policy established to take care of that. Lot of hope amongst the fellows because you wouldn't have an employee here digging around five, six, seven, eight years if he didn't have that hope, you know? You get paid, yes, but you're always striving for something else, striving for higher. And if there's an opportunity—we had cases where kids might have had opportunities some other place, but they stick here because they live in hope. That's where we all come from, from the ranks.

Yet, there are shares which the company has not bought and which have not been put up for sale even though their owners are no longer participating in the company. These inactive shares are held by scavengers who have retired, or by a widow of a partner, or under similar circumstances by non-working owners. In the past, company policy would have required that such shares be promptly put up for sale; no one could own a share, except very temporarily, unless he was working. However, under the 1968 share retirement policy, it finally became more economical to have some inactive shareholders for extended periods. Essentially this is because the company does not want to buy them out and thus enlarge its own indebtedness for retired shares.

By 1976, Envirocal had bought back shares to the amount of roughly $700,000, and the interest on the funds used over time to purchase these shares was as much as was considered a reasonable corporate expense (reaching about $100,000 annually). At the same time, the company could not encourage sale of an inactive share to a worker while the court suit was still in process. Moreover, the sale would have the effect of increasing labor costs, substituting a higher-paid shareholder slot for a lesser-paid helper slot. For their part, the inactive shareholders were happy to keep their shares, because they believed that their value was continually appreciating past what an immediate sale might offer. One of the retired shareholders "thinks I am going to make him a millionaire," Stefanelli told me, shaking his head. In any case, there has been a general reluctance to admit new partners.

Recently, a contrary policy was approved by the members, upon recommendation to them by the board. Under that policy, as partners retire, perhaps only one out of four shares will be bought by the company, and the rest designated for new shareholders. Moreover, in the next few months, in expectation of a resolution of the court case,

Envirocal will probably offer a dozen or so shares for sale and increase the number of working partners. When it does so, it should be able to offer them stock in such a way as to satisfy any critics who have believed that the company discriminates racially against prospective buyers. In addition, of course, it will lower the interest costs to the company while it raises the labor costs, with a small overall net increase in expenses.

Such sales will require a variety of prior adjustments. Stefanelli is particularly concerned that the distinction between the work of partners on the trucks and that of helpers must be clear and precise, to satisfy the (conventional) union requirement that differences in pay reflect differences in jobs performed. Partners therefore must have, for example, supervisory responsibilities or some other task in addition to pulling out the garbage. In the past, the difference was very clear, because only a partner collected money from the customers. But since Lenny introduced computerized billing, that significant responsibility has almost disappeared. Thus, it is a real task to construct new responsible jobs within the organization to which shareholders may be assigned. Also, of course, it will have to be company policy that whenever a shareholder is for some reason unable to do a particular job and a non-shareholder is assigned to do it, he will be paid at the same rate as the shareholder. In this manner, the wage structure of Sunset (and other divisions) will become progressively rationalized. A new labor contract will shortly institutionalize such practices.

The projected sale of shares will require that all of these questions be clearly resolved ahead of time. Then, in addition to any expectations of appreciation in the value of the shares, a prospective shareholder will know that he is in effect still buying a right to a particular level of job, the pay for which will make it reasonable for him to take on the monthly payments for the mortgage on a share. But from the company standpoint, the purchase of such shares must be carefully balanced with the opening up of real job slots. This is one constraint on the sale of shares.

Another constraint, according to Stefanelli, lies in a sort of public "psychological barrier" to paying high wages to garbagemen. A major increase in the number of shareholders would mean that the usual man on the truck will be paid on the higher wage scale. Even if it were economically feasible within the current regulated rate structure to return to the pattern of most of the Sunset garbagemen being partners, it would raise serious public questions. For example, why should a garbageman get $25,000–$30,000? (Right now, with maximum overtime, top salaries are about $24,000, but any renegotiated union contract, soon due, will raise that.)

It is true that San Francisco and its environs are recognized as a union stronghold for all occupations, and for that reason wages are maintained at a high level under union contracts. But with the recession of the mid-1970s (and especially with the problems of municipal financing), there is increasing local resistance to higher wages even in San Francisco. And even previous contractual agreements for municipal wage increases have been reversed. In addition, in some unions (in the construction trades particularly), there has been a broad attrition of membership and an increase in non-union jobs in those trades. In short, within the local economy there is a general sense that, across the board, unionists have priced themselves out of the market.

Whether or not San Francisco's unionized wages are too high for what can economically be paid, the fact remains that many people believe that this is so. And many of those are people whose own wages have not risen in line with union levels. For example, street sweepers in San Francisco get upwards of $17,000 (and were due $19,000 under their contract), while many white-collar workers, perhaps with college degrees, get much less. It is in this context, then, that

Stefanelli must find wage increases for Envirocal's partners and helpers.

Envirocal's profits have not been high and have disappeared into the expansion program. Annual dividends have continued to be modest; they were $500 per partner in 1976. Thus, they may not cover substantial wage increases in the future. So if such increases are demanded and agreed to, Envirocal would have to go to the city of San Francisco for a rate increase. At that point, it would be necessary to defend the higher salary levels.

To the extent that the labor is performed by non-shareholders, the wages will appear to local people as not too far out of line. (As of this writing, the new 1977 hourly rate for a non-shareholder will probably average about $8.25 an hour, close to what the previous shareholder average has been. This compares to $11 an hour for drivers of the San Francisco municipal trucks that collect street sweepings. In Oakland, the drivers of garbage trucks for the Oakland Scavenger Company got a raise to $9 an hour in 1976.) But for shareholders (with a comparable hourly increase of about $1.50) the annual salaries would indeed work out to between $25,000 and $30,000, including the usual overtime available to shareholders. Such salary levels can be justified in the current atmosphere only if the job includes route supervision as well as pulling out the garbage.

Under these circumstances, it is extremely problematical whether the principle of shareholding can be appreciably extended. Moreover, as of now, a share would not sell for less than $50,000 and probably would be worth a good deal more if a conventional market for it existed. By increasing the number of shareholders (decreasing again the formal number of shares allotted for each shareholder and creating new shareholder allotments), the price of a partnership could be brought down. But even at a level at which more prospective partners would find it practical to put together the necessary down payment, the wage rates needed to support the mortgage would push against the public's idea of a reasonable ceiling for a garbageman's wage. And the partners must consider that.

The argument may be made, and indeed must be made, that Sunset's productivity justifies higher wages. In 1976, the charge to the householder for the usual 32-gallon can per week was $3.65, for collection *and* disposal. Translated into annual figures, this works out to about $45 per ton in 1976 for all of San Francisco's residential collection and disposal costs. (Total disposal costs, which include royalties of 32 cents a ton to the city of Mountain View and such things as cost of the land, street improvements required by Mountain View, and so on, are now $14.10 per ton, compared to $6.50 in the first Mountain View contract in 1969.) The comparable figure for New York in 1975 was $51.50 a ton, including disposal costs averaging $6.50 a ton. In fiscal year 1969–70, New York was paying $47 a ton for collection and disposal, of which the disposal alone accounts for about $7 a ton. So New York was paying more then than San Francisco is now paying many inflationary years later. All the same, to sort out what these figures really mean when they have not been gathered comparably is like trying to find your lost wedding ring in the Mountain View garbage dump.

It is almost impossible today to create precise standards for overall inter-city comparisons. In any case, it would certainly be a long-term research project, which to date has only gingerly and episodically been attempted under either public or private auspices. In the meantime, one must go by rough calculations and relatively unsystematic appraisals of work practices. On such bases, today, there seems to be fairly general agreement that San Francisco still has a bargain. Yet, there remain tough questions about how the returns on that productivity should be distributed. To what extent should the larger community share in the productivity of its garbagemen and their unique tradition? It may be possible, for example, to increase production on many routes, and in that case should rates to the householder be reduced? Hypothetically, productivity could be increased to the point at which Sunset exceeded the allowed profit and would have to make refunds. To what extent do the citizens have a right to expect Sunset to work in that direction? Stefanelli himself has raised these questions in a thoughtful review of company responsibilities.

It should be clear, at this point, that the cooperative partner structure of Sunset has not translated easily into the Envirocal format, and as the company evolves further, there are new problems. It was not, however, the holding-company structure itself that brought the problems. Even before Envirocal was incorporated, Sunset's program of modernization, expansion, and acquisition strained its traditional ways of doing business. For example, equipment modernization, as I have pointed out, caused two far-reaching changes. First, it reduced the number of men required to do the same length of route (or even a larger route), and it reduced the range of responsibility for bill collection. From that stemmed the initial policy of reduction in the number of partners. Second, the major financing requirements forced the company into finding new ways to arrange for money for the changing needs of the business. Thus, leasing took the place of outright purchases and introduced a set of new concepts of money management.

Financing Sunset/Envirocal's operations "is a story in itself," Lenny once said. "The standard form of finances in the organization," he related, "was historically the old Italian philosophy: Never borrow money; save up and pay cash for it, then you don't have to pay interest. No one understood the complexity of leverage with interest, or that type of stuff. So we always paid cash for everything. [Before 1965,] there was very little debt in the company, so the banks always required twenty percent down when you got equipment."

But the banks or other financial institutions were conservatively loath to loan big money on long-term loans to a group that had not developed a modern credit record.

When Stefanelli became president, Sunset had just entered into its first major financial arrangement. It had been necessary to borrow money from an insurance company to purchase a tract in the Sierra Point area of Brisbane for the fill-and-cover operations. The loan agreement was the size of a major legal reference book. "They had a deed of trust on just about everything in this company, and you couldn't even change your toilet paper without getting their approval on it. You couldn't declare dividends. . . . We couldn't lease trucks. We couldn't do anything, because they were so worried that we weren't going to pay them back that they tied down every asset and every resource and every extraordinary expenditure of funds within the company. . . . And we couldn't even pay it off . . . until 1970, and even then there was a very heavy prepayment penalty."

At the time of the loan, the same insurance company had been handling Sunset's various insurance policies and that of the scavengers' welfare program for some time. As a former insurance agent, Lenny was incensed at the nature of the loan agreement with a company that had had such a lucrative insurance business with Sunset. "So I just ignored it," he reported. He went ahead and leased trucks and broke other covenants of the loan agreement, because "it was ridiculous. I said, 'Let them call the loan in.' I could finance the son-of-a-bitch anyplace, what the hell?" The insurance company shortly capitulated, withdrew all its covenants, and restructured the loan to cover merely a part of Sunset's real property; and so the loan continued more sedately and will eventually be fully repaid by 1979. "And now, you know, the insurance company wants to lend us all sorts of money now, because we are such good payers." Ironically, 160 acres of tidelands bought initially for $4,000 an acre, with the

Stefanelli explains the business to William Ward, Bank of America's vice-president for equipment finance.

insurance company's financing, can never be used—an albatross sired by the gulls of Brisbane.

Today, Envirocal has a $750,000 line of credit with the Bank of America, which they use once in a while for a few days or weeks to cover a cash flow problem—for example, to close a deal when they temporarily do not have all the cash necessary. For acquisitions, Sunset (and then Envirocal) has always carefully figured the projected incomes to determine that the revenue of the new division would support repayment of any debt that would have to be incurred. The down payment, so to say, is made from funds regularly reserved for expansion purposes, and the borrowed money is repaid from the revenues of the income-producing new division. No fancy juggling is required.

Of course, there are certain advantages for any garbage company with a long-term franchise or contract. And Envirocal (and Golden Gate) capitalized on that asset to finance SWETS, the transfer system that connects San Francisco's garbage collection to the Mountain View disposal operation. By relying on the city to permit a rate increase to finance the transfer center, the two companies obtained an unsecured $2 million loan from the Bank of America for a five-year term. The five-year term was linked to the guarantee of five years' disposal rights at Mountain View, the cost of which the city permitted the companies to include for purposes of a rate increase. In fact, the necessity to establish transfer operations to truck San Francisco's garbage thirty-some miles to Mountain View is the major reason why the rate for a 32-gallon can in San Francisco rose from $1.60 in 1966 to $2.40 by 1973. (Discovering a good thing, Mountain View raised its prices for San Francisco garbage after the end of the initial five-year contract, occasioning much of the rise to the 1976 figure of $3.65 per householder can.) But Sunset/Envirocal had to take very little risk as it converted smoothly from the Sierra Point site to Mountain View. All this is not to say that Envirocal has always made money. Indeed, the first full year of its operation, the corporation lost, by one computation, about fifteen cents a share—mostly due to liquidating the unprofitable demolition company. But its general history is one of careful, smooth financial progress.

Stefanelli sees no particular reason to look for further expansion opportunities outside California. To him, the models of the Bank of America, the world's largest, operating essentially within the state, and Pacific Gas and Electric Company, the biggest private utility, operating only in northern California, illustrate what is possible right at home. The problem is to see where the opportunity will come next, says Stefanelli. ''The garbageman philosophy is that you have to look at and evaluate the things that you can't see on a balance sheet.'' For example, take the acquisition of the South Valley division, Gilroy. ''There's a section of road between San Jose and Gilroy which I would say is about ten miles long, and they call it Blood Alley [because of auto accidents]. . . . People are getting killed right and left on it, and nobody wants to move into Gilroy [and commute], although a lot of people *have* moved down there, and that's the way it has been for five years [with state resistance to reconstructing that section of the road]. Well, when we bought the company, I visualized that just out of so much public pressure, eventually they would have to build that thing, and once that freeway was built, that area would just grow leaps and bounds. And the governor just approved it the other day [reversing his previous stand].'' With each new home that will be going up in the environs of Gilroy, Envirocal gains a customer.

Envirocal will continue to do more than merely relieve the householders of the wastes they produce every day. Although Stefanelli himself is not particularly eager to buy out any more collection companies, Envirocal will undoubtedly develop other related interests. For example, the Mountain View area is horse country, and manure disposal is a problem, so Envirocal will probably establish some sort of containerized manure removal service. But resource recovery will be the major thrust of the company in the near future. The scavengers always knew there was gold in the dross of castoffs and garbage cans, and Envirocal is even now planning for a major expansion of its resource recovery operation—a venture so large that it cannot be managed without state or federal help. By 1983, Envirocal expects to be engaged in an energy conversion operation, very likely a steam generation plant burning San Francisco's refuse, working in conjunction with the electric utility and other major partners. The project is probably a $100 million affair.

Lenny is not fazed by the figures: ''It's the same as we

did before, except we've got more zeros at the end of the figures now. . . . I can look back to the first staggering time when I bought my first truck. . . . It scared the living daylights out of me to take the responsibility to authorize a $25,000 expenditure. I mean, that was like all the money in the world to me at the time, and yet now. . . .''

All of this actually amounts to a very conservative financial strategy. It will continue to serve the purposes of Envirocal, so long as it adheres to what Lenny Stefanelli insists is the "garbageman's philosophy." That philosophy does not seem to be so very different from any savvy businessman's. As Lenny talks, it comes out very clearly as an astute assessment of the future, of market growth, and of how to get in there early, although sometimes there is almost a bit of poetry in it. Musing over what California has to offer, he once described flying over the state at night, when he sees the lights sparkling down below, "and every light you see, there's a garbage can to go along with it too, you know. And if you can find a vehicle to put it together, I just think then you *could* build the system to provide the people the service they require, that is environmentally necessary, and at the same time enlarge and perpetuate the same philosophy that made the company great to begin with."

Sometimes Stefanelli is not so optimistic. In an introspective vein, he has not always been sure about Sunset's growth. He is more and more critical about the wastefulness of America's materialism, even though that wastefulness makes his business, and he has linked Sunset's own development to the American materialist pattern. "You want to eat more than you can consume," he explained once, saying that the company "has become a monster." Envirocal is not without its costs. "You sort of visualize these things that are coming, and, in my judgment, . . . eventually the shareholder as we know it today, working on the route, making that kind of money—it's just a matter of time. It's going to be eliminated,'' he said. ''The monster has changed us; it's gotten away from us.'' But then he will get excited again about the new ways in which the entire garbage collection and disposal process can be re-worked into a rational recovery system. And he expects the San Francisco scavengers to lead the way.

Ten

Work, Ownership, and the Worker Cooperative

THE story of the Sunset scavengers illustrates certain basic social and economic problems in our society. At the same time, it symbolizes or suggests solutions to at least some of these problems. Immediately, for example, the experience of the scavengers in a dirty work occupation should help us to think about the future of all kinds of low-level work throughout the society. Also, the way the benefits of ownership are spread among the workers at Sunset leads to the general issue of how the fruits of our economic system may be equitably distributed through shared ownership. Additionally, the company history raises questions about the viability of a cooperative or other shared ventures in the web of cultural, business, tax, and legal relationships that characterize the American economic system. I want to consider each of these three broad policy areas—dirty work, expanded opportunities for ownership, and the viability of cooperative ventures—in the light of the Sunset experience.

As our society becomes increasingly dependent upon filling more and more jobs in lower-paid and seemingly lesser-skilled occupations, we shall have to discover what it is that attracts or repels recruits for these jobs. There seems to be less and less interest in the lower-level jobs just as they are beginning to increase in number. Higher levels of education generally throughout the society are a product of increased aspirations among the less advantaged; and more education urges aspirations even higher. More broadly, the political and social climate has encouraged us all to expect more out of our society.

Thus, those who might have more readily accepted lower-level jobs in earlier years (especially the racially and ethnically disadvantaged job-seekers) are less inclined to take such jobs today; and, if they must do so, they are more prone to the pathologies of discontent: absenteeism, turnover, higher rates of injury and illness, and so on.

Also, energetic younger people have been relied upon in the past for the hard distasteful work, but long-term population trends toward a decreasing proportion of youth in America mean that fewer of them will be available to take the dirty jobs. Moreover, as our society takes better care of those who are temporarily or permanently out of luck (through retraining and other unemployment benefits, retirement plans, rehabilitation and welfare rights for the disabled, and so on), fewer and fewer people will be forced to take jobs that they would avoid if they could.

There are a number of reasons why we must expect a continuing high demand for workers in just those jobs which are less and less sought. Despite the advances in technology, the number of these jobs will continue to grow. First, we have entered a long-term era of restricted energy resources (and perhaps a tighter capital market). This means that it will be less economical to eliminate jobs by using some kind of new machinery that will inevitably gobble up scarce energy resources. And capital may be too expensive anyway to invest in the design or purchase of such equipment. Technology will not progressively eliminate the lower-level jobs.

Second, as we continue to demand more and more services (greater than the increased demand for goods), we inevitably move into jobs that are not as amenable to mechanization. This, too, probably proliferates the kind of routine work that is regarded as unattractive.

Third, there is no likelihood of a future decrease in the major kinds of dirty work, because most of them involve the basic necessities of life. For example, much food production depends upon stoop labor on the farms of our nation, and we do not seem likely to switch to foods that do not require that kind of work. Also, daily onerous chores in the care of the infirm and the sick cannot be wished away. And construction and maintenance of housing require some of the hardest tasks of unskilled laborers. Even the manufacture of clothing seems to depend upon the use of many low-skilled stitching-machine operators.

Refuse collection is an outstanding example of the kind of important work that will not go away. It is part of the whole class of fundamental services and activities which can no longer be left to the conventional playing out of the labor market. As distinguished from food, clothing, and shelter, refuse collection (and, to some extent, the care of the infirm and the sick) directly involves public provision of services, usually municipal. Thus, in one way or another, refuse collection has a special connection with city finances.

The near-disastrous financial emergency of New York City was a hard way to learn a lot of things about municipal finance in America. But it also happened to lead to some ideas about the problems of recruiting and keeping employees for dirty work jobs.

For many years, a job in the New York sanitation department has been regarded by many as a prize. The last time job openings were announced, in 1974, a record of almost 69,000 men took the civil service examinations to qualify for what could be, at most, a couple of hundred slots that year. This astounding statistic was, it is true, very much greater than for the recent previous civil service examinations, given usually about every four years.

New York City Sanitationmen's Entrance Examination

Year	Number Taking Civil Service Test
1957	11,728
1961	8,524
1965	25,156
1970	17,462
1974	68,845

The 1974 figure probably represents the insecurity of blue-collar workers in a recession period. Nevertheless, the numbers taking the qualifying tests over the past years document the general attractiveness of the job.

Probably the major reason why sanitation work in New York is so fiercely sought has been the militant and politically astute leadership of John DeLury, for over forty years the head of the local union. He has concentrated on bread and butter issues so that the wages of his men have kept pace with blue-collar work generally (in 1974, the starting salary was $9,870, with increases over the first three years to $12,886). The combination of a tough, respected leader, a living wage with excellent pension benefits (DeLury pioneered early retirement, after twenty years, for refuse workers), and good job security—all these have made recruitment an easy task. It is probably no coincidence, either, that most of the recent commissioners of the department have risen through the ranks from picking up refuse themselves. (Incidentally, it was their support, especially in testifying at state hearings that a man is physically spent after sixteen or so years of the work, that made early retirement a reasonable demand.)

Clearly, then, it is possible to make the job attractive, but, in the context of tight municipal budgets, a crucial attraction has melted—namely, job security. In 1975, New York City fired over 1,400 sanitationmen, probably including all or most of those whom it hired from the 1974 civil service examination list. Moreover, the attrition rate since the firings has been almost double what was expected, reflecting the loss of attractiveness of the job. In the search for economy, the city also discovered wasteful supervisory and assignment practices. The vigorous defense put up by DeLury and by department staff did not dissipate the finding that morale and work practices had to be improved to provide better service at less cost.

In addition, since 1970 the department has operated under the threat posed by a report to the mayor which claimed that private firms could do the job better and cheaper. There were questionable assumptions in the report and an unexamined likelihood that the workers themselves would lose benefits that have made recruitment easier. Nevertheless, a new study under the direction of the same researcher, now at Columbia University, has recently reinforced the threat by concluding that, nationwide, municipal organizations usually give poorer, more expensive service than private firms operating on contract with city governments. Unfortunately, the statistics from this study have not been fully reported and are difficult to interpret safely. It is also a fact that each year some cities give up the contract system and move to a municipal department system, on the grounds that the former gives them poor service. But the general trend is towards private contractors, even according to the nationwide association of municipal public works departments.

In any case, the debate over a public versus a private system for solid waste collection is by no means confined to New York City; and wherever it occurs, it brings up thorny questions of accounting and public social costs that get buried in the practices of private business generally. For example, it is difficult to calculate or even trace narratively what happens to older workers who move out of the conventional private refuse firms for reasons of health and injury; but it seems likely that in public departments workers of comparable age and disability retain their jobs. Part of the productivity of private firms is undoubtedly due to their generally younger work force, compared to the municipal departments.

If a strong union with intelligent leadership can, as in the case of New York City, move refuse workers into a more protected situation, with disability benefits and early pensions rather than the societal ash heap as a future, the same kind of unionism ought to be able to protect workers in private firms. The question, of course, is, Does it? The answer to that is not clear. But, for that matter, municipal unions in other cities are not necessarily adequately protective of *their* membership. Nevertheless, municipal workers, as voters, usually have alternative sources of influence through the political system to mobilize support for better wages and benefits.

The advantages and disadvantages of both private and municipal organizational forms require further intensive study. Significantly, for the purposes of the story of the Sunset scavengers, in the spring of 1976, the mayor of New York and his productivity council discovered the San Francisco experience, and so they proposed an experiment for two of the city's sanitation districts: Turn over each of these two districts to its own cooperative business organization composed of volunteers from the current municipal employees. Whether the experiment will ever be launched remains impaled on the complexities of union–city relations, pension fund problems, and the worries of conventional private carters. Union leader DeLury, for example, has thundered: "I don't want to make any comments on idiotic suggestions. [The plan is] not even going to see the daylight."

Nevertheless, because considerations of municipal finance set constraints on what workers can get from a city directly, the Sunset model offers an idea for any city to avoid reducing services when it seeks to cut its costs without cutting wages or benefits for the workers. Converting to cooperatives might

be a good solution, according to some analysts in the New
York City government.

The cooperative member can own his job, so to speak,
and achieve the security that municipal civil service status
ordinarily implies. By his own efforts, he can maintain or
improve the wages that the civil service salary would have
provided. Health and safety rules can be the responsibility of
the man himself; he does not have to be dependent upon
supervisors or outside monitors to recognize the hazards and
do something about them. And, of course, a more direct
relationship between performance and rewards can help
assure a high quality of service to the city. At the same time,
as the Sunset experience documents, the member can be
proud of his job, maintaining self-respect in an occupation
that has been designed in more challenging ways. (I believe
that the Sunset workers told me clearly enough that variety
and challenge is an important ingredient of the job. I differ
on the basis of this evidence with those—like Irving Kristol—
who insist that the blue collar worker is generally interested
only in pay and not in the work itself and who therefore
conclude that job design and "job enrichment" is an irrele-
vant preoccupation of middle-class sociologists and personnel
specialists.)

If a whole set of problems inherent in the need for more
workers for lesser-skilled occupations seems addressed by the
Sunset model, so too does another fundamental question
that is posed for any society. How shall people share equitably
in the fruits of the general economic system?

The pluralistic structure of American society makes the
process of sharing in economic rewards a matter of contest
and competition. Adversary relations require one group to
organize explicitly against another. Thus, the unions are the
tools by which a worker demands his share from the managers and owners of public and private enterprises. But the
Sunset model allows a different sort of participation in the

fruits of the American system: it expands access to ownership and the returns from ownership.

In the instance of Sunset, most of the economic rewards of ownership are indirect—that is, a higher wage rate, more job security, and the nest egg of an appreciated share upon retirement—while direct distribution of profits has been at a minimum. Nevertheless, it is clear that, economically speaking, the scavenger-owner gains considerable monetary benefits from being an owner, not to mention his noneconomic rewards. Sunset, then, can be regarded as one model of ownership for an increased participation in the economic returns of the American enterprise system.

The significance of this model is highlighted by the fact that the wealth of this country is concentrated in a very tiny proportion of its people. One-fourth of all personally held assets are owned by one percent of the population, and in the instance of business stockholdings, about one-half of one percent of Americans own about fifty percent of all outstanding stock. Such statistics have begun to generate more concern than ever before, and in early 1976, the Joint Economic Committee of the U.S. Congress published its hearings and staff studies on expanded ownership. Because of the recognized stature of the committee and its significance in national economic planning, its work on ownership deserves close attention.

The committee considered that broadened ownership in the United States really must mean ownership of corporate stock rather than other sorts of assets. Their reasoning was that stocks are probably the easiest way to spread asset ownership, but also expansion of corporate ownership would mean a healthy capital injection into that sector and would benefit the economy as a whole.

The central technique considered by the committee was the so-called ESOP or employees stock ownership plan. The ESOP is essentially a program for individual firms to award stock bonuses to its own employees on a regular basis and in such a way that the firm benefits by tax treatment of that contribution and by the equity funds generated through the new stock. However, as the hearings and studies showed, ESOP has not demonstrated its general usefulness over other stock bonus plans, although it has had certain limited advantages for corporate finance for companies that might have difficulty floating stock in the ordinary marketplace.

The committee less intensively considered two or three minor proposals for expanding ownership of productive (including service) facilities through corporate stock holdings, but, interestingly enough, did not look at the cooperative format for this. Perhaps this is due to the common misconception of a cooperative as limited to parts of the agricultural sector; and to the fact that such cooperatives are often groups of firms rather than of individual farmers.

On the federal level generally, small and worker-owned cooperatives receive short shrift. For example, even in the agricultural sector, federal services for the small cooperatives have been restricted, while services to the larger agribusiness groups expand. Also, the Small Business Administration has been administered in such a way as to deny aid to cooperatively owned businesses. Indeed, although tax laws of the country have long encouraged the larger agricultural cooperative, they could not be applied to non-agricultural worker-owned service and production firms until as late as 1962.

What the committee concentrated on, the ESOP, contrasts sharply with the status of cooperatives. The ESOP rests, in part, on a generally applicable statutory provision that permits a company to make tax-deductible contributions to employee-benefit trusts; but it is even more directly supported by specific provisions of the retirement income legislation of 1974 and the tax reform legislation of 1975. With such support, ESOPs are still indifferently successful; and one respected commentator (Peter Drucker) has called them "financially unsound to the point of recklessness."

The Sunset experience shows that even without special tax benefits it was possible to maintain the productive interests of worker-owners in a non-agricultural cooperative. The opportunity for ownership typified by Sunset deserved further encouragement rather than restriction by the operation of the tax code.

Now, of course, the evolution of Sunset into Envirocal may make the point moot for Sunset. However, Sunset is not just a single illustration of this means of expanding ownership. The same cooperative format has also been used traditionally in the Northwest by plywood manufacturing firms, which are totally worker-owned. These, like Sunset, link worker-ownership to high performance. But in the case of the plywood cooperatives, this high performance has been parlayed into tax advantage. With the assistance of careful output analysis by consulting economists, the plywood co-operatives have fended off Internal Revenue Service attempts to reduce them to the tax status that Sunset was forced to accept some forty years ago. By carefully documenting that the owners are more productive than the (usually temporary) non-owner workers in the same firms, higher ''wages'' to the former could be presented to the IRS as being not taxable as distributed profits. More recently, the companies have avoided taxation on the revenues for all compensation of the owners—by defining that compensation as a ''patronage refund'' similar to the refunds of consumer cooperatives. (Of course, each worker-owner still pays his own personal income tax on proceeds from the firm.)

In essence, the plywood cooperatives have successfully argued that the owner-workers are merely getting the value of their additional efforts refunded to them. Perhaps Sunset might have been able to do the same thing in its altercation with the tax agents, but that is water over the dam. The point is that, despite federal inattention, the cooperative format is a practicable means of broadening the ownership of capital in our society, and whatever it takes to remove the obstacles to that objective ought to be undertaken.

Because cooperatives have, after all, been around for a long time and have certainly been significant in the economic life of other nations (such as Canada, Sweden, Israel, and Tanzania), the question has to be raised, Why is this form of economic organization so rare in the United States? Surely the reason is not just the discrimination of the tax laws, however constraining these have been. The explanation must lie deeper in the structure of our society and its value system that produces, among other things, the tax code; and it is in the social and cultural system that we must look for clues to understanding the possible place that cooperatives of worker-owners may have in America.

Again, the history of the Sunset Scavenger Company offers a tool to consider both problems and solutions. Several specific events highlight the dangers in and to the cooperative form in our society. The most outstanding signpost was, of course, the IRS dispute of the 1930s, and passages from the new bylaws written after the settlement in 1934 offer insight into the problem. Although the new bylaws formalized the required change in status, the members did not take the defeat lying down. They went on at length about what the situation truly was in their own eyes:

Heretofore in the amended bylaws and in the minutes of this corporation, the term "member" was frequently used instead of the term "stockholder" or "shareholder," for at no time have the stockholders regarded this corporation as an entity separate or distinct from its stockholders or as anything other than their tool or servant. They have always . . . spoken of themselves not as stockholders but as members and partners. For the sake of uniformity and out of an abundance of caution, we shall use throughout these amended bylaws the term "stockholder" or "shareholder" instead of the term "member," although we feel, insist and claim that the term "stockholder" or "shareholder" misrepresents the true relation existing and which has ever existed between the owners of the stock of this corporation and this corporation and the relation of the so-called stockholders among themselves, and that the term "member" truly represents and describes that relation, for this corporation was intended to be by its ninety-two original organizers and stockholders from its very inception an association solely of boss scavengers and solely for the benefit of boss scavengers and decidedly not for the benefit of drones or speculators; in other words, they were an association of workers who intended to form and carry on a cooperative corporation where every member was a worker and actually engaged in the common work and where every member did his share of the work and expected every other member to work and do his utmost to increase the collective earnings. This corporation [originally] took its present form of an ordinary corporation for profit, it might be said, from compulsion rather than choice, because the lawyer who drafted its articles and attended to its organization advised the ninety-two founders and original stockholders that a cooperative corporation such as they desired was not provided for by state law but that they could form a corporation in its present form and thereafter use and carry it on in the cooperative way they desired, and if any question arose the courts would ignore the form and adjudicate the corporation to be what it was in essence and in fact, in other words, what they had regarded it in their dealings with it; in short, if they carried it on as a cooperative corporation and dealt with it as such, the courts would ignore its form for profit and adjudicate it to be a cooperative corporation. Relying and believing in those representations and advice, the present corporation was formed and from that day to this, as its history will abundantly attest, it has been carried on, dealt with and regarded by all its stockholders as a cooperative corporation and in no way a corporation for profit.

If the social and legal structure of the cooperative is discouraged and a substitute structure encouraged, the substitute will finally emerge with all of its appurtenances and psychological baggage. It is but a short step, then, for the participants to drift into the whole range of conventional corporate behaviors, the whole range of conventional internal business practices which go along with the corporate form. And the traditional social benefits of the cooperative finally disappear.

Despite the protestations of those 1934 bylaws and despite any feelings then in the men themselves, the fact is

that today very little is said at Envirocal (or in the years of
Sunset just before Envirocal) about the cooperative form.
The members may be referred to as partners, but usually
they are called shareholders. Neither Sunset nor Envirocal
has been referred to as a cooperative or even as a partnership
in trade journal articles. This can only be so because it is no
longer important to the company to be so designated. Thus,
kinds of interpersonal and social attitudes and expectations
that are evoked by the very terms "cooperative" and "partnership" may be expected to disappear with the virtual
disappearance of the terminology.

The next event that vividly demonstrates the societal
pressures and expectations and values that shape or distort
the cooperativism of Sunset was the specific Sunset decision
taken in 1967 to restrict the entry of new members by retiring
shares from the next year on. Clearly, this decision had a
reasonably overt stimulus—the reduction in manpower needs
with the conversion from open trucks to packers. But it
would also have been a reasonable alternative to plan for a
reduction of non-member helpers (who in any case have a
higher attrition rate) and to maintain the tradition of an
open door for the sons of members and for those who are
just beginning their lives in a new country.

The fact that costs would be cut further by using helpers
at a lower rate than the partners would get was, of course,
influential in the Sunset decision. But, again, this marks a
reversion to conventional business thinking that omits both
the costs and the benefits (usually so hard to measure on a
corporate balance sheet and therefore so frequently ignored)
of the different psychological and social meanings of working
in a firm. If productivity is related to ownership in Sunset, as
the partners will testify, then the proportionate increase in
helpers versus owners would surely reduce productivity. Such
a reduction, however, would be masked by the savings from
technological improvements (the new equipment) and eventually by the fact that helpers will be generally younger and

healthier than the aging partners. In any case, with the reduction in the number of shareholders, the return to each shareholder could increase despite minor productivity losses.

I do not mean to suggest that there is something in the cooperative form itself that would specifically sensitize members to social and psychological cost/benefit factors which mere corporate shareholders would not recognize. There is, it is true, in the history of the cooperatives here and abroad a strain of ideological altruism—an emphasis upon the good of others who are joined in a common enterprise—which requires a kind of sensitivity to those others. That emphasis does not appear in the ideology of conventional business and corporate life. But whatever the effect of an ideology and whatever the extent that the ideology actually appears in and governs (or used to govern) Sunset members, I would point instead to quite a different source of encouragement to think of the other guy rather than just of the returns to one's self: specifically, the fact that each man must depend on the other for the amount of money that becomes the common pot. That interdependence is more evident to members directly working with each other than it is to workers who are more isolated and fractionized in their work setting and whose efforts do not increase the returns for each other. This is, of course, well recognized by job design and industrial management specialists who have long been studying work group effects.

In the rough-and-ready context of scavenger work, however, as Freddie's views and actions illustrated, there was a built-in readiness among the men to respond to each other and the organization in what Lenny called "the psychology" of shared ownership and working together.

Zero-sum thinking (whatever you get is precisely measured by my loss, and vice versa) is a natural outgrowth of the competitiveness of the ordinary business world. Indeed, one firm's contract is truly another firm's restricted market. There is no way around that, and it must have its generalized effects upon the mentality of those who participate in it. Cooperatives would tend to mute that, although they would still be susceptible to some of the same competitive business pressures, such as the loss of a contract to another firm's successful bid.

Sunset, however, has long had a virtual monopoly on services for its section of San Francisco, and that has offered the men a major security; thus, they have less need to invoke the zero-sum approach. The monopoly, in fact, did not entice the company into gouging the customers (at least during the period I observed and so far as I know to this day). Generally speaking, the local regulatory processes as well as the sense of responsibility in the men and the company itself have prevented abuse of Sunset's monopoly position. However, as Sunset (in the form of Envirocal) ventures further into the world of commercial services and bids on contracts for other communities, it will become more vulnerable to the modes of thought that govern its competitors.

In fact, the initiation of Envirocal can be considered still another historical event of importance in this whole context. Envirocal was a necessary tool if Sunset was to expand. Expansion itself was a response to the conventional assumption in the corporate world that bigger is better. As the profit and asset statistics, reported earlier, document, Envirocal has prospered, and so too, presumably, have the individual Sunset shareholders. Yet, as the already classic federal government review, *Work in America,* reported, the productive and other effects of worker-ownership are diffused by increased size of the firm. And the Joint Economic Committee repeats this finding with respect to the effectiveness of ESOPs. Thus, the urge toward bigness, inherent in the conventional corporate world, seems likely to reduce the benefits to Envirocal of its original cooperative format.

Expansion as a goal of modern corporations is not the only potential threat to the benefits of the cooperative model. The practice among modern expanding corporations of corporate diversification is another. For hedging the risk of a single line of services or products and for reducing tax liabilities by buying a business that has a temporary accounting loss, or for other reasons, diversification recommends itself in corporation life. But diversification operates along with size to diffuse the beneficial effects of worker-ownership. As a conglomerate, Envirocal increases the levels and degrees of specialization that were at a minimum in the simpler and smaller structure of Sunset. Such specialization separates the men from each other. No longer are they more or less able to do each other's work, to pitch in and help out the way Pasquale and his crew helped Freddie's crew when Ernie hurt his back. No longer will it be as easy for Lenny to rotate men through the other jobs at headquarters so that they will see what they are like and therefore appreciate those who are doing something different from their own work on the trucks.

The psychological distance caused by larger organizations and the specialization that goes with increased size are multiplied by the conglomerate approach to business development. As a matter of fact, both size and specialization have been recognized as dangers by some of the plywood cooperatives. They have watched as some of their fellow cooperatives have grown, reduced the number of member-owners, moved into other lines, and finally sold out at attractive prices to other corporations. For some worker-owners, that can be a desirable course of development, for others it is anathema. In any case, the fact is that the cooperative is subject to pressures which are difficult to resist when the opportunity comes for expansion and diversification. That opportunity, if seized, brings with it inevitable changes in the patterns of working and in the uses of ownership assets.

These remarks should suffice to demonstrate the universal situational influences that any cooperative must experience and their potential for transforming the cooperative into a conventional American business firm—if, indeed, it survives at all. What I was able to learn about the scavengers of Sunset makes such pressures and changes appear to threaten what is prideful and efficient in the cooperative organization. If Sunset is vulnerable and succumbs to these pressures, there is no reason to suppose that others may not also. Certainly, the experience of the plywood cooperatives indicates their vulnerability.

Are there ways to encourage cooperatives to maintain their shape and benefits rather than to exchange them for others? Sheer information is one counter-influence. Watching the disappearance or degeneration of some of the plywood cooperatives was stimulus enough to some of the other plywood cooperatives for them to make the conscious decision to avoid the same path. Decisions to restrict the hiring of non-member helpers, relying solely or almost solely on member-owners for the work to be done, and decisions to restrict expansion in the number of owners at any one cooperative are two actions that a single organization can take for survival. There are, however, costs to such decisions that make them unlikely, unless those costs can be reduced. It should be the task of social policy to consider the counterbalancing costs and benefits and to seek a creative resolution which includes more than simply providing the information so that knowledgeable decisions can be made by any individual cooperative and its members.

For example, expansion in and of itself is a natural response to an increased demand or market or to complications in the market that require a larger capability. A cooperative that loses an old customer because it was not large enough to produce in sufficient quantities when the customer's demands changed may decide to hire a large number of helpers the next time—and keep those helpers on as long as there is work for them to do but refuse them full membership in case the market should shrink. For the plywood field, that is reasonable behavior, but for municipal garbage collection it may be so only under some circumstances. For instance, competitive bidding periodically called for by a city for relatively short-term garbage contracts would encourage cooperatives to rely on helpers more, but long-term franchises under regulatory utility commissions would not.

Unexpected requirements for new capital (as when Sunset had to pay off five years' worth of back taxes and penalties) may propel a cooperative into expanding its membership beyond the size that allows each member to be sufficiently acquainted with every other member and to keep specialized roles to a minimum. Yet, there are ways around this too. The new corporate articles for Envirocal, for example, envision that new capital may be brought in by non-voting "Class B" stock, in much the same manner as any corporation might use non-voting preferred stock as a way to raise equity without diluting control. However, since a company may need capital but not have the attractiveness to sell such stock, other capital-generating techniques may have to be used. It could be federal policy to underwrite one or more techniques by guarantees or reduced taxation or other provisions that would assist a basically sound cooperative to raise funds for new collection or disposal equipment or procedures.

Expansion or appreciation of the cooperative business can, without any deliberate intention of the members, result in share prices that are too high for young new members. A successful cooperative may in that way force itself out of cooperative status into something closer to conventional corporate status with outside owners. Anyone with enough money to invest $100,000 in a garbage workers' cooperative probably would prefer a different job and a different investment. Even if his cash down payment were only $10,000, that would be $10,000 that could otherwise go as a down payment for a house—a likely concurrent need at the career stage of likely recruits. Yet, to reduce the sales price of the shares may be technically very difficult while protecting the interests of the current shareholders. Again, the costs of such price reduction may be lowered by careful consideration of how the proceeds are distributed to the standing shareholders upon a severe reduction in the price of shares. For example, the standing shareholders might exchange high-priced shares for low-priced shares plus bonds on which taxes are reduced, especially with respect to capital gains. In short, federal policy can encourage rather than discourage the continuity of cooperative share-owning by new workers by instituting a procedure for engineering equitable ways that older worker-owners may benefit from the appreciation of their assets while maintaining a low share price.

The natural urge to expansion may also be deliberately shunted by social policy into the proliferation of new cooperatives rather than the growth of existing ones. Each cooperative could obtain advantages by spinning off independent new entities. Moreover, there can be ways of permitting or encouraging a group of cooperatives to deal with each other and with customers to handle larger business orders or other matters that no one of them could alone. The Federation of Southern Cooperatives and the Southern Cooperative Development Fund are examples of organizations of worker-owned cooperatives for handling common problems. SCDF, for instance, is a joint financial instrument to offer advantageous new capital to cooperatives in low-income areas, while FSC maintains a staff of technicians to assist individual cooperatives which cannot afford, for instance, a full-time accountant to handle special bookkeeping problems.

Finally, there are many possible ways by which state or federal economic development programs can be designed to help generate capital for worker-owned enterprises. For example, there can be procedures to generate private sector low-interest loans for workers who wish to purchase a share in an existing worker-owned cooperative or to join in buying out or beginning a productive firm. Such programs of assistance will require that we recognize that worker-ownership strengthens our economy and is compatible with it.

I have suggested here some of the issues that are raised by any attempt to promote worker-owned cooperatives as a means of bringing new meaning to work and broadening participation in the fruits of a healthy economy. In no sense can these few suggestions be considered a systematic program. Such a program can only be developed by intensive consultation with and among leaders of the smaller cooperatives, who can speak from daily experience. Yet, today, there is not even a general census of cooperative firms in our country, nor any mechanism by which their progress or failures can be monitored.

The story of the garbagemen of the Sunset Scavenger Company leads deep into the innermost processes of our society, raising questions about the nature of work and the possibilities of equitable rewards in an expanding economy. Participating in the mainstream economy while following the different currents that go alongside the conventional courses proves to be an exceedingly complex matter. Yet, to the extent that we wish to preserve and strengthen the range of opportunities for all citizens while meeting the basic economic and productive requirements of our society, we shall have to analyze more closely what happens when proud men and women try to work together to meet those requirements.

Appendix:
Methodological Comments

HERE I want to set out some of the facts and procedures of the methods I used to conduct and report this case study, together with some comments on one of the major methodological problems. These notes are designed only to try to satisfy those like myself who, as social scientists, want to know enough of the details of the way the investigator went about his work so that they may better assess it and its validity.

I went to Sunset cold, introduced only by my own previous letter expressing an interest in studying the company and asking for an appointment. (I had written Golden Gate, too, and actually went there for an interview later.) My initial contact with Sunset was on May 11, 1966, when I first met Stefanelli, and my last site visit (as of this writing) was on January 17, 1977, when I went to see the managers (Lou Pitto and Joe Renati) of two of the Envirocal subsidiaries south of San Francisco and toured the disposal area at Mountain View. I had met Lou Pitto ten years previously, almost to the day, when I worked with him and his crew on their truck route.

The accompanying table summarizes the numbers and kinds of observation and interview visits. In the text of this book, I have already described enough of my observational practices on the truck, but comments on the other encounters are necessary here. An interview at the company headquarters was not just sitting and talking for an hour or so. Usually it would include a walking or

SUMMARY OF ON-SITE OBSERVATIONS*

	On the trucks	Other (offices, dumps, etc.)
1966	4	5
1967	1	1
1968	1	—
1969	1	1
1972	1	1
1973	—	2†
1974	1	—
1977	1	3
Total	10	13

*Usually each of these represents several hours of site contact; "on the truck" observations, with one exception, represent at least the full day's work period.

†Interview-observations by Raymond L. Russell, III. All others by SEP.

driving tour to introduce or re-introduce some aspect of the company operation, and most often the contact would include at least one other person and generally half a dozen or more other people. The research contacts then might last for several hours and include a lunch, a drink after the work was formally over, an after-work committee meeting, kibitzing at a card game in the company board room, and such other formal or informal encounters. Thus, for a relatively small number of days of encounters, I was able to see a fairly complete round of activities, as these centered on the company.

I did not at any time see people outside the context of my study; for example, I did not have social engagements or interact with families. Partly this was deliberate, a kind of compartmentalizing of my relationships to keep them clear; but partly, I believe, it also had something to do with my own personality limitations (an uneasy incapacity to break compartments of work and play). At best, this has meant that it has not been hard to limit the book to true work-related aspects of social interaction, though I have not been exhaustively inclusive of them. For example, there are company events such as ''Old Timers' Day'' or ''lunch at the dumps'' that I have not participated in.

The fact that I left San Francisco some months after I began the study also made it more difficult for me to take the leisurely time that simply enjoying other people's company requires. I was always sandwiching in my later contacts and observations on quick trips back to the city from the East Coast, trips usually made for some other purpose and offering little free time. And yet, I never came back to the city without going out again on Freddie Fontana's truck, always for their whole day—with one exception, my last visit in January, 1977, when I joined them late on the route. Ordinarily, then, I would just turn up at the doughnut shop where the crew (and other crews) waited for the trucks to pick them up. Yet, even with such irregular, short, and infrequent contacts, one cannot maintain a relationship over so long a period of time without a growing feeling of identification and just plain friendship, however limited the kinds of interactions. The dedication of this book is in those terms.

If I planned a contact for what I may loosely call an interview, it was to answer a specific set of questions which I had considered and listed beforehand. Sometimes I would consult my list of questions during the encounter, to make sure I had not forgotten something. Even so, I would sometimes find that I got back home with a wealth of information but that I lacked one crucial item which I would have to obtain at some future time.

With Lenny Stefanelli, it was always easy to snap on the recording machine and then ignore it, except for making sure it did not run out of tape. Those tapes were transcribed, and the transcriptions and the transcribed notes that I made on all other occasions, together with other case materials, comprise a file of about ten to twelve inches of typescript pages, the raw data on which the book is based. It should be evident that some significant aspects of my encounters would occasionally evade getting embodied in my formal records, and, indeed, perhaps a half dozen times I have recalled one or another particularly vivid episode, decided on its relevance, and then looked back to the records of that day and discovered I had not set it down. That is an unnerving experience, but I gather I share that with other participant observers who also cannot set down the whole necessary richness of their encounters in the course of a study. However, such lapses do not seem to get reported ordinarily, and I want to make sure that I report them here, especially for the benefit of students who may feel that all social science is as systematic and routine as published reports make them seem.

Of course, as a social scientist, I have tried to present my materials in a way that does not distort what I believe to be true on the basis of the inquiry I have conducted. Yet, the objectivity of the social scientist is sometimes challenged most in those instances in which he knows the most. That is, continued association over time with a subject organization or set of respondents establishes reciprocal obligations that will not arise in a quick in-and-out inquiry. Journalists face this problem, and, if they are on one beat over many years, they may become captive of the people or agencies or institutions they cover.

I have certainly developed a strong positive feeling for Sunset and its people, and I have probably not been able to fully correct for my own bias in favor of the company, though I have tried to do so. For example, if I checked out potentially uncomplimentary data with an informant and could not obtain direct confirmation, that did not mean that I would not use such data; I might assess a denial as more confirmatory than convincing. Also, I have consciously tried to resist the natural impulse to present the men and the company simply in the admiring terms that I have personally felt. Whether I have been successful or whether (as my colleagues on the larger study worry) I have leaned over backwards to correct for my positive feelings is for the reader to judge.

In one instance, I have deliberately not reported a minor uncomplimentary episode. I was told that it would present problems to the company today to rake over those old coals. I accepted that, for I believe that presenting those particular events would not have provided the reader with any meaningful additional insight—merely a potentially interesting aside. Even to mention this non-report probably gives it undue prominence from the standpoint of the story of Sunset. I want to mention it, however, because it is methodologically instructive.

When one has gained entry (and the privilege of publication) regarding any on-going institution, particularly one (like a business) in which any published information can have financial repercussions, one can be caught between wanting to report something and feeling bound not to do so. Again, journalists often face this problem but can sometimes finesse it by quoting named or unnamed dissident sources. Most, however, will not place the right to publish above the obligation to keep confidences, in order to obtain background information that can be helpful without being directly used. (Similarly, I have been privy, for example, to recent labor contract strategy in San Francisco which I do not report as such but which helped me deal with the general issue of pay and management-labor relations.)

Of course, the study of any organization can place it or its members in jeopardy, and for that reason the leaders of an organization often ask a right of review. [See Erving Goffman's comments on studying patient life at St. Elizabeths Hospital, in *Asylums* (Garden City, N.Y.: Doubleday, Anchor Books, 1961), especially pp. ix–xi.] Aside from the correction of obvious errors, the review by Sunset of my manuscript occasioned only a request for the one change I have mentioned. I had no hesitation in accepting the request, since it seemed so minor. Perhaps, in fact, it was merely a symbolic sacrifice for any uneasiness, expressed and unexpressed, mine or theirs, about other touchy things I *did* include. In any case, it seemed a small price to pay for the intimate access I had and the right to do what is rarely possible in social science studies of real institutions: that is, to use real names instead of a variety of anonymities that obscure empirical or theoretical connections that could otherwise be made.

With a previous book, I had to quietly endure a reviewer's misidentification of the institution I studied and his misinterpretation based on the misidentification. Since the real identity could not be revealed, I could not show its significance in the book nor correct the reviewer's criticism. In the instance of Sunset, readers will have a better chance to check me out, and differences will not be due to my deliberately misleading the reader in order to protect the anonymity of the subject organization.

In this connection, it is important to note that the initial version of this manuscript was cast with assumed names and disguised identities of place and organization. It was a great relief and actually a methodologically releasing decision to discard that tactic. I was able to write in more detail about many issues when I could write it true to life. It was a decision made with the specific concurrence and encouragement of Lenny Stefanelli. I rewrote and reorganized, using additional materials made possible by his encouragement on that decision. I believe that the book is more useful now with full identifications, and I pass on the experience for the benefit of other social scientists.

I believe we may too often handicap ourselves by assuming that those whom we study will not tolerate what we want to publish. Perhaps so, but perhaps it may be helpful to use the two-stage review process that I used by chance. That is, write first in the standard disguised identities format, and test out that version with the institution or organization. As a dry run, it protects confidences and allows a long, considered process of judgment as to whether the organization will accept a change in the rules of the game and permit full identification. The next review version will, of course, be more revealing, but the previous review will have made the identified version less novel—a familiar portrait, warts and all.

One final important feature of the inquiry I made: after 1973, I had the advantage of having younger colleagues also making case studies of garbage collection organizations. They worked full-time on certain other selected organizations, and what they discovered there and talked about with me helped fundamentally to clarify issues regarding Sunset and to correct errors that might have otherwise gone unnoticed. That sort of sharing of a common enterprise in research is a major methodological aid.

If these notes on my methodology leave some questions unanswered, as indeed they must, I would welcome and respond to any inquiries from students and others who may want further orientation to the research. And, of course, I would be appreciative of anyone's corrections of any misstatements of fact that I may have made in the book. I do not plan to write another book on Sunset/Envirocal, but I intend to keep right on following what happens to the company and the people there, and I will want to keep my facts straight.

Epilogue:
Twenty Years Later

B Y 1977, during my last interviews before this book was originally published, it was abundantly clear that Sunset was entering a new era, projected four years before by the 1973 transformation into Envirocal. Lenny Stefanelli said that he "visualize[d] these things that are coming, and in my judgement . . . eventually the shareholder as we know it today, working on the route, making that kind of money—it's just a matter of time. It's going to be eliminated. The monster has changed us; it's gotten away from us." In a sense, Lenny Stefanelli had, it would seem, helped create that monster by his Envirocal strategy, but the social and economic conditions of solid waste management in San Francisco and the country were not to be overridden, even by the most talented of leaders for the scavenger co-ops.

Twenty years later, in this epilogue, I will emphasize three arenas in which transformative changes took place: The leadership, the company format, and the work itself. Of course each arena overlaps the other two, and none can be discussed discretely. Let me therefore simply recount more or less chronologically some of what happened to Sunset; and let the action in each arena appear as it might in a three-ring circus.

By the mid-1970s, the ethnic domination of Sunset by the old Italian families was being challenged by the new social and legal rules in America and California. The civil rights lawsuit against Golden Gate on behalf of their Hispanic and black helpers, as noted in chapter 8, came to include Sunset plaintiffs, and eventually workers at Oakland Scavenger Company, the third of the large Bay Area co-ops. It ground on, as legal cases do, but eventually in 1979 Stefanelli and the Sunset plaintiffs found an out-of-court settlement for themselves that satisfied company and plaintiffs alike.

Lenny told me some 18 years later that he was still very proud of the settlement, especially in comparison to what had happened to Oakland. Sunset agreed to reverse its stock buyback policy and open the purchase of shares to helpers again, turn and turn about for Hispanic, black, or other helpers, with the company itself planning to retire only one share for each three new partners. At better than $50,000, shares were expensive then, but they opened the door to a higher wage scale for the buyer. In addition, the plaintiffs as a class received about $450,000 in cash, which, to the benefit of the company too, could be charged on its accounts as retroactive pay to the employees concerned. That meant that a major part of the settlement expense could be charged against the company's bona fide labor costs and figured in for any rate adjustment requests for the city to approve. In short, Sunset could charge off its settlement.

It had, in any case, come to be burdensome for Sunset to continue buying back the shares of retiring partners. The costs were not chargeable as expenses to be recovered in some future rate increase, and they represented a drain on capital that might be better invested in equipment or further acquisitions. By contrast, the higher wages that the former helper received now as a partner could be amortized in rate adjustments. The final settlement turned out to be an instance of doing well by doing good.

All this was in considerable distinction to what happened with Oakland Scavengers, where the battle was fought all the way for many years by the encrusted president and his partners: "No one is going to tell me who I can hire," he had told Lenny. The ultimate court decision in 1987 came to $12 million in damages. However, by that time, Oakland had sold itself to become a subsidiary of Waste Management, thus shedding its cooperative status; so there was no question of non-Italians buying into a partnership. That, no doubt, was part of the reason that the plaintiffs got such a major cash pay-off.

The sale to Waste Management had provided that the previous owners of Oakland would be responsible for any settlement that cost more than $2.5 million. So the former partners (not the company) were individually liable for paying by far the major portion of the settlement; it worked out to $300,000 apiece. They had already exchanged their shares for Waste Management stock which, as the case wore on, rose astronomically, so each former partner was able to pay his $300,000 out of personal profits from stock appreciation; but it was still an enormous price to pay for their resistance.

Over the 1970s and 1980s, Sunset continued to grow and prosper as Lenny Stefanelli had predicted. The handsome financial status of the company came to depend primarily upon a variety of real estate deals (especially regarding disposal sites) and fortuitous acquisitions of small but lucrative California and other garbage companies that Lenny was ingenious at seeking out. It was, he had told me long ago in 1966, the only way Sunset could make any real money, because it was limited by its city charter to no more than 5 percent profit solely on revenues from collecting and disposing of the garbage. Past experience had shown that this allowed no substantial dividends, and any rise in wages had to meet local standards.

On the one hand, the net worth of the company continually expanded, especially in the population (thus market) growth and the torrid real estate atmosphere of California. By the 1980s, the company changed its rules to allow retiring scavengers to keep their shares rather than sell them back to the company, almost the only likely buyer. By then the price was more than $100,000, but it was much less than a share might be worth if another company should someday want to buy out Sunset the way Sunset had bought out so many others. So the number of working partners continued to decline from a high of over 300 to perhaps 200 in 1986, even though many other, retired scavengers formally remained partners and often participated actively in company affairs. In December 1986, Sunset partners learned that the Oakland scavengers had sold their company to Waste Management. Furthermore, later that same month Golden Gate sold itself to its own Employee Stock Ownership Plan, each partner receiving $645,000. All this confirmed Sunset partners in their hopes for a better return on the appreciation of their shares.

Wages as well as company value had also steadily risen. Even though these were tied to local union scales and to the city rate increases, Lenny was adroit, as even his opponents conceded, in petitioning for rate increases when they could best be justified and awarded. In 1977 the "boss scavengers" made somewhat more than $25,000, but by 1985, 20 years after Lenny had taken the helm, many partners working the trucks could make $65,000 a year—the salary allocated also to Lenny. Some scavengers were actually making a few thousand dollars more because of heavy overtime, but Lenny himself was restricted by his board to one Saturday each month of paid overtime, no matter how much time he might actually put in. Thus, he would ordinarily rank in income no more than seventy–something among the two hundred–plus scavenger partners. That was true up to his very last days with the company, in mid-1985.

He always hoped that his fellow board members would "show me some appreciation for all I was doing" and increase his salary; but remembering what had happened to his predecessor, he never requested a greater amount than what was based on equal pay for all partners. Eventually, the car that the company periodically bought for him was upgraded to a new Cadillac, and he drove it around proudly with a license plate that read "RUMENTA"—Italian for "garbage." But even that cost him dearly among his partners. He grumbled to me passionately on this topic, imitating an Italian immigrant rhythm for what he claimed was a weekly complaint from one of the board members: "'We all equal in this company. You got a Cadillac car, I don't got a Cadillac car. Equal is equal.'"

Occasional rumors even had it that he was making barrels of money on corrupt side deals, and he had to endure that. At the end of his years with the company, bad feeling among some of his former partners led to an attempt to repossess the car and even its license plate and to hire lawyers to investigate whether he had embezzled funds. (The prestigious law firm especially hired by the company reported back that there was no reasonable evidence of such problems and warned the company to drop the accusations.) In the 1960s Lenny had laughed when he told me about the "bunch of old ladies" and the rumors that he had to dissipate, but when he actually left the company in 1985, it was no laughing matter.

When I saw him in 1997, I asked him about the rumors of his financial activities. He explained his personal finances: On a tip from one of his wife's cousins many years before, he had made a crucial stock investment which multiplied its value many times, and so later he had the capital to make a land deal that was also lucrative. No doubt, this was a

mighty reason that he had never been attracted by the extremely high salaries he was periodically offered by other
bigger companies during his Sunset Scavenger days. His
acumen in making advantageous deals for Sunset had earlier made his family's status secure. Nevertheless, it was an
entrepreneur's pleasure in the freedom to build his company ever more powerful that was clearly the real key to his
acceptance of the modest scale of compensation he received at Sunset. What in the end contributed to his readiness to leave the company was primarily his disappoint-
ment at not being able, time after time, to get the company
board to accept the deals he brought to them.

* * *

The story of Leonard Stefanelli's departure in mid-1985 is
worth telling in detail because it is deeply imbedded in the
structure, culture, and economics of the cooperative. He
had told me in the 1970s that the only solution to the problem of the increasingly valuable partnership shares would
be ultimately to take the company public; and he worked to
that end for years. He was ambivalent, though, about jetti-
soning the cooperative structure and explored for a while
the potential of establishing an ESOP structure. However,
he determined that there was no way to finance a buyout of
the partners by an ESOP trust, again because of the 5 percent profit ceiling of the city's rate setters; the cost of the
financing would not be chargeable within the allowable
expenses for rate-setting.

In 1982 he and Gal Campi, Sunset's financial officer then,
conceived another solution that would concurrently solve
the same problem for the other two major Bay Area cooperatives—Oakland Scavenger Company and Golden Gate
Disposal Company. Joining together the three of them
would consolidate a revenue of "a quarter of a billion dollars," he marvelled to me years later. A combined company

could become a juicy prospect for a buyout but in any case a powerful industry combination. The financial figures on a potential merger needed to be worked out so that the equality of all partners would be maintained and at the same time clearly recognize that the shares of partners in the other two companies were worth considerably more, because each of them had fewer partners than Sunset would bring to the deal. "It could have been done," he insisted. While the stocks would be exchanged for shares in the consolidated firm, each company could continue under its current management.

When he arranged a meeting with his counterparts at the other two co-ops to go over the finances and prospects of the merger, they were not interested in the figures. Other questions came to their minds. As he reported it, one asked who would be president of the amalgamated co-op, and the other asked what color the trucks would be painted. Lenny says he insisted that he did not seek to be president, and that the trucks could continue to be painted with local logos for each district; but the conversation petered out. Years later he was still disgusted with what he saw as the parochialism of his counterparts.

Having to be content with the smaller but still considerable canvas of Sunset, Stefanelli continued to draw big plans, pushing expansion possibilities, but he began to get less and less concurrence from his board. "I lost control of my board; little by little my supporters retired or were voted out." Turnover on the board gave a majority of votes to a circle of partners who hung back, seemingly resenting the president's ever-wider vision. The newer board members built support for themselves through a social club that met regularly at a restaurant to plan strategy. Stefanelli kept losing votes on his projects, sometimes as close as six-to-five.

The board majority complained that he was not concerned with the ordinary operations of the company (he felt he was putting the emphasis on the right priorities); that he

was running around too much with politicians (his influence put the company in good stead, especially at rate-setting time, he would argue); that he wasn't spending enough
time on company business (he told them even if they paid
him a million dollars, he could not be spending more time);
that he sought publicity, gave too many talks, visited the
pope, went to the White House as a member of an advisory
group, and so forth (and he wondered why they were not
proud of the prominence of their company and its chief
executive). The new board majority organized itself to
speak for a substantial group of those who were discon-
tented with Stefanelli's type of leadership.

Central in this group was Livio Cristanelli, who came to
prominence and high regard as chairman of a committee
that had revised the pension arrangements, a move that
vastly improved everyone's returns. He was Italian, but not
San Franciscan; he had come, like Ernie Samietz, from coal
mining in a mountain state. But he fit into the perspective of
the partners. For example, in 1983 he joined others to criticize Stefanelli's desire to hire a finance specialist at a salary
20 percent higher than any of the partners. The new officer
would receive $65,000 plus the use of a car. Lenny's choice
for this job was Michael J. Sangiacomo, a gifted young financial specialist, a certified public accountant. Lenny
sought Mike Sangiacomo as Envirocal's chief financial officer at more than his own or other salaries were at that time
(they rose to $65,000 in a couple years) because he knew
the burgeoning and complicated company needed more resources in financial planning than he could offer, or that
anyone else in the company could provide; and he knew
that the company had to pay for a top man. It should count,
he thought, that Mike's father and Mike's mother's father
had been scavenger partners at Golden Gate. Nevertheless,
his recruit had to go before the board for a stiff grilling.
Lenny was pleased at Sangiacomo's quiet and smooth handling of the hard time he was given; the board in the end

approved him, but it stung them that he would make so much more money than they or the other partners.

Lenny had always wanted to be a part of Sunset, a part of the Italian camaraderie that he had witnessed, growing up on "Dago Alley," as Freddie Fontana fondly called the old San Francisco neighborhood where he and most of the other scavengers came from. Freddie and his brother Pasquale befriended the young Lenny who had missed out on a father's interest. "We practically raised him, I guess," Freddie told me. Stefanelli became a garbageman helper right out of Polytech High. Eventually a partner, he married Virginia Campi, the granddaughter of Emilio Rattaro, the first president of the co-op. While he worked the trucks, he went to night school and studied business, although it all seemed so academic. But when he was elevated from the garbage truck to be president of Sunset at 31, suddenly "all I learned in school got to be real."

He changed the atmosphere of company meetings. Where, under his predecessor, it had been dangerous to criticize, he was ready to listen to anyone say anything. Not that it was all Stefanelli's doing that the company changed. Former board member Rich Borghello, an area supervisor today, recalls, "When decisions were made, it wasn't just his voice, it was the board's voice." But Stefanelli worked hard to meet everyone's needs, to be available. Indeed, years later, Livio Cristanelli would tell me that Lenny's "door was always open."

Stefanelli himself recalled that the partners and helpers alike would come to him with all sorts of personal problems. In a kitchen table interview, he and his wife Virginia remembered the many desperate telephone calls: A teenage daughter was pregnant, could he do something? "I got a bad traffic ticket, can you get it fixed for me?" A family wanted to adopt a baby, but weren't getting anywhere; could he help? "I can't handle my husband anymore, can you help me get him into alcohol rehab?"

Virginia shook her head, "[He was] a regular godfather." She thought that in the end it wore him out. "Deep down, he had had it up to here." But Lenny felt it was more the disappointments with repeated board disapprovals of his proposals. After 20 years in the presidency, "I lost interest." He no longer worked so hard to smooth the edges of things. Always energetic and restless, he had often taken up hobby enthusiasms. In the mid-1970s he even kept a pig someone gave him as a joke and raised it as a pet out at the landfill and bred it too; and of course that made a lot of humorous news for the company. Later there was gold-mining with a couple of scavenger partners that he would do on weekends. He had begun spending time on a hobby of guns, which he sold from time to time, mainly to other scavengers at cost. He even got a special gun dealer's license, of which there were only four in the state, to sell automatic rifles. (One day at lunch with him in an inexpensive restaurant frequented by scavengers, city workers, and minor politicians, I followed his conversation about guns with our young waiter. They apparently knew each other well, from Lenny's coming to the restaurant, and the young man was interested in buying a revolver for target practice.)

The last straw though came out of a disciplinary case that angered the board. One of the traditional functions of the Sunset board had always been discipline decisions, back to the days when the bylaws specified that a partner who "slandered" another partner or "neglects a horse" would be fined, even suspended. In this case, a partner had apparently been involved in a conflict of interest when he had fostered a contract between Sunset and a company he apparently owned part of. Lenny and the rest of the board had no doubt that he had violated the rules, but Lenny told the board that they did not have sufficient evidence to prove it and would have to go slow on the matter.

The board ignored his advice, fined the man $15,000, and suspended him for one month. The partner filed a grievance with the union local, and the first step in the process was a hearing before two union representatives and two company representatives (one of them being Lenny), with a fifth person, the president of Golden Gate with whom Lenny was close. Unfortunately Lenny was going to be out of town when the hearing was scheduled (indeed he was to be with a certain important politician whom he felt was key to the company's future), but he told his Golden Gate counterpart the story and asked him to vote with the other Sunset representative, so that it would be a two-to-two stand-off and the matter would merely go to arbitration and thus be out of everyone's hands; then the company and its board would not be blamed for whatever was the ultimate result. But the Golden Gate representative did not follow Lenny's suggestion, and the vote went three-to-one, the grievance upheld. The board was furious at Lenny for his political date and for not being at the hearing and making the thing right. They demanded his resignation as president.

Ernie Samietz probably expresses what the rank and file thought: "We did not know what was going on. It could have been building for a long time in the board. It surprised me. It seemed like he was doing good all along. He was good for the guys on the truck." Ernie and Freddie and Lenny used to socialize quite a bit after work. But for one thing, rank and filers rarely take a really active role, and "maybe the board could see something else." And again, there were those rumours about his finances, and didn't he, for a time, use company diesel fuel for his mining equipment? Yet in the days that followed, Ernie never heard any specifics of complaints against Lenny. So it was that Sunset and Leonard Stefanelli parted.

It was clear that Lenny himself had been loosening his attachment to Sunset. He had already decided not to run again for his board seat in the next election. His wife had felt that at the last company dinner the signs were there that he no longer had a respected place among the movers and shakers at Sunset: Contrary to all previous practice at company social occasions, there had been no table reserved for him, as president, and for his family party. She didn't want to participate in company celebrations anymore, and he had "lost interest," although he still was bringing his ideas for company expansion to the board.

But to be asked to resign, from the company that he had spent his life at since a teenager, after 20 years of successful leadership in making the company into a $100–million firm! "It was the darkest day of my life," he brooded in that kitchen interview. The board told him that he could not work at all in management anymore; he was to go back to carrying the can; he could not even be assigned to driving a front-loader. He tried to wangle some other assignment, but in the two weeks notice he had been given, he could make no deals.

He talked it over with Virginia. He had never been without a job before. How could he explain it to the kids? "I could go back to carrying garbage," he told her, and for a few days he thought he would. "Yes, physically, you could," she had said, even though he was 51, and 20 years away from the vigorous life he had led as a scavenger in the Fillmore district. "But I don't want you to." She was afraid that the animus toward him could get dangerous. "You know, someone near the edge mentally can decide to hurt you, even kill you." So she objected forcefully. "I may be a housewife and not know much to get a job with, but I can clean toilets, and I will. You're not going back to the trucks." That was a bit of an exaggeration of family needs; after all they were living in a house that they had put a down payment on when he first became president. After 20 years, they would basically have owned it by then—one of those pleasant row houses so common a feature of San Francisco, with a lemon tree and trimmed shrubs, in the old established district of Merced Manor. And they had other resources. Still, Virginia reported that he worried about looking for work: "I had never seen a look like that on his face. He was frightened. He had never been out of a job before."

Virginia insisted that he go out everyday in a regular suit and tie, in case any of his old associates saw him. Initially, getting work in the industry was not easy. The company apparently told prospective employers that he was under investigation. Finally he got a consulting job for a nearby city and very successfully managed some ticklish problems of a contested contract transition between BFI and Waste Management. Soon thereafter the president of Waste Management came to San Francisco and recruited him as West Coast regional vice president, at almost three times his salary at Sunset.

Things looked good, but Virginia's fears seemed to come true. They started to get threatening phone calls and letters. The example of the crazed assassin of San Francisco's beloved mayor, George Moscone, was all too prominent as a model. The letters and calls became weirder and pornographic. It became more and more frightening. It went on for more than a year, but somehow the FBI finally tracked down the culprit, the unbalanced son of a scavenger whom Lenny had mortally offended at one time. The young scavenger pleaded guilty in federal court, and the harassment ended.

Waste Management was a haven, and Lenny worked for them for ten years, 1986–95. Almost immediately he made the deal for them to buy Oakland Scavengers and, over time, to buy out several other companies to increase their western regional holdings by a half-billion dollars in revenues. But he eventually became weary, he said, of being second-guessed at corporate headquarters in Chicago. He felt that the company was no longer being run by people who knew the garbage business, but by accountants and MBAs interested only in the financial reports. In late 1995 he got a job with a real garbageman, Richard Granzella, president of Richmond Sanitary Services, in the upper Bay Area. Stefanelli became Vice President for Special Projects and generally backs up the president in planning for the company. There Stefanelli exercises his penchant for deal making and delights in raising the net worth of the company in lucrative projects. The company recently bought a critical landfill site and will soon be accepting trainloads of refuse from two California counties up the coast near the Oregon border, with a potential of making $50,000 a day profit, he claims. Lenny is fulfilled in his work: "Today I am the happiest son-of-a-bitch on the face of this earth."

Why did Sunset and Lenny sever connections? Virginia says it was a generational change. Those Lenny's age or younger did not appreciate what their fathers and uncles had done to put the company on the launch pad from which Lenny took it up. They had never worked the open trucks, never seen the packers take over the hardest tasks, never watched while computers were installed to relieve everyone from evening duty collecting the bills, never worried through the inception of the environmental movement. The previous generation were the ones who had supported the revolution and installed Lenny. But now they were mostly gone. Their sons and nephews didn't see it the same way. They had it too easy.

It must be conceded that the company had grown big with subsidiaries and other interests; it was no longer simply a matter of interrelated families from Dago Row. But Virginia, like some others, still sees it as an Italian enterprise that could have brought even more respect for the Italian community. Why wouldn't she take that view? Granddaughter of a founder, daughter of a scavenger, cousin of scavengers, wife of a long-time scavenger president, cousin of a former president of Golden Gate—all Italian. When I raised the question with her as to why the board members (mostly Italian) couldn't see that Lenny's projects would be prizes that other companies would snap up when Sunset let them go, Virginia had her own answer. "You've got to remember that Columbus couldn't get any ships from the Italians."

Livio Cristanelli succeeded Stefanelli in the churning days after his resignation. Years later Cristanelli would have a softer focus on his predecessor. "He did a lot of good for the company. He went to the politicians and got the packers and a better wage for the workers. I can't really knock him. We all make mistakes. I think at the end he was tired of it. You do get tired of things." But at the time, feelings ran high, and uncertainty was a haze in the atmosphere. For example, was Sangiacomo too much identified with Stefanelli, and would his days too be numbered? But Lenny urged him to stay put. "They'll need you." And they did. Within six months Cristanelli wanted to explore the ESOP solution again, and Sangiacomo's financial skills were crucial. He was made chairman of the ESOP committee and led the planning. If the partners took a cut in pay and the company merged ten routes with others, maybe it could be done; maybe there was a way to make the payments on a leveraged buyout.

Golden Gate (in its holding company format of Norcal Solid Waste Systems) was in the process of becoming an ESOP, so why couldn't Sunset? In December 1986, Golden Gate was bought by the ESOP that its board set up and called simply Norcal Waste Systems. It was a leveraged buyout that paid each scavenger shareholder about $645,000, which included a note for $200,000. That certainly looked good to the Sunset board, although with more Sunset shareholders a Sunset share, of course, would not go anywhere near that high. Beyond that, because most of Golden Gate's customers were businesses, it was not regulated in its rates by the city; it could negotiate rates with customers and was not bound by the same 5 percent profit ceiling that Sunset was. This meant that Golden Gate shares were fundamentally more valuable.

Nevertheless, by June 1987 a plan for a Sunset ESOP to

buy shares at $271,000 each was ready for a vote. In the meantime, however, partners were hearing that other companies, BFI, Waste Management, a company in Canada (Laidlaw), might pay more. After all, only six months before, Waste Management had bought the Oakland Scavenger Company for $700,000 a share.

Things were getting complicated for launching the ESOP. Perhaps the most complicating thing of all was that Waste Management's offer was being promoted by its regional vice president. It was considerably more than any of the other offers, but did it mean that Lenny Stefanelli would be at the helm again? Eventually Waste Management made a formal offer of $312,000 per partner's share, half of it in stock and half in a seven-year interest-only note. It looked good, but it did not get much consideration from the board. In the end, the board formally recommended no one proposal but merely submitted them all to the shareholders. The ESOP proposal was ultimately approved by a vote of 72 percent.

However, as Lenny had figured long before, an ESOP would stretch the credit resources for a regulated company, and Sunset began to have troubles arranging the details of financing. The banks preferred to see a really overwhelming majority of the shareholders approving the plan, maybe 85–90 percent. So Sangiacomo worked up a re-design. By August the ESOP was refigured at $273,750, and the board approved it, seven-to-four, again rejecting the Waste Management offer. Cristanelli conceded later that Lenny's involvement "might have hurt Waste Management's chances." Others tell me that in hindsight they now know they would have done better with Waste Management.

The shareholders had to vote again in November, and Waste Management upped its price to $332,000. By this point the partners were uneasy, but they rejected both Waste Management and the ESOP. Instead an eleventh-hour proposal from Norcal came in at $305,000, half in cash and half in a note at 9.6 percent. On the vote put to them, Norcal was accepted by 78 percent of the 274 partners.

On October 3, 1987, the *San Francisco Chronicle* business section trumpeted "1 S.F. Garbage Firm." Under a picture of the two presidents concerned, Livio Cristanelli and Leo Conte, the headline read, "Envirocal To Be Sold For $83.6 Million." Envirocal was dissolved, and the two original San Francisco cooperatives were finally joined as subsidiaries of one employee-owned company.

In contrast to the original cooperatives, Norcal was owned by all the employees, not just those dealing with the garbage. Thus, the Sunset office staff (including those scavenger wives like Marlene Cristanelli in company jobs) and all others in subsidiaries who had traditionally been excluded from ownership now had a new status. Each year they would see stock deposited to their accounts, proportionately in accordance with their salaries—as the company paid off the debt it incurred to buy the co-ops. Most Sunset office staff were extremely pleased with their new employer, at least at first; later, aggrieved because they had not received a raise in a long time, they joined the scavenger union (Teamsters Local 305) and then struck, but in about two hours the company settled the strike to their satisfaction.

Although everyone at Norcal would participate in ownership, no one, not even the former partners, would have any say in choosing the management and direction of the business, or even the trustees of their own Employee Ownership Stock Trust that held and voted their shares. Like many ESOPs, Norcal had been organized to be closely managed by Golden Gate's original board members and officers, who appointed the ESOP trustees. Those trustees in turn appointed the board who in turn appointed the company officers. It was a circular control mechanism, but no one seemed to care much at the time.

Some old-timers may now regret the time when they could berate their leaders in a meeting and make demands for equality. "Norcal is run like any other company, BFI or whatever. Of course, that was what we got paid for, to give up what we had," Jack Sullivan points out. He had retired in June of 1987, kept his share, and then sold it in November that year as Norcal took over. "I paid $14,000 for my share when I first got in, and I had a pretty good living all those years." And in the end he, like others of his generation of scavengers, realized a major appreciation through the $305,000 price per share.

The Sunset partners were well satisfied with settling any worries about how to get their highly appreciated equity out of the company. Many who continued to work for a short time for Norcal and then retired early (perhaps fifty scavengers in all) could collect their Sunset pension (with prime health benefits) which, incidentally, was better than Norcal's own; and they would also cash in any Norcal stock deposited to the trust account for them. "That was good for me," Ernie reported. And Livio Cristanelli, who remained president of the Sunset subsidiary for five years and then retired at 61, was highly satisfied with the extra $10,000 he got from his Norcal stock account.

The partners got a shock in January 1991 when Norcal stopped paying on the loans allocated to all the previous partners, both those who had sold their Golden Gate shares and those from Sunset. Norcal had overextended itself in bank borrowings for the ESOP and for all of its operations, including real estate, and had defaulted on a bank payment. That triggered a series of defaults. The company was in serious trouble. However, rank and filers are apt to feel that trouble is the managers' problem, especially if they have no say in who is managing. The former partners from both Golden Gate and Sunset showed little patience when their interest payments were interrupted. Late that summer, they filed lawsuits against the company, each one putting up $2,000 for legal expenses.

In the meantime, Norcal's management was struggling

with its own stresses. Just at the time in late 1987 that Norcal had been trying to buy Sunset, a dangerous investigation by the FBI began to look at potentially illegal political pay-offs. The (long-time) president at that juncture seemed to be the focus of investigation, and as it proceeded, the directors became more and more nervous about what would happen. Coincidentally, the company was struggling with its debt load, and the banks were nervous too because they had looked on unblinkingly as the onerous debt grew; they might be held responsible in a stockholders' lawsuit.

The trouble had been coming for a long time. The managers earlier saw that the company would have to liquidate many of its real estate holdings. "We had medical buildings, shopping centers, a lot of property," Cristanelli recalled. The management was not happy with the chief financial officer's handling of the problems, and Cristanelli suggested that the company put Mike Sangiacomo in the job. In August 1988 Sangiacomo was promoted from his job as general manager of the Sunset operations under Cristanelli, and he entered a new fray. His work brought him considerable recognition among the management and bank representatives and was to stand him in special stead as the company lurched through more crises.

In late 1990 a couple of the former Golden Gate directors, part of the Norcal management committee, started to engineer a call for the president's resignation, especially as a means of insulating the company from the FBI investigation which was still going on. At first the president merely resigned from the board and went on leave from the CEO position. Sangiacomo was asked to take on the task of interim president, while some jockeying among the directors for the permanent post ensued. But most directors and the ESOP trustees, egged on by the banks, wanted none of the previous board members. A new and more financially sophisticated leader was required. Suddenly in January 1991 Mike Sangiacomo was elevated to the job with full powers to pull the company out of its slide.

It was the culmination of the new history of the scavengers, bridging the gap between "the old days" and a new mode of operation. Mike's father, Battista Sangiacomo, had worked for the Scavengers Protective Association, the company that eventually took the name of Golden Gate Disposal. He started as a helper in 1937, two weeks after arriving in this country from Italy at the age of 27. Someone gave him the name "Mike," but when his son was born, he gave him that name for real. When the young Mike was eight years old, he began working on occasion with his dad. He would write out his father's bills for him, and later he joined him in the task of collecting the accounts on his father's route in Chinatown. But the older "Mike" wanted his son to get an education. College followed and then further training and certification as a public accountant.

The son might have gone to work for Golden Gate then in its accounting department, but they required all new hires to begin on the truck. As Lenny reported it, the father, though he had retired by then, absolutely refused to countenance his son working the trucks now that he was college-educated; and the son went on to become the chief financial officer for a food processing company. It was when that company went out of business that Lenny recruited the younger Mike for Envirocal, a job that, seemingly, led almost inexorably to the presidency of Norcal at a time when that company desperately needed a financial specialist who knew what the world of garbage was all about.

Right away the major task for Sangiacomo as president was to increase company revenues substantially. "Most of our collection and disposal businesses were not performing at a decent level," Mike recalls. So he requested rate increases at almost all of them and was generally successful. Norcal also closed or sold some of its units that were probably never going to be particularly successful, like a portable toilet company, or an asbestos removal company (which had begun work just as the California real estate industry hit bottom and few could afford property improvement like that). And finally, Sangiacomo reluctantly sold four performing subsidiary garbage companies in order to get a new life from the banks.

Meanwhile, the suit by the former partners pressed forward, and Sangiacomo had to juggle that, too. The Sunset suit had legal and financial priority, so it was critical to settle before the old Golden Gate retirees could get their just deserts. Some of the Sunset partners were ready to give Sangiacomo the benefit of the doubt, as the new president. Ernie Samietz and Jack Sullivan with another scavenger wrote a letter to the Sunset plaintiffs, urging negotiation and an end to paying so much money for lawyers. (The lawyers for all sides are said to have ultimately received over $2 million in fees, but that may be just one of those rumors.) At any rate, Sullivan, for one, was afraid that the fringe benefits like the pension and the lifetime medical insurance which were part of the original selling agreement for all Sunset partners was threatened by the financial troubles. He asked for feedback from the partners and got 150 replies that encouraged him to work with others to set up a negotiation meeting. Of course, not everyone was positive about his ideas, and he got some irate telephone calls to the effect that he was betraying the partners' interests. He persevered.

In late 1994 several current and retired scavengers, including Jack Sullivan and Joe Pesce (who had all along urged the Waste Management offer), met for an all-day negotiation session with Cristanelli and Sangiacomo, together with the lawyers for all sides (including those for the nervous bankers). A "special master," appointed by the judge in the case to hear the dispute and try to mediate it, held the meeting in his office in Palo Alto. It was a marathon session, according to one participant, running from early in the morning to late in the evening. Apparently Mike himself talked for about an hour and a half to present the situation as he saw it (he doesn't remember that although others seem to recall it). At any rate he convinced the plaintiffs of his sincerity in trying to work out the situation. At the end of the day, there was a handshake on the general terms of a settlement. The ultimate agreement for ending the suit included a reconfirmation of the fringe benefits for the life of all partners, a payment up front of $20,000 on accumulated unpaid interest and a note for the balance of the unpaid interest of $38,000, and, finally, a new note for the balance of principle, which at the option of Norcal could be paid up early at a discount.

Mike Sangiacomo was not only a wizard at resolving that dispute; he was able to negotiate very soon thereafter a major rate increase from the city (11 percent). That, among all the other actions, put him in a position to refinance the company's debt. In November 1995 a Wall Street firm sold $175 million of ten-year bonds at 12.5 percent. With the proceeds, all the Sunset and Golden Gate partners (and all other defaulted obligations) were paid off completely. The company had finally sailed out of the storms. Today Sangiacomo is said to receive $675,000 in salary and other benefits.

As Sangiacomo concedes, the company remains highly leveraged, but that is not so different from a lot of sound companies. "We plan carefully, and we can make ends meet," he points out. A very new 11 percent rate increase from the City of San Francisco in February 1997 will help. Further rate increases are on the horizon, but they are not likely to rile Norcal's customers. It is important to remember that San Francisco still has cheaper collection and disposal costs than the rest of the Bay Area. The cost to the householder of a 32–gallon can each week is now at $11.90 per month (and scheduled to drop back to $11.72 in a year's time). And the company continues to assume the responsibilities for meeting the city's state-mandated recycling goals, which in itself implies considerable expense, despite the return on the recyclables.

What is the most important issue that the company must continue to deal with? Mike thinks the biggest challenge is, in fact, making the ESOP work. Other problems may be taxing, like the payments on the debt, or a generally litigious corporate world, or employment laws that get tighter, and so on; but those are no different for Norcal than for the rest of the business world, he feels. What is different is the definition of Norcal as worker owned. Even though the format is quite different from the old cooperatives, the same question remains: Can the company survive in an economic environment that does not encourage what Lenny undiplomatically and perhaps all too graphically persisted in calling "a quasi-capitalist-communist company"? Yet the Soviet Union never had much tolerance for cooperatives or true worker-owned companies, nor have they ever flourished in capitalist United States.

* * *

What has all this meant for the man on the truck? Much of the work remains the same. For instance, entry to perhaps 80 percent of the apartment houses still requires that the scavenger have a ball of keys with him on the truck. The charges for climbing up or down from street level are more specific than the old charge of so much for each flight of stairs, and of course they are more expensive but still outstandingly reasonable: $2.40 per can for any distance between four and seven feet or $3.21 for each eight feet (rates effective in 1996). These days, some customers in a second floor flat might be more apt to think about bringing their garbage to street level, but the scavenger is, as Freddie had always said, ready to do any service as long as the bill is paid.

There is a mixed feeling about whether the company, in turn, is sufficiently demanding of some customers where the challenge of pulling the garbage out is too high—for example, when the cans weigh more than the regulation maximum of 60 pounds, or the stairways are too rickety. One scavenger may say that the collectors will be more ready today to suggest that a staircase is too dangerous; and that the climbing service will be discontinued until a repair or redesign is made. Another may contend that while it is acceptable in the company to decline a particular dangerous can, later in the day the company will merely send someone else out who is willing to do it, rather than make a fuss with the customer. Perhaps route or area supervisors hate to make customers unhappy by complaining to them. Said one scavenger: "There ought to be some way in which the complaint can be made directly" to a safety authority, without requiring the supervisors personally to get after the customer. An increased sensitivity to safety is undoubtedly a part of a nationwide recognition of worker concerns since the rise of OSHA (the U.S. Occupational Safety and Health Act).

OSHA (and state regulations) have also changed the way in which a work break might be taken: No more drinking on the job. You can be pulled off the truck at any time and given an alcohol test; similar testing for drugs is just another sign of the changed habits of this nation. In my February 1997 interviews I was the audience for some wistfulness among the old-timers about the rules against alcohol, but no one really objects; they know it is for the best. And the rules are enforced equally. Even while I was learning about all this, I was told about a top Norcal manager who just left the company because he failed a cocaine test.

Safety precautions mean that there is less opportunity for what can be seen on the routes as a choreography of the can, as I have described it. There is less physical work with the carrying cans today, and the best choreography is viewable at city celebrations, where Norcal's garbage can drill team is always a hit with its precision movements.

Most cans now have rollers and are not carried. Twenty or thirty years ago, I got the impression that rollers were

The Norcal Drill Team performs, followed by garbage trucks.

deemed to be almost sissy. Now everyone uses them, and the packer trucks have devices that catch up a can rolled against the truck opening, and lift it, tip the contents in, and then set it on the ground, as the scavenger stands and waits for his can to be returned; for him now there is a lot less emphasis on how to lift, swing, hold, shift, tip, lower. But that by no means suggests that even this work is leisurely, for the new dumping mechanism works very quickly. And you can still see the scavengers practically or even actually running, with their roller cans pushed in front of them, darting in and out of apartment houses and the single-family row houses of San Francisco. Moreover, there are plenty of occasions in which the cans still have to be lifted and carried over surfaces where they will not roll.

Today many routes are perhaps four times the length of the routes when I first went out on the trucks in 1966, yet the worker can still quit and go home when he has finished his route. The 43–year veteran Joe Pesce snaps, "The routes may be longer, but they are easier." The increase in route length is workable with the better equipment. Moreover, because of an increase in separate curbside collection for recyclables, there is less from any one customer to put in the packer. A scavenger is still paid for an eight-hour day, whether or not he actually spends that length of time, so long as the route is taken care of. The average hourly rate is $20, with a yearly salary of something over $40,000. The lowest-paid helper on a curbside truck gets $16 an hour, or about $33,400 a year, plus substantial benefits, including the company share deposits to his account.

I write here "his account," but there is one woman who has an assignment on a curbside truck; another works the special jobs truck, picking up large items, like mattresses or dead animals on the city streets; and another woman, Joyce Hume, a young grandmother in her fifties, has been working the packer trucks for about 10 years. The women collectors are rare exceptions, but in general women make up about 10 percent of the total work force, including some in managerial posts—which is probably a major accomplishment, considering the original male scavenger culture, as well as the kind of work involved which puts a premium on the physique of men, and, too, a laudable company practice of promoting from inside the work force.

Another obvious difference from a generation ago is the fact that Asians and Pacific Islanders are among those working the trucks, and they, along with black and Hispanic minorities, make up about 40 percent of the work force. When I visited the Sanitary Fill offices the last time, there were a black woman and a Hispanic woman as receptionists. What a contrast from the days described to me by an old-timer, Bennie Behrmann: In her initial interview for a three-month clerical appointment, they asked about her skills; and when she admitted that, as a young stay-at-home mom, she had few, they asked if she was Italian and, upon learning that she was, hired her, saying she would be trained on the job.

She became a mainstay for the company, working in many different capacities as a customer service representative and is still there more than thirty years later.

Mike Sangiacomo asserts that the company takes seriously its responsibility to mirror the community in which it is situated. He is proud of the accomplishments in minority hiring and at the same time sees the need for an even greater effort. The company's high status in the community stems in part from its hiring policies, but at least as important is the tradition of service. Paul Giusti, who has a long family and personal connection with Sunset as a worker on the garbage trucks and who is now the operations manager to whom all Sunset's area supervisors report, cites many evidences of community support. He notes that when Norcal was going through its worst financial times, one vendor (their printer) told them not to worry about his account and just to pay him when it finally became more feasible. Paul is proud that other business firms have spontaneously recommended the company to the city for new tasks, recommending that it can always be trusted to do the job right. He and others feel good at community meetings where some minor things get criticized but overall there are always "good vibes for us." More than one interviewee cited the fact that the city voted 76 percent against a referendum that would have opened up recycling contracts to others besides the scavengers.

The company participates in perhaps five different parades each year around the city. Other firms and organizations, of course, do so too, but the scavengers still hold a special place in the affections of the city, as the *San Francisco Chronicle* is apt to attest. Parade watchers will cheer as Norcal's contingent goes by. In addition to the garbage can drill team, the company sports a recycled instruments band, and, of course, the antique garbage trucks—like "Old Red" from Sunset's 1930s or even a horse-drawn truck from an earlier period. These are pressed into service to carry neighborhood children and their families along the parade route. Sangiacomo himself and other old and new employees in the company join the riders on the trucks. All this community support and interaction remains an integral reward for the scavengers and their colleagues.

Kenny Stewart, who manages the long-haul operations, takes responsibility, on his own time, for restoring and maintaining the antique trucks for the company. There is a lot of fun for him and his partners in that task, but on the two occasions that I talked with him recently, he led me to re-discover that there remains still plenty of opportunity for considerable enjoyment in the regular work of the scavengers.

Maybe Kenny is different, but I doubt it. "Even as a little kid, I was excited when the garbage trucks came," he told me. When he grew up, he worked at a family-run business for some 15 years, but when it folded, he looked for work at Sunset. In 1983, he began by accepting occasional day work driving long-haul 50 miles to the Altamont landfill, or sometimes driving loads of city sludge from the sewage plant—another of Sunset's contracts for the city—to a Gilroy site, about 75 miles to the south. "You showed up every day and waited for work. Whether you worked or not depended on the tonnage for that day or if people were off sick or something." For three years he did this occasional driving until finally he was hired full-time in 1986. By 1989 he was dispatcher for the long-haul work, and then in 1995 he became manager of the operation. For him now, "It really feels good to be part of the company."

"The idea that you can move up" is a special advantage now in the company, he says, although that policy is new because "for a time they hired from the outside." He knows he can be a better manager because he has been a driver. His work force numbers about 70, of which around 50 are equally former Golden Gate or Sunset workers, so there is very little turnover. He himself says, "I plan to be a 30–year man." And one reason is almost a repeat of what Lenny Stefanelli told me 30 years ago, as I have reported, in the chapter on "What's Good About This Job?" At that time Lenny said: "I thought I'd be a garbageman all my life because every day there was something different." Kenny told me why he cherished his job: "Everyday it's something different."

Joyce Hume will tell anyone that the work suits her too, even though she has not been able to find other women who might be recruited. For her part, she has chosen to be assigned to different routes as needed, rather than take a permanent assignment to a single route. This has allowed her to know just about everyone who has carried the can during her 10 years with the company. "It's kinda fun that way," she says, and she stresses the same rewards of the job as I heard before from the men—for example, being outside instead of sitting at a desk, which she did before Sunset. Also, since she has worked so many of the routes, people realize that she knows their experience, and they may come to her for advice. She finds a real satisfaction in standing up for others.

Seven children tended to interrupt her college studies (where she was a sociology major), but she continues her sociological interests by volunteer work on behalf of the homeless and other needful San Franciscans. And she maintains her good physical condition by regular home exercise, because she has plenty of respect for the physical stresses that the work entails, not just for her but for "some of those guys who act macho" but can scarcely walk or stand straight by the time they are retiring. Nevertheless, "God willing, I'm going all the way" on the trucks to retirement.

I got a fascinating comment from Joyce that no one else in the company had ever even alluded to. She points out that the scavenger who pulls garbage out of a citizen's garage, home, apartment house, or whatever, is always "invading other people's space, big time" and so must take that into account. She tries to make sure that her invasion is not threatening. I do believe that many other, male scavengers probably are careful also but do not have her sensitivity to articulate it. So the enjoyment of the job brings with it some psychological responsibilities too.

For the worker on the truck there is still plenty, even if limited customer contact. Stories still abound about favors done along the route, like climbing in a window to open the door for a housewife who had locked herself outside. "And when someone loses something in the garbage, we try to help them out." Art Cooper, a veteran of almost 20 years, tells a hilarious story about chasing a rather large, well-beaked bird around a customer's living room in order to get it back into the bird cage. Occasionally some issues about billing have to be settled along the route—despite (or maybe because of) computerized bills—although such problems are usually handled by the "area supervisors" who manage a group of routes for all sorts of customer relations problems.

Incidentally, no other Northern California company in the garbage industry has these trouble-shooters, but Norcal considers them crucial to community relations, even though the company must always defend the cost of these positions in rate hearings. The area supervisors are "management." There are also "route supervisors," men who would previously have been called "boss scavengers," pulling out the garbage the same as the helpers but in charge of the truck, and holding responsibility for customer relations. They are not considered management, and so they have union pay rates, very recently raised to about $23 an hour.

The biggest change in the work is the concentration on recycling. As I have reported, the scavengers of San Francisco had a long tradition of rigorous practices of salvage and re-use. But in 1989, a state law codified a stringent demand for all citizens and municipalities throughout the state to carry out a Herculean recycling program. Cities are required today to be recycling 50 percent of the waste stream by the year 2000. The main responsibility for this task in San Francisco falls to Norcal, and the cost is integrated into the rate system. Thus, about one-half of the most recent rate increase was due to recycling expenses. The current percentage of materials recycled from the waste stream is more than 30 percent, and the company anticipates making the target by the millennium. Kenny says, "We are always finding new ways to recycle and be cost efficient."

Since 1987 San Francisco has had a curbside recycling operation. Beginning about 6:45 in the morning, a special one-person or two-person truck will follow the same route as the garbage packer to pick up separated cans, mixed paper, and the bins of green, amber, and clear glass. These are sold by Norcal, and any profits show up as a rebate on the bills of the householders who participate. A separate set of trucks recovers cardboard from commercial clients.

However significant these activities are, they seem the least of Norcal's recovery activities. A trip out to the installations on Tunnel Road reveals many more impacts of the recycling demands on disposal techniques and on the culture of the company. What Lenny used to call Il Palazzo della Immondizia, the palace for garbage, which Sunset originally built merely to dump the refuse from packers into transfer trucks for the trip to the disposal site, is today a hive of new recycling activities. Heavily gloved men sift through the refuse as it passes along a belt-line before them, and anything that can be recycled is separated out. Outside and nearby, a totally separate belt-line operation takes place to deal with the heavier materials that are brought in from construction-area debris boxes. Wood and metals are segregated from concrete, for example, and bricks have a special place in the process. Up to 50 percent of these demolition and construction materials are now being recycled.

Also, the company claims to have the largest mixed paper program in the country. The paper is sorted according to market demand. For example, bales may or may not include magazines, according to what a buyer may seek. More astonishing is the program for paints. Containers of re-usable paint are differentiated by oil types versus latex, and colors are combined so that there are three ultimate colors to choose from: grey, off-white, and "Norcal beige"—this refers to a particular brownish color that is actually commercially made and so named and sold by an unrelated paint company. However, Norcal makes the cans of its recycled paint available free to anyone who wants to pick them up from a "shop" where various other recyclable liquids (including cleaning materials like Lysol or Pinesol) are labelled and accessible on shelves for the "customers."

Householders bring hazardous wastes to a collection center, where refuse workers sort the materials as acid, poison, and so on. A full-time chemist is employed to check unlabelled or questionable materials. What cannot be handled by Norcal is destined for other companies that specialize in hazardous waste processing and disposal. And of course there is a final but acceptable residue of this entire process that is sent off in long-haul transfer trucks to a landfill.

In late 1986 the city renewed its contract jointly with Oakland Scavengers and Sanitary Fill Company (the long-time subsidiary of the two San Francisco co-ops) for the transportation and acceptance of what was then an anticipated 15 million tons of refuse a year, to be dumped and covered at the Altamont landfill, 50 miles east of San Francisco. At the time the city manager estimated that the site would last "for a quarter century." Today it is assumed that the life of the site is vastly extended because of the rigorous recycling program.

The most attractive of all the recovery programs is what was originally called "The Garden of Hopes and Dreams." This is a sculpture garden that has been constructed on the crest of the hillock that separates and screens Sunset's disposal and transfer areas from the residential district nearby.

Everything in this attractive garden comes from recycled materials, especially what has been rescued from debris boxes. This includes the plants, the trees, the crushed concrete walkways, and, of course, the sculptures that artists have contributed from found materials.

The company has an artists-in-residence program in association with the garden. The artist is provided with a studio and a small stipend for two or three months and given free run of the recycling program to select any items or materials. The artists are chosen by an advisory council made up of citizens from around the city—not including anyone from the company itself. Sculptors, painters, and even a performance artist have been chosen, the latter rescuing musical instruments or near-instruments and fabrics and other materials for costumes for her presentations. At the end of the residency, the company is allowed to choose up to two pieces of the artist's work for exhibition, and some items are even now hanging in Mike Sangiacomo's office.

When the garden was first opened in 1991, one feature was a poured cement stream, in which children had been invited to write their thoughts—hence, the garden's name. About three years later the company petitioned the city manager for permission to change the name to honor the city's long-time solid waste manager, who had recently died from AIDS. It is now the Joseph E. Johnson Memorial Sculpture Garden.

Sangiacomo is very proud of the garden, but what he takes most satisfaction in is what he sees as his task and trust to preserve an employee-owned company. No, it is not the same as the old co-ops, but it deserves and gets widespread support from its employee-owners, he feels. "We have a tremendous number of employees who really want to make the company succeed. The form of ownership is ideal for the nature of our business. And our people are proud of what they do, not just in San Francisco but around the state [in Norcal's other subsidiaries]."

The Johnson Memorial Garden—all recycled materials and plantings—is the site for Norcal's artists-in-residence program.

Mike asserts strongly that he has a responsibility to the worker-owners to keep the company strong. "And I feel some social obligation for the people to come"—for the workers of the future to have a chance to claim ownership too. There is constant pressure from both inside the company and outside for a buyout, and it is not an easy task to handle the special problems of the ESOP. People retire every year, and they are due payment for their stock accounts (installments may be stretched over a maximum five-year period). Of course, only a profitable company can buy back the retirees' shares, and also only a profitable company can make those shares valuable. There are reciprocal limits. A retiree cannot cash in shares until age 62; and even though the shares might appreciate if left in an account indefinitely, they must be sold back fairly soon after the employee reaches retirement age. Still, the ownership stake can be an attractive addition to the regular pension plan, as Livio Cristanelli and Ernie Samietz reported. But the value, as with any stock, fluctuates with the company's fortunes.

Sangiacomo recognizes that there are some long-term scavengers who have a different point of view on where the company is today. Indeed it is not hard to find some who are highly critical, claiming that too many of the newer managers never rode the trucks and do not care about the workers. Perhaps the most criticized aspect of the company is its governance structure. Control is closely held by the board and trustees who are reciprocally appointed. And more than one scavenger, retired or still working, claimed in effect, "It's all one man now." Even Mike Sangiacomo concedes a potential problem in the reciprocal relationship of trustees and directors: "It all seems so intertwined," he says. But he insists that both legal and ethical obligations protect the worker-owners.

In a group interview I held with mainly long-time scavengers (most of them now at various middle-management posts), I found a sturdily maintained pride in the company and confidence for its future. At the same time, they volunteered that "[top] management is more in control" now than earlier when the scavengers elected their board of directors and the elected board then appointed the officers. Paul Giusti pointed out that there is a stability in the current governance structure that is good for the company, considering all the financial and legal stress that it had to go through. "The bankers probably set it up that way, knowing the history of Lenny [and his predecessor]. I guess they didn't want Mike ousted the same way."

The group members discussed how Norcal trustees and directors had in fact made a basic change in company leadership when Sangiacomo's own predecessor was asked to resign, so the same could happen again if it was necessary: "If people [today] thought things weren't right, we wouldn't stomach it." Another participant in my group interview, John Legnitto, the relatively new manager for the Sanitary Fill subsidiary, noted that he had been appointed as an ESOP trustee and took his fiduciary responsibilities to the worker-owners very seriously. Even though he had not previously worked for Norcal, he had had an association over the years in other capacities as an accountant and insurance representative; and he felt a strong sense of identification with the people who are the real base of the company.

Yet this same group conceded, "It was more family before." That same theme of a loss of a family feeling among the work force was often cited in other interviews too. "I don't even know some of the managers today. I used to know everyone, but they get these guys coming in here. . . ." And in earlier times, "we used to go to the first communions of each other's kids. Now you can't relate. The wives [of those without previous connections to the companies] don't want to. They aren't that much into garbage. I don't know if the wives think the garbage part is insulting, or what." Or: "It's just a business now. It doesn't matter what your product is. It's just a business."

In the group interview, though, Paul put the psychological situation in a larger context, namely, of the changes that San Francisco as a city has undergone.

The whole city has changed. It used to be more of a blue-collar city; now it's a white-collar city. And the price of real estate! No one can afford to live in the city anymore. Previously we [scavengers] were seen as peers of [many of] our customers—carpenters, plumbers, and so on. They were maybe third generation San Francisco, and we were too—natives. We were San Francisco—that's why we had that relationship. Nowadays, so many people come here from elsewhere, from the East Coast. And they wonder, "Where does the garbageman fit into the hierarchy?" They are nervous about us until they can figure it out. It may take them a couple of years, because on the East Coast, the garbageman is not held in the same regard as here. Once they get the picture, it's okay, but: You get [a] reaction from a [new] customer, when you say, "Hi!" And they seem [to be saying], "What are we doing talking to each other?" And then after a while they figure it out.

Donnie Lopez, who is dispatcher for the debris box operations, saw something else that makes a difference. "Now there is [often] only one person on a truck. It's not a team. So people need to get acclimated to the idea of teamwork with the rest of the company." And Paul added, "It's also a generational change. The younger kids today, they are in it for a different reason." And then he laughed, "I sound like my father!" But they all agreed that there was certainly a different attitude in the newer workers that the old-timers had to deal with. "You had to earn respect [by your work]," Donnie said. "We have to expect the new ones to do that. So we must pass it on." Paul recalled, "When I got my own truck, it was a great thing, a great responsibility. No boss looking over my shoulder. The pride has to be passed on."

The question that the group wrestled with was how to assimilate the newcomers if they do not initially share the same perspective? Although some will never take up the team approach and commitment, "Hopefully, there are enough people who want to," says Leo Maionchi, a route supervisor on a packer. And they all agreed on characterizing the positive transformation of one younger colleague who changed from a non-caring perspective to a real commitment. It happened "when he became a shareholder," said Paul, and they all agreed again. In this interview, no one but me seemed to be fazed at Paul's term "shareholder," so I questioned what he really meant. After all, everyone is a shareholder at Norcal and becomes fully vested after five years—that is, permanently holds full title to his earned stock account if he stays with the company for at least five years.

Paul chuckled, "I used the old terminology [for someone who supervises a truck] because [before] only a shareholder could be a supervisor. And I still say 'boss scavenger.' I just meant he changed when he became a supervisor on his own truck." Thus, the transformation happened when the younger man, as with Paul himself, had no one looking over his shoulder.

I sensed in general in my interviews some sort of underlying feeling of personal independence in the workers. Significantly, it was the old terminology that was appropriate in this group to express the transformation of their younger colleague. They concurred, "It takes longer than the five years [required for vesting] to get that psychological feeling"—maybe even up to fifteen years to become "a shareholder" and truck supervisor. For one thing promotion from helper to driver to route/truck supervisor requires seniority. When reaching the supervisor level, the old habit of salvage is invoked: "Your first job as a [route/truck] supervisor is to find a good briefcase in the garbage to keep your paperwork in!"

The group agreed that not only was it possible to pass on some of the old ways but that was what was actually happening in many cases. Only in one regard was there a prob-

lem, workmen's compensation. It seems as if the younger
workers have less tolerance for minor injuries or aches and
pains. "These new guys get a little scratch, and they go off
for two months [on workmen's compensation status]." The
older workers had learned to live with a minor injury or
strain. "It's a whole cultural thing. If you cut your hand, they
used to say, 'Piss on it and wrap it up.'" However, the group
also agreed that that attitude could be taken too far, and one
recalled a hard worker years ago ("no one could keep up
with him") who cut off his thumb in an accident, wrapped it
up, and put it in his pocket to get medical attention after the
day's work was done; but it was too late then for the doc-
tors to re-attach it.

Other interviewees who had not lived the tradition of
working no matter what happens to you took a different
line with me. Even after some years with the company, one
still worried that truck supervisors and area supervisors
hated to make customers unhappy by complaining about
safety conditions. That meant that the collector had to undergo stresses that he shouldn't—cans that routinely exceeded the 60–pound limit, staircases that were rickety.

The workmen's compensation situation has been made
more complex because of recent statewide changes in the
laws and procedures. Due to such changes in the last two
years, Robert Morales, secretary-treasurer of Local 350,
which is 90 percent made up of workers on the trucks, considers the system virtually unworkable. It is not just the process of becoming eligible for workmen's compensation: To
go back to work, he complains, requires inordinate red tape
and paperwork and the employee has to be certified by "a
qualified medical examiner." He feels that the insurance
companies and the lawyers are running the system, not the
employers, though the latter have to pay for it. "The red
tape is beyond explanation," he sighs.

Morales characterizes the whole garbage collection industry as having been taken over by accountants and law-

yers. This means that grievances are more difficult to re-
solve. "In the old days, you could call up and say, 'Hey, you
know this guy, can't you just put him back to work?' But not
anymore." He finds this is true even for Norcal, "especially
Norcal," which is no longer run in the old family-style.

In general, the participants in my group interview conceded that "things are not as tight-knit" in an emotional or
feeling sense as they used to be. But they saw this as being
offset by some positive things—by the access to ownership
for all employees (not just for the scavenger partners), by
the advantages of increased diversity, and by the needed
infusion of fresh blood. Leo Maionchi, 26 years with Sunset
and Norcal and now working as a route supervisor, says, "I
was there in the old times and that was fine, but the business has changed" and needs new ways. Moreover, it
seemed to him and others from their own experience that
since many managers now are coming up internally from
having been on the trucks, as managers they can pass on
the tricks of the trade that they had learned from their own
families. One participant in the group interview, Joe La
Mariana, manager for commercial client relations, who had
come into the company from outside, felt a positive difference in his colleagues; he emphasized a high group morale
that he had not experienced in jobs elsewhere, including
another Bay Area garbage collection company.

Of course, La Mariana is not alone in appreciation of
what Norcal has to offer. Art Cooper recalled the time when
he first came to work for the company as a collector/helper
and discovered so many co-workers who had been there for
a dozen or more years. He had said to himself then, "'Man,
I don't expect to be here that long, no way.'" Today he
laughs disbelievingly at himself, "But here it is almost
twenty years!" In addition to his work as driver for a truck
that handles roll-off collection bins, Art has become an integral part of the company by founding and running the recycled instruments band, which performs with the Norcal

contingent at public occasions, like the Chinese New Year parade.

Such positive feelings and good morale surely can help dissipate lingering questions about the end of cooperative democracy inherent in the particular corporate structure of Norcal. The peer pressure of people who work closely can help undergird the sense of workmanship and, also, the sense of fiduciary responsibility that a non-elected ESOP trustee might exhibit and that is expressed in Mike Sangiacomo's concern for the workers of the future.

However, not all was so well with the company despite the warmth of feeling expressed by many of my interviewees. Two months, almost to the day, that I ended my last field trip, there was a strike. True, it only lasted two days, and also true, probably no one expected it to last long. It began early on a Thursday morning and ended the following Friday evening, so residential collection service resumed the following Monday. The city of course took a strong hand in the negotiations between Mike Sangiacomo and Bob Morales, secretary-treasurer of Sanitary Truck Drivers and Helpers Local 350. Mayor Willie Brown has had close ties to labor, but also Norcal had once been a client of his before he became mayor, while he was speaker of the California legislature and influential for them there—a matter that had come under scrutiny during the FBI investigation. At any rate, he and his staff became intimately involved in some shuttle diplomacy in the 30 hours of ultimately fruitful negotiation. The mayor, renowned as an irrepressible optimist and bon vivant, announced a resolution of the dispute at 8 P.M. on Friday and went off insouciantly to a dinner date with a couple of movie stars, and Mike Sangiacomo and Bob Morales rightly praised each other for ending the dispute so quickly, with an unprecedented five-year contract.

Nevertheless, the event was an unsettling rumble of discontent. One of my last Sunset interviewees had predicted the strike to me (though I must say that at the time I chalked that up mostly to his long-standing discontents with Norcal). The employees had been without a contract for almost four months. But the last sticking point was fairly limited—improvements in pension benefits. Morales emphasizes the fact that now those who retire at 54 or thereafter will have their full family health insurance paid by the company until age 65. This, of course, was the Sunset benefit that the partners maintained when they sold their shares to Norcal, a benefit that the rest of the company did not have until this strike. Since all other issues were resolved, the company and the union could scarcely have resisted a settlement for long. But beyond that the question still arises as to why the worker-owners were so willing to go off their jobs (the strike vote was 95 percent).

News reports had it that in 1940 there was also a two-day work stoppage. I had been surprised to read in my own local paper, by an AP story, that this was "the first strike in 57 years." First time I heard of any previous strike. But Mike Sangiacomo corrected the account by a letter later on to the *San Francisco Chronicle*. The 1940 two-day stoppage "was staged by four employees of an engineering firm who unloaded railcars at the landfill. Garbage collection continued on those two days. I checked with someone who should know—my dad. He worked as a garbage collector in San Francisco from 1937 to 1971." Thus, the 1997 strike was indeed unprecedented. (As I have reported in chapter 8, there was a mutually rewarding strike in a Sunset subsidiary in another city.)

The *San Francisco Chronicle* reported that Mike Sangiacomo found the 1997 strike traumatic but told a reporter that Norcal was like a family, "We squabble a lot, but service will be back to normal." The *Chronicle* had earlier reported: "Some sources close to the workers said anger over the [original company] wage offer is fueled by their long-standing feeling that they have no voice in running the garbage firm, even though the company has been employee-owned since 1987." One could try to imagine who those "sources" might be and recognize that they might not be as supportive of the company as many of the interviewees I saw; but company governance is an undeniable issue, as even some of the most positive of my interviewees had brought out.

Mike's letter that was published later on in the newspaper said, "It was our first strike, and we intend for it to be our last." He explained it: "The strike taught us . . . that management and employees must communicate better, and the CEO should lead the way." "Communication," of course, covers a wide range of issues in worker-management relations, and what improved communication can mean is critical. Any strike is a communication—usually concerning dissatisfaction about compensation. But when the workers are fairly well compensated, the strike is bound to mean something more, even if compensation is an overt complaint. It means some kind of dissatisfaction with the very nature of the work, and improved compensation will not fully assuage the needs that have underlain the discontent. In the instance of the scavengers, it is possible to look at the communication (as the newspaper article suggested) as some sort of discontent with the degree of self-direction.

Eventually retirement will come to all those who remember the times when you could stand up in regular partner meetings and criticize a board member or company officer. That communication among the partners was important. Will there come a time when their successors among Norcal's workers explicitly look for more options in expressing their ideas about how the company is run? Will the human resources embedded in the various levels of company leadership create new ways for interaction between line workers and the managers?

Today the specific function of the ESOP for Norcal workers is not to establish the sort of sense of ownership and

commitment that real participation in the direction and supervision of the company can give. As my interviewees reported, they see the ESOP primarily as offering a supplement to the pension plan. True, it is a supplement based on
profitability and thus encourages the best efforts on the part
of all. Yet the urge for self-determination that most people
experience is quite different. It can be a strong force for
change in the patterns of communication and participation.
What new forms might that self-determination urge take
when people work in a company that calls itself worker-
owned, especially if it has come out of a tradition like the
San Francisco scavengers? Will the future of Norcal, freed of
the stresses of its early crises, offer a new avenue for self-
direction that will satisfy the scavengers in a way that regular improvements in compensation will not?

In the United States, worker ownership has been the subject of considerable private and government research. There
have been enough studies at this point for some general
trends to emerge, according to specialists like Raymond
Russell, my early colleague in a comparative study of garbage workers in the United States and now professor of
sociology at the University of California, Riverside. In technical reports he has written that worker ownership apparently has only an uncertain effect, according to the body of
that research. On the one hand, just plain profit-sharing or
gain-sharing generally leads to a permanent 3 to 6 percent
increase in productivity. But the same kind of increase in
ESOP firms occurs mainly when the employees also have
other ways to be involved in the company—for instance, by
participation in decision making. Participative management
itself has been shown to have a close relationship with
pride in work, greater effort on the job, and a rewarding
sense of special knowledge. And participative management
is one potential outcome of ownership in the workplace.
But it is not a necessary outcome, as the Norcal case demonstrates. So far no one has been able to separate the ef-

fects of ownership itself from the effects of participative management, especially in the instance of the ESOP—in which personal performance and reward is not as closely linked as in the simpler gain-sharing setting. That would tend to suggest that shared decision-making ought to be included in any ESOP structure in order to get increased benefits for the company.

On the other hand, ESOPs do seem to have a positive, though mixed effect upon their companies' finances, as measured in a variety of ways. Further, earlier research seemed to indicate that a cooperative format—at least in Israel's economic context—can have productivity and profit results, even lower costs of administration. Later reports are less sanguine, seemingly because of changes in the Israeli economy, and cooperatives in general are disappearing there. Perhaps even more to the point, my own attempt with colleagues to compare scavenger cooperatives with other Bay Area formats for garbage collection did not reveal statistically firm evidence for personal benefits (such as levels of reported self-esteem), although other benefits (such as a sense of personal reward) were documented.

In short, today we are not much further along in our confidence about knowing either the positive or negative effects of ESOPs, worker cooperatives, and worker ownership than we were 20 years ago. That in itself would seem to be a reflection of the social and economic context in which these phenomena appear. That is, the United States in particular remains a society in which, in practice, such forms of economic democracy seem to have very limited value or are indeed devalued. So they invite less attention in academic and other research than the conventional corporate world gets. It is not a far reach from there to an explanation that lies in the individualistic ethic of our culture, by which economic status and progress is the responsibility solely of the person concerned and not to be shared in a common enterprise. For Americans, political democracy remains isolated from democratic forms for economic activity. The two seem to be independent dimensions.

The portents of any change in this isolation of the two dimensions of democracy are vague. The most recent economic history of our society is characterized by the planned export of jobs, the downsizing of work forces, the contracting out of integral tasks, the increase in part-time and temporary employment, and the growing disparity between those who have and those who have not or have very little, especially the great gaps between top management salaries and their workers' pay. All these features suggest that a different ethic of economic activity is needed, and "the discontents of democracy" may indeed be engendering a new look at economic effort. The growing phenomena of community development corporations as tools for the self-revitalization of marginal neighborhoods is one relatively new form for joint economic activity, and the histories of such firms as the Sunset Scavenger Company offer pointers for other directions we might take to find more satisfying accommodations to the global market economy.

The Sunset scavengers and their successors and partners have uncommon resources for re-inventing themselves. They struggle to realize the opportunities open to them. That is surely what all of us are engaged in. We do it better together.

Notes and Sources

Chapter One: A Personal Inquiry

Straightforward descriptions of refuse work are understandably rare. A devalued occupation receives little attention. However, there are two recent and especially good sources, as mentioned in the text. John R. Coleman, *Blue Collar Journal* (Philadelphia and New York: J.B. Lippincott, 1974) offers an intellectual's firsthand experiences working for a few weeks as a garbage collector. His experiences dovetail with my own, down to some uncanny details. For example, in another city where I continued my participant observational studies of refuse work, working on the trucks, I too, like John Coleman, had to deal with householders or passers-by who would avoid my eyes, an experience I did not have in San Francisco. Coleman's independent confirmation of some of my own observations has been reassuring.

The other best source is the vignettes reported by Studs Terkel in *Working* (New York: Pantheon, 1974). These come in the refuse workers' own words. Like most of the other work descriptions Terkel provides, they are wonderfully articulate and insightful, although very brief.

Also useful is Edward J. Walsh, *Dirty Work, Race, and Self-Esteem*, No. 23, Policy Papers in Human Resources and Industrial Relations (Ann Arbor: University of Michigan–Wayne State University, Institute of Labor and Industrial Relations, 1975). Walsh made a comparison of the self-esteem of refuse workers in two cities and obtained some interesting results. He determined that black workers in Detroit were more self-respecting than their white counterparts, and he explained this by suggesting that for the blacks the job was more rewarding vis-à-vis the lesser chances of their fellow blacks for any sort of job. For the whites, however, working as a sanitationman was comparatively more threatening, for it raised the issue of why they could not have done better. The same tests of self-esteem in Minneapolis bore out the Detroit findings. Walsh's is a provocative effort to observe the effects of dirty work on self-esteem, but what he chose to use as measures of self-esteem makes his findings technically questionable. However, the concept of self-esteem is a very tricky business, and no measure is without its limitations. See L. Edward Wells and Gerald Marwell, *Self-Esteem: Its Conceptualization and Measurement* (Beverly Hills, Calif.: Sage Publications, 1976). So until someone does better, Walsh's work remains significant. For a general and layman's look at self-esteem and dirty work occupations, see Elliot Liebow, "No Man Can Live with the Terrible Knowledge That He Is Not Needed," *New York Times Magazine,* April 5, 1970.

While it may be hard to believe, not everyone fully shares the position that refuse collection is "dirty work" and that it involves some assault on one's self-respect. I have found only one formal and sympathetic recognition in trade or related publications that there is any status problem whatsoever for the man who carries the can. This was a comment in a manual of the National Safety Council, urging "upgrading the image" of the worker by decreasing injuries and illnesses, "thus giving to the occupation a dignity that it has never had before" (*Public Employee Safety Guide: Refuse Collection* [Chicago: National Safety Council, 1974], p. 18). Compare a British government report: "If . . . a social stigma attaches to the job of refuse collector, as several organizations told us, we think that totting [that is, salvaging and sale of articles found in the refuse] may well be a contributory factor." And they speak no further. One gathers that, contrary to my own findings, in the opinion of this task force for one of Her Majesty's ministries, the stigma is really due to the collector's practice of salvaging; and they and others recommend that individual salvaging be stopped. See *Refuse Storage and Collection* (London: HMSO, 1967), especially pp. 89–90, 111, and 118.

There is no major cleavage between their opinion and the stance of the American handbook for municipal refuse departments, which avoids looking directly at the problem of self-respect either in its discussion of personnel practices or elsewhere. See *Solid Waste Collection Practice,* 4th ed. (Chicago: American Public Works Association, 1975), especially p. 9. Also, in parallel with the British government opinion, many U.S. cities have ordinances against salvaging from household refuse put out for collection, apparently preferring that reusable or repairable items be assigned to incineration or the dump rather than be rescued. Again, there is a different tradition in San Francisco, where salvaging has always been an integrated aspect of refuse collection.

As I am suggesting in this book, the status and work of the refuseman can and will vary, depending upon local circumstances and historical changes. In San Francisco, part of that local and even national context was the counter-cultural events in the Haight-Ashbury at the very time I began my study and went out on a truck in that district. My comments on the relationship between the events in the Sunset Scavenger Company and the national crisis expressed in the Haight-Ashbury experiment rely on Helen Swick Perry, *The Human Be-In* (New York: Basic Books, 1970).

The origin of the sociology of dirty work lies in the writings of Everett C. Hughes. No one has substantially improved on his formulations. See his papers reprinted in *Men and Their Work* (New York: Free Press of Glencoe, 1956). They may also be found in his *The Sociological Eye* (Chicago: Aldine-Atherton, 1971), which includes "Good People and Dirty Work," dealing with morally reprehensible occupations.

A student of Hughes, Erving Goffman, has occasionally dealt directly with dirty work also. His exquisitely detailed and analyzed illustrations of social interactions in protection of the self, especially when engaged in potentially demeaning activities, make his work especially important. See particularly *The Presentation of Self in Everyday Life* (Garden City, N.Y.: Doubleday, Anchor Books, 1959) and *Stigma: Notes on the Management of Spoiled Identity* (Englewood Cliffs, N.J.: Prentice-Hall, 1963).

Behind my concern for the meaning of self-esteem among workers in any occupation is my debt as a social scientist to the writings of Harry Stack Sullivan, who made the concept central to his psychiatry of interpersonal relations. See his *Conceptions of Modern Psychiatry,* 2nd ed. (New York: Norton, 1953), *The Interpersonal Theory of Psychiatry,* edited by Helen Swick Perry et al. (New York: Norton, 1953), and *The Fusion of Psychiatry and Social Science,* edited and with introduction and commentaries by Helen Swick Perry (New York: Norton, 1964).

The growth in numbers of refuse workers (and other unskilled occupations) is documented by U.S. census figures for 1960 and 1970, as reported in Table 221 of the U.S Bureau of the Census, *1970 Census of the Population: Detailed Characteristics, U.S. Summary* (Washington, D.C.: U.S. Government Printing Office, 1973).

The standing of refuse work in frequency of injuries is hard to assess from published data. National Safety Council figures vary widely from year to year, and the Council warns against comparing one year's figures with another. The latest Council statistics (1975) put refuse workers second to firefighters in frequency of injuries, but in 1972, for example, municipal refuse workers were listed as having twice as many injuries as firefighters. See *Work Injury Rates* (Chicago: National Safety Council, 1976).

Completely different methodologies have been used at the Department of Labor. For example, the reports of the Council cover mainly municipal departments plus the companies of two of the major agglomerates—according to personal communications from Council staff and the safety director of one of the agglomerates—but in its latest survey the Department of Labor limits itself to private industry. See *Handbook of Labor Statistics 1976,* Bulletin 1905 (Washington, D.C.: U.S. Government Printing Office, 1976), p. 13. I gather from Table 155 of this publication (pp. 320–327) that workers in "sanitary services" are about fifth in incidence of workday-lost cases of on-job injury.

The methodology now used by the Department differs so much from that which it has previously used that no precise comparisons with its own earlier statistics are possible. For what it is worth, however, it may be interesting to know that the Department's 1970 survey showed the refuse industry as number one in frequency and fourth in severity. See *Handbook of Labor Statistics 1972,* Bulletin 1735 (Washington, D.C.: U.S. Government Printing Office, 1972), pp. 361–372. The survey of specific health problems of New York City refuse workers is reported in Joseph A.

Cimino, "Health and Safety in the Solid Waste Industry," *American Journal of Public Health,* 65 (1972): 38–46.

For a review of the variations in organizational forms for refuse collection and the statistics for municipal versus private firms, see Dennis Young, *How Shall We Collect the Garbage?* (Washington, D.C.: Urban Institute, 1972).

The Solid Waste Management Office of the U.S. Environmental Protection Agency is gathering more specific and detailed statistics on refuse organizations and workers, including injury rates. The work of that relatively new government bureau is gathering momentum and has begun to provide essential information never before available. A major and general bibliography is *Solid Waste Management: Available Information Materials,* Report SW-58.19, U.S. Environmental Protection Agency (Washington, D.C.: U.S. Government Printing Office, July, 1973). See also Thrift G. Hanks, *Solid Waste/Disease Relationships: A Literature Survey,* Public Health Service Publication No. 999-UIH-6 (Cincinnati, Ohio: U.S. Department of Health, Education, and Welfare, 1967), especially pages 119–129.

Chapter Two: "In the Old Days"

My discussion of the history of San Francisco's garbage collection is taken from several sources discovered by Raymond L. Russell, III. These are mainly an article by the city engineer in 1929, M. M. O'Shaugnessy, "Solving San Francisco's Garbage Problem," *Municipal Record* [of San Francisco], December, 1929; a note entitled "The Garbage Question Revived," *The City* [a monthly publication of the non-profit San Francisco Bureau of Governmental Research], vol. IV, no. 9 (September, 1924), pp. 110–112; and a city council document "Prepared by the Special Committee appointed to investigate and report . . . ," entitled "Refuse Collection of the City and County of San Francisco, California," January 28, 1919.

These historical materials shed little light on the reasons for the original amalgamation of scavengers in a large cooperative. A report of the California Refuse Removal Council, Northern District, suggests that the City of San Francisco somehow threatened the scavengers into settling their differences (and organizing cooperatives), but the account is casual and contains inaccuracies that cast doubt on it generally. See Easley and Brassy Corporation,

Solid Waste Management and the Bay Area Future (San Francisco: California Refuse Removal Council, Northern Division, 1973), p. 5.

It may be that a general post–World War I trend towards cooperativism in Europe had some effect. It is possible that the ferment of cooperative activity in Italy at that time was transported to the San Francisco Bay Area. See Odon Por, *Guilds and Cooperatives in Italy* (E. Townshend, trans.; introduction by A. E.; appendix by G. D. H. Cole; London: Labour Publishing Company, 1923). However, neither I nor my colleagues in our wider study of refuse collection cooperatives have found any particular evidence of ideological commitments to cooperativism. In fact, there seems to be a singular lack of articulated ideology supporting the scavengers' choice. The early bylaws assert the value of cooperating but do not present this as in any way linked to a movement or a recognized ideology.

One particular cultural fact was an important predisposing influence. The scavengers have generally been Northern Italians, mostly from Genoa. It is said, in fact, that in one of the scavenger companies the bylaws provided that only Genovese would be admitted. No such explicit rule was true at Sunset, but in the presence of Italians of Genovese extraction, one scavenger told me that he was the first Sicilian who had bought in as a partner. The in-group processes, carried over from the Old World, must have influenced the immigrants to join their fates in a common enterprise, while their fierce (and armed) independence (and perhaps even distrust of each other) must have made it essential that each would be an equal partner. Sylvia Pellini MacPhee has reviewed the elements of the Italian-American culture specifically to determine its assets and liabilities for economic cooperation at the community level. See her *Changing Perspectives of Italian-Americans* (Cambridge, Mass.: Center for Community Economic Development, 1974). She emphasizes the transplanting of peasant culture traits to the New World.

In the San Francisco Bay Area and nearby, there are six major cooperatives in refuse collection work. The first consolidation of independent operators into a major cooperative was probably Sunset, followed closely by Scavengers' Protective Association, now Golden Gate Disposal Company. Often, partners would leave one of these groups and strike out on their own, perhaps with others, going to an outlying community to start a refuse business. Thus, the whole area is populated by refuse company partnerships of three, four, seven, or however many Italian owners (or their heirs), with close connections by family and history with the original cooperatives, from whose example, of course, the other cooperatives also stemmed. However, the largest of all is one founded about the same time as Sunset, the Oakland Scavenger Company, which now employs over 600 men in refuse collection. Oakland has been called the "nation's largest single contractor," serving 300,000 clients in Alameda County. See "Nation's Largest Contractor Has \$9.1 Million Development Proposal," *Solid Wastes Management,* vol. 17, no. 9 (1974), 26, 60, 114.

The trade journal articles that single out some aspect of the Sunset operations, especially in conjunction with its Golden Gate collaborator, appear fairly frequently. Among them have been "Electronic Scales Speed San Francisco Disposal," *Waste Age,* vol. 7, no. 6 (1976), 14–15. Harold Gershowitz, "League of Cities Survey Is Unsoundly Drawn," *Solid Wastes Management,* vol. 13, no. 9 (1970), 48, 91. "Hauler Group Surveys Available Landfill Sites," *Solid Wastes Management,* vol. 17, no. 2 (1974), 12–13, 38, 40, 42. Gershowitz, who is now senior vice president of one of the major national agglomerates, especially praised Sunset for its low costs and landfill operations. Interestingly enough, none of the trade journal articles note the cooperative structure of the company.

The larger companies in the nine Bay Area counties have been unionized, but there are still a couple of the cooperatives that are non-union, as well as, of course, the smaller partnerships. Although the scavenger locals are not mentioned, Donald Garnel, in *The Rise of Teamster Power in the West* (Berkeley, Calif.: University of California Press, 1972), provides some of the background and reasons why they were organized when they were, in the 1930s.

Chapter Three: The Scavengers' New Broom

Stefanelli's concern about the gulls was stimulated by a rather obscure article by Bruce Brugman, "Garbage and the Space Age," *Cry California,* 1 (1965–66), 18–24. The scavengers felt and continue to feel threatened by any but favorable press attention—as any business is likely to feel. *Cry California* was a new publication and soon disappeared. Yet, Stefanelli was not only aware of its article but irritatedly quoted its more lurid passages. To use one of Stefanelli's favorite expressions, Sunset was "ironically" being threatened by gulls, who are themselves scavengers, of course.

Chapter Four: A Day of Routines

A joint master's thesis by Diamond and Schein provides a very detailed analysis and a specimen protocol of the movements and tasks of New York City refuse collectors. The issue they were concerned with (does what an informant tells the researcher about an activity dovetail with what the researcher can observe about the activity?) meant that the researchers were not particularly interested in garbage collection per se; and they used a very specialized approach for recording their observations (an approach provided by Marvin Harris, *The Nature of Cultural Things* [New York: Random House, 1964]). Nevertheless, their study is probably the earliest formal social science research on garbage collection routines per se. See Sydney G. Diamond and Muriel Dimen Schein, "The Waste Collector" (Master's thesis, Columbia University, Department of Anthropology, 1966).

Chapter Five: Encountering the World

When the scavengers used their spike hammer to "improve" a householder's garbage can, they might seem to be dealing improperly with someone else's property. But they have a certain kind of support from a body as august as the National Safety Council, which advises such holes in the bottom of cans. See *Public Employee Safety Guide: Refuse Collection* (Chicago: National Safety Council, 1974).

Chapter Six: Discontents

My statistics on types of injuries come from a study commissioned by the Solid Waste Management Office, U.S. Environmental Protection Agency, and are not publicly reproduced. The basic report (prepared by Applied Management Sciences, Inc.) is available from the agency's "open file" as "Solid Waste Management Manpower: Profile and Analysis," January 16, 1973, (SW-124.of); see especially Tables IV-12 and IV-13. For comparisons with other industries, see references cited in Notes and Sources for

Chapter One. On stress effects, see Robert D. Caplan et al., *Job Demands and Worker Health* (Washington, D.C.: U.S. Government Printing Office, 1975).

The troubles encountered by scavengers in collecting their accounts are perhaps matched by owner-operators of the very small refuse companies (one-, two-, or three-truck companies) that still collect about 11 percent of America's wastes. They made up about 57 percent of the private companies active in the field in 1971. About 60 percent of all private companies and 100 percent of small private companies contract directly with their customers rather than with a county, municipality, or the like. Their customers are mostly commercial accounts whose bills are therefore probably more easily collected; of course, they too may use mailed bills rather than collecting accounts in person. See Dennis Young, *How Shall We Collect Our Garbage?* (Washington, D.C.: Urban Institute, 1972).

The relative statuses of occupations in the United States have remained fairly stable, with the garbageman at or next to the bottom rung. See Robert W. Hodge et al., "Occupational Prestige in the United States, 1925–1963," *American Journal of Sociology,* 70 (1964): 386–402. The recent expression of confidence in garbage collectors compared to other aspects of government and the private sector was reported by the Subcommittee on Intergovernmental Relations, U.S. Senate Committee on Government Operations, *Confidence and Concern: Citizens View American Government— A Survey of Attitudes* (Washington, D.C.: U.S. Government Printing Office, December 3, 1973).

Chapter Seven: What's Good about This Job?

Wage and other statistics are taken from the study done by Applied Management Sciences, Inc., for the Solid Waste Management Office, U.S. Environmental Protection Agency, available at the agency as "Solid Waste Management Manpower: Profile and Analysis," January 16, 1973 (SW-124.of); see especially Figures IV-2 through IV-9.

On the rewards of dirty work, see the work of Everett C. Hughes cited in Notes and Sources for Chapter One. Compare Ray Gold, "Janitors versus Tenants," *American Journal of Sociology* 57 (1952), 486–493.

Chapter Eight: Challenges to a Way of Work

The so-called sanitary-fill method of disposal is inherently vulnerable. Garbage always seems to stir up deep feelings generally; and unless the operation is hidden to all but the workers concerned, passers-by even from a distance can conjure up vivid fantasies of odors, pestilence, and vermin. Critics of the fill-and-cover procedure may unconsciously or consciously play upon our fears and disgust—certainly major factors in the status we assign the garbageman generally. The word ''sanitary'' applied to a landfill operation is an obvious attempt to counteract such fears.

In the instance of the scavengers' Brisbane operation, this sort of primitive aversion, a modern-day taboo, may have suggested to one critic that the ordinary size of waterfront rats along the tidelands was somehow related to the disposal area (''rats big as pups''), as was the occasional and ordinary demise of gulls (''sea gulls falling dead from what they eat at dumps along the San Francisco Bay''). The quotes come from an article by Bruce Brugman, ''Garbage and the Space Age,'' *Cry California,* 1 (1965–66), 18–24.

One hundred and sixty acres of the proposed Brisbane landfill area, for which the scavengers paid $4,000 an acre, remain as occasionally submerged tidelands, and Brisbane will not permit diking already approved by the Army Corps of Engineers. Ironically, the tideland flats are much smellier than the fill-and-cover operations ever were—a natural feature of tidelands in the Bay Area—but, of course, they undoubtedly have some compensatory ecological value for the flora and fauna of the area.

My statistics on pounds of waste generated per capita in the United States are taken from two sources. The 5.5 pounds per capita national average was computed by the 1968 National Survey of Community Solid Waste Practices, cited in Arsen Darnay and William E. Franklin, *Salvage Markets for Materials in Solid Wastes,* Publication SW-29c, U.S. Environmental Protection Agency (Washington, D.C.: U.S. Government Printing Office, 1972); see especially pp. 3–4. See also *Solid Waste Collection Practice* (Chicago: American Public Works Association, 1975), which gives a slightly smaller figure for 1974, 5.3 pounds. That figure probably was a result of the recession. According to a recent report in a trade journal, projections by the Environmental Protection Agency show increases generally until 1990. EPA uses a different method of determining "post-consumer solid waste," that is, the waste from households, offices, trades, and services (excluding manufacturing, construction, agricultural, and certain other wastes). Their (preferred) "material flow estimation method" is based on government and trade association statistics on production, foreign trade, and consumption of all major raw materials and final products. This is adjusted for scrap losses, product lifetimes, recycling, and so on. By this method, 1971 produced 3.3 pounds per capita each day, and 1973 produced 3.5. See Frank Austin Smith, "The Quantity and Composition of Post-Consumer Solid Waste," *Waste Age,* vol. 6, no. 4 (1976), pp. 2–10.

A footnote to the saga of the "old *barraca*": In 1977, Lenny had another company car—an enormous black Cadillac equipped with a radio-telephone. The company still was not paying him any more than any other partner, but he certainly enjoyed the Cadillac.

Chapter Nine: Envirocal: The Cooperative's Conglomerate

The formal date of incorporation for Envirocal was November 21, 1972, in the State of Delaware; but it was a year later that the Sunset partners took the corporate shell and made it real.

"Garbage Gets a Glamour Image," sang an article in *Business Week* (March 4, 1972), p. 44. "The outfit that started it all is Houston-based Browning-Ferris Industries, Inc., the fastest growing of the garbage chains. . . ." BFI sold construction equipment originally, but it shifted into garbage collection and bought a couple of dozen companies, including the San Mateo Scavenger Company, a cooperative like Sunset, operating south of San Francisco. BFI tried stringently to decentralize decisions to its local divisions, but former owners of San Mateo who are still working with the company complain now about the loss of their autonomy.

At the height of the glamour period, *Business Week* saw only two potential problems: excessive administrative overhead and competition with the Mafia. The article quoted one chain president as saying, "The garbage business just isn't that sophisticated [to be able to use big central staffs and computer analysis]." And although that president and "other garbage chain executives deny they have run into organized crime, the denials are sometimes less than convincing." Conversely, Envirocal's computer operation has been successful; and the administrative staff does not seem excessive, though it rose from three in 1965, before Stefanelli was elected, to eleven in 1976. Revenues also rose from about $6 million in 1965 to about $25 million in 1975, with 786 employees in the latter year as compared to 440 in 1965.

As for the Mafia, Envirocal has so far experienced no trouble. There were one or two incidents and threats of violence during a brief strike at one subsidiary just after Envirocal bought it, but that was a unionization dispute. The biggest problem Sunset has always had is trying to keep itself from being stereotyped as a Mafia operation just because it has been primarily Italian-American. Even presumably sophisticated folk (among my acquaintances at the University of California) assumed that the scavenger was a Mafia type, because when he came ringing the doorbell to collect accounts, he might wear a silk suit and drive a Cadillac. (Such stereotypes had probably suggested in earlier days the policy among the scavengers that forbade the ownership of expensive cars, but that policy was no longer in effect by the time I was studying scavengers.)

A moment's thought is all that is necessary to dispel the Mafia question. The cooperative structure of Sunset is a clear barrier to the motivation and exploitation inherent in the way organized crime runs its sector of the refuse industry. And unless Sunset's structure is drastically revised (by, for example, going into the public stock market), the company will remain invulnerable to the stain that runs through the refuse industry in many other parts of the country.

The procedures used by Envirocal for acquisition of new companies has helped maintain its freedom from any underworld taint. Although the prior owners of a new company might sell in a transaction that included an exchange of stock, as had occurred in a couple of instances, the new partners still had only the same equal share as any of the shareholders of Sunset/Envirocal. The selling parties actually tended to be people who were getting along in years, and they did not maintain their shares for long. There has been one recent exception: a young heir to the owners of a company has been accepted as a (presumably long-term) partner in Envirocal with the expectation that he will remain in a managerial position in the family firm that will now be a division of Envirocal. (Incidentally, this new division is the first assay of the scavengers outside of Northern California. The buy-out, concluded in early 1977, was of a relatively small firm in Oregon, near the California border. Its geographic proximity to Envirocal's northernmost California subsidiary [headquartered in Redding] made it at least seem not to be a real departure from previous policy, and, moreover, it was near enough for adequate administrative supervision.)

The importance of the knowledge of line workers in an organization, for the solution of its problems, has been reported by Max Elden of the Work Research Institute, Oslo, Norway, in a paper entitled "Bank Employees Begin to Participate in Studying and Changing Their Organization" (January 15, 1976). The paper was presented at the third Conference of People for Self-Management, Washington, D.C., June 10–12, 1976. Elden reported that the introduction of new technology (an "on line" computer system) spurred a study at the first branch of a bank that was starting to introduce the new technology. Both management and line workers (such as tellers) articulated the same problems in the branch, but the line workers could suggest more solutions, and their solutions were more concrete. The lower the level of the worker, the more complex the theory of bank problems and solutions—and the more the problems were seen as interrelated and interdependent. In short, the line worker was more able to use a systems approach!

Statistics on the costs of municipal refuse collection differ according to the sources. For 1969–70, I have used what the administrators of the New York City collection service have reported for that city, since they were not likely to overestimate their costs when they were comparing alternate services. See *Private Cartmen and the Department of Sanitation,* A Report by The Environmental Protection Administration, Jerome Kretchmer, Administrator, and the Department of Sanitation, Herbert Elish, Commissioner (New York, January, 1972). The city report indicated that private cartmen could in effect underbid the city only by their practice of paying workers less. According to the federal Environmental Protection Agency, the 1975 figures obtained from the city indicate that New York is holding the line against cost increases, with the cost per ton having increased only $4.50—even though EPA estimates that overall in the country costs have doubled since 1973. From 1973 to 1976, San Francisco's costs had risen 50 percent—partly because of a change in disposal arrangements. New York's recent economical performance may be explained by a drastic reduction in sanitation department employees.

The National Commission on Productivity has published some helpful materials on refuse collection; its approach is mainly to recommend particular technical procedures (such as size of crew or type of equipment). The chairman of its specialist advisory group was William F. Farnam, Public Works Director for Inglewood, California, a particularly productive municipal department. See especially the Report of the Solid Waste Management Advisory Group, *Opportunities for Improving Productivity in Solid Waste Collection* (Washington, D.C.: National Commission on Productivity, 1973). A rather interesting management point of view on getting municipal workers involved in productivity measures is provided by the Labor-Management Relations Service of the U.S. Conference of Mayors, National League of Cities, and National Association of Counties. See their "Negotiating for Productivity in Sanitation" (1973), as prepared by George W. Brooks. The Urban Institute in Washington, D.C., and the National Solid Waste Management Association have also conducted productivity studies from both the private firm and public sector point of view.

On the issue of recruitment, the experience and policy of the Inglewood, California, sanitation department is significant. Only high school graduates who intend to get trained for other jobs are accepted. And it is up and out for them, as a matter of city policy. Salaries are good. In 1973, they began at $719 a month, with a maximum of $877 a month. Average length of service (except for supervisory personnel) is three years. See *Solid Waste Collection Practice, op. cit.*, pp. 83–86.

Chapter Ten: Work, Ownership, and the Worker Cooperative

For a general perspective on the growth of dirty work jobs in our society, I have relied upon a report submitted to the National Planning Association, *Upgrading Low-Level Employment: A Major*

National Challenge (Washington, D.C.: National Planning Association, 1975). On the issue of whether or not workers would be concerned with job content as well as pay, see Robert L. Kahn, "The Work Module," in *Work and the Quality of Life,* ed. James O'Toole (Cambridge, Mass.: MIT Press, 1974), pp. 199–226. Irving Kristol's objection to emphasizing job content is reprinted in his "Job Satisfaction: Daydream or Alienation?" *The AFL-CIO American Federationist,* vol. 8, no. 2 (1973), 11–12. See also in the same journal issue William W. Winpisinger, "Job Satisfaction: A Union Response," pp. 8–10.

The figures for New York City sanitationmen's examinations were provided by Morris B. Shiechel, Director of Recruitment and Employee Incentive of New York's Department of Personnel. The comparative report on New York's municipal costs versus New York's private carters was prepared under the direction of E. S. Savas, then a deputy city administrator. See John F. McMahon and Herbert R. Gamache, *Refuse Collection: Department of Sanitation vs. Private Carting* (New York: Office of the Mayor, November, 1970). Later, at Columbia University, Savas has continued his studies, described in a 1,071-page report of research to the National Science Foundation, as reported in the *New York Times,* November 23, 1975. A 20-page summary is available: E. S. Savas, "Evaluating the Organization of Service Delivery: Solid Waste Collection and Disposal," Columbia University, Center for Government Studies, October, 1975. The city probably first became aware of the San Francisco scavengers through an article in *New York,* July 12, 1971, "Can Free Enterprise Speed Up Our Garbage Collection?" by Nick Kazan. *New York Times* articles on the proposals for local cooperative-serviced districts have appeared on April 29, 1976, and thereafter. The DeLury quote comes from an article on October 17, 1976.

Statistics on the switches back and forth between private contracts or the municipal department model throughout the United States may be found in *Solid Waste Collection Practice,* 4th ed. (Chicago: American Public Works Association, 1975), p. 237. For data on the older ages of municipal workers compared to private company employees, see Solid Waste Management Office, Environmental Protection Agency files: "Solid Waste Management

Manpower: Profile and Analysis," January 16, 1973 (SW-124.of),
p. 4.5.

Statistics on ownership in the United States (and other useful
data) appear in [Robert D. Hamrin], *Broadening the Ownership
of New Capital: ESOPs and Other Alternatives,* a staff study prepared for the use of the Joint Economic Committee, Congress of
the United States, June 17, 1976 (Washington, D.C.: U.S. Government Printing Office, 1976).

A useful compendium is John McClaughry, *Expanded Ownership* (Fond du Lac, Wisc.: Sabre Foundation, 1972). Interestingly
enough, this research report was jointly funded by the Economic
Development Administration (U.S. Department of Commerce)
and the Ford Foundation. More specifically and currently, see
Marty Thompson, "Employee-Owned Companies: A New Look at
an Old Phenomenon," *Mergers and Acquisitions,* vol. 11, no. 1
(1976), 4–13.

A very specific examination of the implications of the ESOP
approach for worker control of their own firms is provided by
Katrina V. Berman, "Employee Stock Ownership Plans (ESOPs)
and Implementation of Worker Management," *Association for
Self-Management Newsletter,* No. 19 (July–August, 1976), pp.
2–10. For a general evaluation and discussion, see W. Robert
Reum and Sherry Milliken Reum, "Employee Stock Ownership
Plans: Pluses and Minuses," *Harvard Business Review,* 54 (July–
August, 1976), 133–143. For a useful perspective on what ownership of conventional stocks may or may not mean to the individual
worker through ESOPs or pension funds, see Peter Drucker, "Pension Fund Socialism," *Public Interest,* 42 (1976), 3–46. For comments on ownership in *Work in America,* report of a special task
force to the Secretary of Health, Education, and Welfare (Cambridge,
Mass.: MIT Press, 1973), see pp. 106 ff.

Federal discouragement of the cooperative form outside of
agriculture can be documented in a number of ways. For example,
it was not until October 16, 1962, that nonagricultural cooperatives
received the same tax breaks, by the passage of Public Law 87-834.
I have a copy of an amazing letter from a Small Business Administration bureaucrat in which he admonishes a business applying
for assistance with the words that the applicant is a cooperative

and therefore "un-American" and not eligible for SBA assistance. The federal anti-poverty agency (Community Services Administration) has long tried to get SBA to change its practices discriminating against cooperatives. SBA continues to refuse such assistance, although PL 92-424 and 93-644 would seem to require it. See Lloyd C. Lee, "No New SBA Rules for CDCs," *Economic Development Law Project Report* (September/October 1976), pp. 1, 30. (This publication is issued by the Earl Warren Legal Institute, 2313 Warring Street, Berkeley, Calif. 94704.)

The story of the plywood cooperatives has been told initially by Katrina Berman, an economist who worked with some of them on their arguments for cooperative, nontaxable status. See Katrina V. Berman, *Worker-Owned Plywood Companies: An Economic Analysis* (Pullman, Washington: Washington State University Press, Economic and Business Studies Bulletin, No. 42, 1967). See also Carl Bellas, *Industrial Democracy and the Worker-Owned Firm* (New York: Praeger, 1972). And see Paul Bernstein, "Run Your Own Business: Worker-Owned Plywood Firms," *Working Papers,* 2 (Summer, 1974):24–34.

Researchers at the University of Michigan Survey Research Center are now compiling a census of cooperatives for a major study. The leaders of this effort include Stanley Seashore and Arnold Tannenbaum. The latter has published a significant study dealing with some of the themes of this book. See Arnold S. Tannenbaum et al., *Hierarchy in Organizations: An International Comparison* (San Francisco: Jossey-Bass, 1974).

Worker-owned cooperatives and worker-ownership generally have occupied the attention of members of the Association for Economic Democracy (Box 802, Ithaca, New York 14850), although their concerns extend to workplace democracy or worker control beyond or in the absence of ownership. Three national conferences of this group (formerly called People for Self-Management) and its newsletter have produced many significant papers and reports of studies in the United States and abroad. An associated group, the Federation for Economic Democracy (c/o IGP, Suite 607, 2100 M St., N.W., Washington, D.C. 20063), specializes in problems of financing cooperatives and other worker-owned enterprises.

Many of the details of the sale of Oakland and Golden Gate come not from my interviews but from those of Raymond Russell conducted in the late 1980s. He reported his work in an unpublished paper prepared for presentation at the annual meetings of the American Sociological Association, San Francisco, August 11, 1989, entitled "Sunset for the Scavengers: The Politics of Degeneration in Democratic Firms." I have used his report as well as his interview notes, although my own additional information alters some conclusions for me.

The local newspaper, the *San Francisco Chronicle*, is a major source for the most recent events detailed in this chapter, particularly regarding the strike of April 24 and 25, 1997—about two months after my last field trip. On April 26, after the strike was over, the newspaper ran an article that indicates that the burden of the keys is still a part of the work, reporting that "Mario [a scavenger interviewed by the *Chronicle* reporter] carries 19 bundles of keys—about 1000 in all." Also, the paper reported in an April 25 article that "by one account [Sangiacomo's total compensation] is as high as $675,000." Sangiacomo himself cites public figures available for the previous fiscal year, at $350,000 salary plus $147,500 bonus. The drill team's prowess is featured, with a picture, in a *Chronicle* article by Sam Whiting, February 20, 1997, in the context of the traditional parade through Chinatown to take place the next day on the occasion of the Chinese New Year's festival.

The state law mandating recycling of 50 percent of the waste stream by the year 2000 is known as Assembly Bill 939.

Probably the most recent survey of research reports on the effects of ESOPs appears in Roger T. Kaufman and Raymond Russell, "Government Support for Profit Sharing, Gainsharing, ESOPs, and TQM," *Contemporary Economic Policy* (1995) 13: 38–48. See also Raymond Russell, "Taking Stock of the ESOPs," in Cornelius J. Lammers and Gyoergy Szell, eds., *International Handbook of Participation in Organizations*, vol. 1 (Oxford University Press, 1989; pp. 50–60). And see also the items cited in Russell's foreword to the present book. Problems in the very idea of the worker-owned firm are discussed in Stewart E. Perry and Hunt C. Davis, "The Worker-Owned Firm: The Idea and Its Conceptual Limits," *Economic and Industrial Democracy* (1985) 6: 275–297. For a recent report on the effects of participative management in comparison to other work arrangements, see Randy Hudson, "Dignity in the Workplace under Participative Management: Alienation and Freedom Revisited," *American Sociological Review* (1996) 61: 719–738. Incidentally, the previous edition of the San Francisco scavenger study was among the 86 reports of the varying work arrangements examined for this analysis.

On the productivity of Israeli cooperatives, see Seymour Melman, "Industrial Efficiency under Managerial vs. Cooperative Decision-making: A Comparative Study of Manufacturing Enterprises in Israel," *Studies in Comparative International Development* (1970–71) 6: 47–58. For an insightful update on the fate of the cooperatives, see Raymond Russell, *Utopia in Zion: The Israeli Experience With Worker Cooperatives* (Albany: State University of New York Press, 1995).

Our comparative study of scavengers and other garbagemen is reported, in part, in Raymond Russell, Arthur Hochner, and Stewart E. Perry, "Participation, Influence, and Worker-Ownership," *Industrial Relations* (1979) 18: 330–341. See also Arthur Hochner, *Worker Ownership and the Theory of Participation* (unpublished Ph.D. dissertation, Harvard University, 1978); and Raymond Russell, *Sharing Ownership in the Workplace* (Albany: State University of New York Press, 1985).

On the conflicting tendencies in democratic values, both economic and political, see a clarifying and provocative work by Michael J. Sandel, *Democracy's Discontent: America in Search of a Public Philosophy* (Cambridge, MA: Belknap Press of Harvard University Press, 1996). He sees hope in the community development corporations or CDCs (pp. 333–334). For my own work on CDCs and what they can offer, see especially *Communities on the Way* (Albany: State University of New York Press, 1987). A review of new forms of corporate relations with workers, including ESOPs, appears in Roger E. Alcaly, "Reinventing the Corporation," *New York Review of Books* (April 10, 1997) 44, 6: 38–45.

Index of Authors

General Index